Constructivism across the Curriculum in Early Childhood Classrooms

Big Ideas as Inspiration

Christine Chaillé

Portland State University

PEARSON

Boston   New York   San Francisco
Mexico City   Montreal   Toronto   London   Madrid   Munich   Paris
Hong Kong   Singapore   Tokyo   Cape Town   Sydney

*For my children: Adrienne Ann Chaillé, my delight and inspiration,
and Dr. Peter McConnell Chaillé, the real scientist in the family.*

Series Editor: Kelly Villella Canton
Series Editorial Assistant: Angela Pickard
Marketing Manager: Danae April
Production Editor: Annette Joseph
Editorial Production Service: Denise A. Botelho
Composition Buyer: Linda Cox
Manufacturing Buyer: Linda Morris
Electronic Composition: Schneck-DePippo Graphics
Interior Design: Deborah Schneck
Cover Design: Elena Sidorova

For related titles and support materials, visit our online catalog at www.ablongman.com.

Between the time website information is gathered and then published, it is not unusual for some sites to have closed. Also, the transcription of URLs can result in typographical errors. The publisher would appreciate notification where these errors occur so that they may be corrected in subsequent editions.

ISBN-10: 0-205-34854-8
ISBN-13: 978-0-205-34854-1

Library of Congress Cataloging-in-Publication Data

Chaillé, Christine.
  Constructivism across the curriculum in early childhood classrooms : big ideas as inspiration / Christine Chaillé.
    p. cm.
  ISBN 0-205-34854-8 (alk. paper)
  1. Education, Primary—Curricula—United States. 2. Education, Preschool—Curricula—United States.
  3. Constructivism (Education)—United States. I. Title.
  LB1523.C43 2008
  372.19—dc22   2007013542

Printed in the United States of America

5 6 7 8 9 10 VOCR 16 15 14 13 12

Photos courtesy of Christine Chaillé.

Contents

Contents

Preface

This book is intended to provide a guide for teachers who are looking for inspiration, teachers who are interested in constructivism and the ideas of Reggio Emilia. Some of you may already be doing many of the things described here and will gain some new insights and perhaps some new ideas. Others of you may just need to have an image in your mind about what is possible, an image that can inspire you to try some new and fresh approaches to curriculum development.

One thing to keep in mind as you read this book is that there are many degrees of being a constructivist teacher, and it does not necessarily take a transformation of everything you do to move in the right direction. A teacher in one of my classes once said that she decided that the *one* thing she could do after reading about constructivism was to turn questions back to children and then to listen to what they say. Once she started doing this one simple and straightforward thing, she found a shift in the classroom culture that made many more things possible over time. Another teacher said that she didn't have time to do the things I was advocating but decided to devote thirty minutes a week to "choice time" during which she could try a few ideas out. She found that these thirty minutes had a far-reaching effect on the rest of the week as students started making connections to other things she was doing. These connections in turn encouraged her to make more connections explicit, and she began to transform, little by little, other aspects of what she was doing during the week. She did this without sacrificing any of the things she was "required" to do, much to her surprise.

Many of the teachers I work with initially remark on how "difficult" it seems to be a constructivist teacher. What they begin to see, over time, is that it is easy to do boring things. It is also boring to do boring things. In doing those things that seem difficult the teacher, in fact, finds excitement and joy. The daily acts of teaching, then, become full of joy, both for the teacher and, most importantly, for the children. Over time, these same teachers make comments about how much easier it is to go to work when it is full of challenge and learning. They begin to redefine "difficult" as "challenging" and "interesting." So, given a choice—easy and boring or challenging and joyful—which would you choose?

After a brief introduction to working with "big ideas" in Chapter 1, Chapter 2 introduces you to one big idea——light—as a way to begin to understand the comprehensive nature of this approach to classroom teaching. Then in Chapter 3 we take a step back and discuss what it means to be a constructivist teacher implementing this approach to curriculum. The next six chapters delve into the remaining big ideas explored in this book—balance, zooming in and out, sound, upside down and inside out, cause and effect, and transformation. These six chapters can be read in any order that interests you. The book ends with a challenge to think about how you can develop and implement big ideas in your classroom and some suggestions for proceeding.

The Hundred Languages of Children exhibit, showcasing the remarkable representational art done by the children in schools in Reggio Emilia, Italy, was originally titled "The Eye Jumps Over the Wall," an apt metaphor for how teachers need to start to think about curriculum. There is nothing that holds back your imagination; and once you let yourself think about things differently you will find yourself doing things differently. Anything is possible where there is a dream. And someday you, too, can put over your classroom door the wonderful inscription seen in the schools of Reggio Emilia, "Nothing Without Joy."

Acknowledgments

Many people have contributed to this book, indirectly and directly. I'd like to acknowledge the numerous teachers and students whose ideas are reflected in the book in many ways, and whose questions and interests have stimulated the writing of this book. In addition to those in Portland, I'd like to also thank the many students and teachers in Sapporo, Japan, and Juneau, Alaska, who have always challenged my thinking, and Amelia Gambetti and all of the incredible teachers, children, and families in Reggio Emilia, Italy. I owe particular thanks to the teachers and children of the Helen Gordon Child Development Center, the laboratory school of the Graduate School of Education of Portland State University, Portland, Oregon, including Will Parnell and Ellie Justice, Co-Directors; Marsha Kennell, studio teacher; and teachers Stephanie Varley, Liz Dickey, Frank Mahler, and Nikki Hume; and the teachers and children of the Creative Children's Center in Beaverton, Oregon, with special thanks to Lucy Chaillé, my good friend and an inspiring teacher; and Brandeis Bailey, elementary teacher in Canby, Oregon. I also owe a great deal to my doctoral student and graduate assistant, Xiaoling Tian, who worked hard to help prepare the manuscript. My colleagues at Portland State University have provided a constant source of support and caring through this long process, including Sara McCormick Davis (now at the University of Arkansas, Fort Smith), Emily de la Cruz, Sandra Wilde, Susan Halverson, and Donna Shrier. Thank you to those who gave helpful suggestions to the manuscript: Betty Ruth Baker, Baylor University; Rhonda A. Brunner, Shippensburg University; Joan Campbell, Santa Fe Community College; Johnna Darragh, Heartland Community College, Kathleen E. Fite, Texas State University; Linda Kay Gregory, Osseo Area Schools, District 279; Michelle Rupiper, University of Nebraska, Lincoln; Emily D. Schmidt, Kennesaw State University; and Nancy B. Stewart, Norfolk Public Schools. Others to thank include MyLinda King, my marimba teacher, who has provided me with a model of good teaching and helped me experience what it is like to learn something new; good friends Susan Schradle, Nancy Hicks, Barbara Surovell, and Linda Nettekovin; and my siblings Alice, Raymond, and Judith McConnell. For the photographs, I'd like to thank Stephanie Varley, Lucy Chaillé, and Will Parnell for their assistance. Special thanks to Lory Britain, the coauthor of my previous book, *The Young Child as Scientist*, whose knowledge of and love for children is a constant inspiration to me. And without the support and patience of Tracy Mueller, my former editor at Allyn and Bacon, and Kelly Villella Canton, my current editor, this book would still be just an idea.

Constructivism across the Curriculum in Early Childhood Classrooms

CHAPTER 1

Big Ideas: A Framework
for Constructivist Curriculum

*O*n a small round table are several flashlights, sheets of colored cellophane paper, and small mirrors. Peter and Adrienne approach the table, and Peter picks up a flashlight, turns it on, and covers the end of it with red cellophane. "Wow," Adrienne says, "there's redness on your shirt!" She picks up a mirror, and Peter shines the flashlight through the red cellophane onto the mirror, as Adrienne moves the mirror around until the light is reflected onto the table again. Peter and Adrienne laugh and exclaim as they move the flashlight and the mirror around to reflect the light onto different parts of the room.

▼◄ ▲ ▼◄ ▲ ▼◄ ▲ ▼◄ ▲ ▼◄ ▲ ▼◄ ▲ ▼◄ ▲

What is it that Peter and Adrienne can learn as they engage in this sort of experimentation? What are the big ideas that underlie their experimentation with light, reflection, and color? What are the connections that we, as teachers, can discern and use to develop meaningful, integrated constructivist curriculum?

These questions will be raised throughout this book, identifying and exploring several different "big ideas"—light is the first one—in an attempt to help you, the classroom teacher, begin to see how constructivism underlies all aspects of children's activities and experiences in the classroom. I will attempt to extend each idea into several different curriculum strands, usually with science as the core, and with mathematics, social studies, creative arts, technology, language, and literacy as the connecting realms. In the process, I will describe an array of possible materials and resources that can help you implement a broad-ranging constructivist curriculum focused around a few big ideas. I'll do this specifically with Peter and Adrienne's explorations of light in Chapter 2, but first I'd like to share the framework that this book is based on.

This approach—a focus on big ideas—is grounded in constructivism, influenced and inspired by the work in the schools of Reggio Emilia. The core value I hold is that children are competent, confident, curious theory-builders; this value is the essence of constructivism. I have also been deeply impressed by how this value is exemplified by the schools of Reggio Emilia. In this chapter, I will attempt to briefly introduce the underlying shared assumptions and values coming from constructivism and Reggio Emilia; my hope is that as you continue through the book these will come to life through the big ideas I have chosen to expand on. The ideas I have chosen for this book are intended to be examples: light, balance, zooming in and out, sound, wacky curriculum, chain reactions, and transformation. My hope is that you will see the approach to developing these big ideas—and the scenarios of teachers and children exploring them—as a model for exploring and developing other big ideas. The approach to curriculum development put forward in this book can serve as a guide for how you could approach any focal point that you may be interested in exploring. In this way, you will be able to adapt the model to the circumstances in which you find yourself.

You may be teaching preschool-age children, or you may be teaching in a kindergarten or the primary grades of elementary school. Each big idea presented here will be explored across the age ranges of early childhood, and I will explicitly address in subsequent chapters some of the developmental modifications that you will always want to keep in mind as you tailor curriculum to your particular age group. I will also be exploring some of the cultural considerations that need to be addressed when you adapt curriculum to the particular group of children with which you work, as well as the cultural issues and considerations underlying the choice of big ideas that are presented here.

As a constructivist teacher, you can weave threads across the curriculum, and, through children's experiences in those connected curriculum activities, their own world can be woven together. They can start to make implicit, if not explicit, connections across all of the varied interesting things that go on in their lives. In doing so they create more solid and deeper ideas that last and are meaningful.

Constructivism: The Theoretical Framework for Big Ideas

As a constructivist from my early years as a student in the 1970s, when I had the honor of studying with Jean Piaget in Geneva, my work has been an attempt to show how good practice in early childhood education can reflect constructivist theory. Although the book I wrote with Lory Britain, *The Young Child as Scientist: A Constructivist Approach to Early Childhood Science Education* (Chaillé & Britain, 2003), uses science as the core, it is really about responding to children who are, by nature, exploring, experimenting, and theory-building in everything they do. The broad implications of being a constructivist teacher go way beyond "science education"; the constructivist teacher does not see curriculum as segmented, and engages in a facilitative interaction that involves listening carefully—in the broadest sense of the word—to children's ideas and interests, as well as taking responsibility for provoking experimentation and problem solving by providing a rich environment in which children's work can take place with respect and joy.

Constructivism is grounded in Piagetian theory (Piaget, 1977) and enhanced by Vygotskian theory (Bodrova & Leong, 1996; Berk & Winsler, 1995). Constructivism is a theory of learning that posits that children construct knowledge through interaction between their own ideas and experiences in the social and physical world. Children come to each experience with a rich background and ideas of their own, and, as they engage in interactions and experiment with their ideas, they develop new theories and ideas. Motivation for learning, from the constructivist perspective, is intrinsic, as children are constantly trying to make sense of the world and expand their ideas. Therefore, from the constructivist perspective, children do not learn through transmission of knowledge and information, nor are they motivated through extrinsic means such as reinforcements and rewards. Those views of learning are grounded in behaviorist theories and are incompatible with the constructivist perspective.

One misconception that is important to address is that constructivism is *not* a method, a curriculum model, or a series of appropriate practices. We cannot look at something a teacher does, or an activity that children are engaged in, and say, "*That* is a constructivist practice or activity." Rather, constructivism is the theory that *underlies* the choices and decisions you make about how you set up the classroom, choose the curriculum, and respond to the children's work and ideas. If you ascribe to the constructivist perspective, then you believe that children are constructing knowledge no matter what is going on in the classroom, and no matter what the theoretical perspective of the teacher. Thus, in a behaviorist classroom, children are constructing an understanding that knowledge is transmitted by someone who is knowledgeable (the teacher) to someone who is not (the child). In a constructivist classroom, children are constructing an understanding that they are building their own theories and constructing their own knowledge through interaction with a knowledgeable adult and other children.

We can, however, talk about practices and characteristics of classrooms that are consistent with constructivism. For example, curriculum frameworks that honor children's ideas, such as the project approach (Katz & Chard, 2000), are consistent with constructivism. Similarly, the practice of giving children time and space to put into practice their own ideas is consistent with constructivism. And some practices and characteristics of classrooms are *not* consistent with constructivism. For example, the use of whole group instruction for a large part of the day is not consistent with constructivism, nor is the practice of using extrinsic rewards and reinforcements for desirable behaviors.

This is a very important distinction, because many teachers are under the impression that if they use particular materials, set up particular activities, or implement a particular curriculum framework they are "constructivist" teachers. Not so; constructivist practice involves a complex interplay of decisions and choices that teachers make throughout their practices.

The Inspiration of Reggio Emilia

When I first encountered the work of the schools of Reggio Emilia in the 1970s, I was struck by how beautifully it exemplified my constructivist beliefs and practices. I am sharing here a few of the ideas that resonated with me, with no claim on my part to be an expert on Reggio Emilia, but rather an educator who has found that these inspirations can deepen our work with children. I also cannot do justice to the complexity and richness of these inspirations in a short space, but can only introduce them. As I said earlier, it is my hope that by elaborating on a few big ideas these inspirations will come to life.

For those of you unfamiliar with Reggio Emilia, it is a municipality in northern Italy that has become internationally known for the infant-toddler centers and pre-schools that have evolved over the past fifty years. Reggio Children (see the website at www.reggiochildren.com), the organization created to promote excellent early childhood education and share the work of the schools in Reggio Emilia, organizes study groups throughout the year—some international and some focused on a group from a particular country. Reggio Children also engages in outreach through conferences and talks throughout the world. One of the tools for this outreach is the exhibit "The Hundred Languages of Children," which shares through pictures, words, and other documentation the work of the children of Reggio Emilia, work that, for those new to the work, is startling in its originality and demonstrated capability of the children (Reggio Children, 2005). Children are provided from infancy on with opportunities to express themselves using many different "languages," including clay, wire, words, paint, construction, and dramatic play, and the resulting documentation of the processes and products of the children's work is provocative to educators from other traditions. The exhibit, other presentations by teachers and *atelieristas* (studio teachers) from Reggio Emilia, and numerous publications on the subject sparked an interest in their work that has grown through the years. There are many resources that can provide further background, including Wurm (2005), Cadwell (1997, 2003), and Edwards, Gandini, and Forman (1993, 1998). Most helpful as an introduction to Reggio Emilia are the videos that are available, including *To Make a Portrait of a Lion* (1987) and *The Amusement Park for Birds* (1994). The video *Not Just Any Place* (2002) provides a comprehensive history of the municipal schools, and in the process articulates many of the values and ideas that have so fascinated educators from around the world.

Here I will just mention a few of the core ideas of Reggio Emilia that have particularly inspired me and that are reflected in the exploration of big ideas. You'll see these core ideas expanded on in different ways throughout this book.

The first core idea is the pedagogy of listening, which implies that teachers learn from children rather than transmitting knowledge. Listening is conceived of in its very broadest sense, involving all of the senses. Sergio Spaggiari, director of early childhood education in Reggio Emilia, in a talk to a Reggio Emilia study tour in 2004, spoke of making a "declaration of ignorance" when we work with children, essentially assuming that we know nothing and have everything to learn from the children we are working with. To be totally present and open to seeing, hearing, and feeling what children are doing and thinking—this is what is meant by the pedagogy of listening. Only when we suspend our expertise, assumptions, and prior knowledge can we be open to engaging with children.

This leads to the second core idea—participation. Teachers, children, parents, the community, and the environment are all part of the dialogue of education. In Reggio Emilia, education is an inherently social and interactive experience; children's engagement with peers, with parents, with their social and physical surroundings, with their community, and with teachers are all valued. Children are citizens with rights, which positions them in an active, powerful role in the educational process. They are citizens in a social, cultural, political, and historical context, which is quite a contrast with the image of the child held by many throughout the world.

The third core idea derives from the two previous ideas—the image of the child as a competent, creative, powerful force to learn from rather than to teach to. This image transforms what we do as teachers in a way that is consistent with the constructivist principles described above. The respect accorded to childhood is summed up in the idea that "culture is created in the preschool," a statement made in many different ways in the work of Reggio Emilia.

The fourth core idea, that of documentation, is a corollary of all three ideas. Through documentation adults are doing (at least) two things. First, they are making children's learning visible—putting into words, pictures, videos, sketches, and artifacts the story of the child's learning process—in collaboration with the children themselves. This deepens and transforms the learning itself, adding another level of complexity to the work of children. It also serves to communicate with all who participate in the educational process what is happening, what children are expressing, what is being experienced in the school. It serves as a way to learn more deeply and to reflect more complexly on what we do with children. Second, they are, in the process of documentation, communicating value to children as well as to any audience of the documentation and showing in a very concrete way that what children do is important and worthy of recording.

There are many more ideas that have influenced me, but for now, these four—the pedagogy of listening, participation, the image of the child, and documentation—

will suffice to introduce the importance of the work of Reggio Emilia for the framework of big ideas presented in this book.

I have provided in this book some of the resources, ideas, and even discussions of the scientific knowledge underlying the big ideas. But, as I said earlier, these are only the beginning and are designed to give you a taste for how the process could unfold. Just like the children, this journey might take you on different paths than the book suggests, so don't see this as a recipe book, but rather as an example of what one or two paths could be.

What Is a "Big Idea"?

Three underlying concepts are important for understanding big ideas: inspiration, connection, and observation.

First, let's think about inspiration. How do you get your ideas? How do we explore, with each other and with children, the issues and topics that can lead to important and interesting experiences in the classroom? While there are many approaches to deciding what goes on in the classroom, much depends on your own interest and excitement about what it is and where it is going. Inspiration is what leads us to come up with new ideas and to be open to what is already in front of us.

It is my belief that at least some of the appeal of the work in Reggio Emilia is due to the powerful inspiration that is provided by what we see happening with teachers and children in their environments. Inspiration is also what helps us to value what we do with children. Again, the work in Reggio Emilia has directed the focus of our work toward that which most of us have at our core—our respect for and ability to learn from children. And children are our greatest inspiration. The focus of this book is to consider some "big ideas" that direct our attention toward that which children engage in deeply. The intention is that the focus on these big ideas will be an inspiration to you, stimulating the application of the ideas presented here but, more importantly, stimulating the development of other and different inspiring big ideas that could provide the basis for curriculum development.

This brings us to the second underlying concept—connection. While there are many interesting and appropriate activities and materials that children can engage in, the constructivist perspective makes an assumption about learning and the progress of child development that involves children connecting the things they do. According to the constructivist, learning takes place when we see the relationships between the many different things that we experience and learn. This focus on connection means that in addition to the importance of living in the moment with children and appreciating the immediacy of experience, as teachers we need to think about the broader context of children's experiences and the connections among and between what they do and what they learn. What's particularly important about connection is that it comes naturally for children—they are constantly striving to make sense out of and construct webs among the many different things they experience and learn. By focusing on connection as a basic concept, we are honoring that which children are doing naturally.

And finally, I come to the third underlying concept—observation. Observation in the broad sense involves participation and reflection, and puts the spotlight on your role in the process of creating the constructivist curriculum. How do we as adults understand the world as the child is constructing it? How can we be in touch with what children are engaged in, attentive to, and thinking about without observing and engaging with children in such a way that we approximate the child's world in how we think about curriculum? While much work focuses our attention on how to observe (i.e., "look at") children, it is also about how to create opportunities where, to use the phrase explored by Reggio Children, we can "make learning visible" (Guidici, Rinaldi, & Krechevsky, 2001). Observation, as so many early educators have discussed, is both an art and a science and is a constant necessity for good teaching. But observation in the traditional sense implies a stepping back and away in order to fully appreciate what children are doing. "Making learning visible," on the other hand, implies the active participation of you as the teacher in trying to figure out what is going on for children. It is similar to, and grounded in, Piaget's early work that sought to actively seek children's ideas about the world through what he called the "clinical interview," a combination of discussion and activities designed to elicit from children their thinking. This notion of more actively or aggressively observing children is important for what is presented in this book.

All three of these concepts place value on relationships, on our caring connection with children. Inspiration is at the heart of why we work with children—because we deeply care about their well-being and their learning, and we take pleasure from our work with children. Focusing on connection requires us to try to see the world from the perspective of children, and this also requires relationship-building. Observation, in the participatory sense I am describing here, also implies relationship, a close partnership with children that involves mutual respect.

Toward a Definition of a "Big Idea"

A big idea is an overarching idea that unifies, inspires, and resonates with children, an idea that is rich with possibilities and permits teachers and children to work together in many ways. One way of talking about what a big idea is is to talk about how it differs from other ways of organizing and generating curriculum and how other people have talked about big ideas.

Big Ideas Compared to the Project Approach

The project approach, as developed and described by Katz and Chard (2000) and Helm (2001), involves the development of curriculum around ideas generated by children and teachers that result in projects, which are activities engaged in by groups of children and that are connected by a topic or theme. While some of the criteria that are described by Katz and Chard may apply to the criteria for a big idea, I conceive of big ideas as encompassing numerous projects. For example, in the next chapter I describe projects embedded in the work around the big idea of light, projects involving the study of shadows and contrast. A project could initiate a classroom's work on the big idea, by provoking interest and intrigue. Children could begin to explore the big idea of light, for example, through the initial activity of constructing and performing a puppet show with shadow puppets, itself a large-scale project. A project could also come out of the exploration of light. So, after a group of children have experimented with flashlights in a dark room, children might become intrigued by mirrors and reflection, resulting in a project on mirrors.

Big Ideas Compared to the Work Coming Out of Reggio Emilia

The notion of "big ideas" is very compatible with the work in the classrooms of Reggio Emilia (Edwards, Gandini, & Forman,1993, 1998; Gandini, 1993). What we are doing by looking at big ideas is focusing on strategies teachers can use to generate ideas and curriculum that lead to experiences such as those that we see in the classrooms of Reggio Emilia and in some of the classrooms in the United States and elsewhere that are inspired by the Reggio Emilia approach (Cadwell, 1997, 2003; Abbott & Nutbrown, 2001; Hendricks, 1997). The nature and diversity of the projects undertaken by the children in Reggio Emilia schools are explorations of big ideas, and the complexity of the processes for their projects can be informative. As I've described earlier, the work in Reggio Emilia embodies many of the principles of good practice that underlie constructivist practice, such as respecting and valuing children, paying close attention to the work and languages of children, incorporating ways of making children's learning visible through documentation and observation, and creating a social and physical environment that honors and respects children and their work, collective and individual. In this book, we are making explicit some of the ways that teachers can be as creative and thoughtful as some of the teachers described in the work of Reggio Emilia. Indeed, the ongoing work in Reggio Emilia serves as a constant source of inspiration and support for constructivist practice.

Big Ideas Compared to Ordinary Moments

One of the other legacies of the work of Reggio Emilia has been articulated by George Forman (2001) and has to do with the acknowledgment of and close look at those times when children do wonderful things and experience powerful learning that occurs spontaneously and without clear precipitation by the "planned curriculum," whether it be the framework of big ideas or the project approach. While I am focusing in this book on the aspects of planning and foresight that can inspire you to develop meaningful curriculum, it is assumed that this environment would provide a rich facilitative environment for the opportunities for such ordinary moments to occur. Because in this curriculum framework you are tuned into children's thinking and actions, such ordinary moments are more likely to be noticed and explored. In other words, it is a question of focus, rather than a difference in goals or values, that explains the difference between big ideas and ordinary moments.

Big Ideas and the "Quest for Essence"

Another way of thinking about a big idea is to think of it as what Brooks and Brooks (2000) talk about as the "quest for essence," or "structuring learning around primary concepts." From this perspective, constructivist teachers focus on big ideas because of the importance of looking at the whole rather than the parts. This emphasis on concepts as wholes rather than breaking concepts down into parts relates to the ultimate goal of education, which is that students will obtain deeper and more meaningful understanding rather than proficiency in disconnected elements. Factual rather than conceptual understanding—learning parts without seeing how they connect and relate to the larger picture—leads to disconnected and ultimately unsatisfying and incomplete learning for the student. The construction of knowledge requires holistic understanding.

An important reason for focusing on the whole rather than parts, as put forward by Brooks and Brooks (2000), is that complex, big ideas allow for children to engage at many different levels. There is a built-in multiplicity of possibilities that cannot occur in the context of learning the part of a larger whole. Broad concepts allow for the range of interests and variations in student background, providing "multiple entry points for students: some become engaged through practical responses to problems, some analyze tasks based on models and principles, and others interpret ideas through metaphors and analogies from their unique perspectives. The environment and the use of broad concepts invite each student to participate irrespective of individual styles, temperaments, and dispositions" (Brooks & Brooks, 2000, p. 58).

This brief introduction will frame the big ideas presented in this book. Let's now launch into one big idea in the next chapter. After that, I'll step back and consider some issues in implementation that might be provoked as you read it.

CHAPTER 2

Light as an Introduction to Big Ideas

Let's return to Peter and Adrienne's explorations of light and reflection described at the beginning of the previous chapter. What kinds of connections can be made across the curriculum? To explore this, it is necessary to think deeply about light and reflection and to examine the nature of what it is children will learn that can transcend the scientific domain. For example, one of the things that you can see children exploring in this context is the nature of symmetry, particularly in the use of mirrors. Symmetry, repetition, patterns: these are ideas that can certainly be traced to mathematics, but they also can be identified as key ideas in much of children's literature, including poetry and stories, and in art and music.

To get specific about light, let's look at how Peter and Adrienne's teacher, Jan, began thinking and learning about this big idea as she thought about what she would do. She began by reflecting on her own knowledge base. She found that, despite an introductory physics class in college, she had little enduring understanding of what light is and what might be related to it. She knew that she had always been fascinated with prisms and rainbows, but would have found it difficult to explain them. She had some memories of a problem with defining light and knew that it was both a wave and a particle, but she didn't really understand what that meant. As a kindergarten teacher, she felt it was developmentally inappropriate to teach such science content knowledge anyway and so was not overly concerned with her own lack of knowledge at this point. And she was not going to let this lack of knowledge or understanding stop her from pursuing this curriculum topic area.

She also was uncertain how much her kindergartners knew about or would be interested in light. She did know that they loved to fiddle with the light switches whenever they had a chance, a prohibited activity! And she had noticed that some plastic mirrors that she had put out for a math patterning activity were popular items, with some of them disappearing. The children didn't seem to use them just for patterning, but were using them to look at other things as well.

She began her preparation by deciding to start with science, and started by providing the children with flashlights and mirrors, just to see if they were interested and what they might do with them. She was curious about what questions they might pursue in their explorations. She also decided to gather some resources for herself, both adult science works on light and reflection and children's books. When she went to the library catalog, she was surprised to find that much of the work under the subject category of "light" was related to art, literature, and poetry! So she gathered some of those materials as well, knowing that as she expanded the connections they would come in handy.

And so her journey began, and as she read, watched the children experiment, and began adding different materials and activities to their ever-expanding exploration of the topic, quite naturally the curriculum began branching out. Let's see where Jan's journey took her. As she watched the children playing with flashlights, mirrors, and cellophane, she observed the following episode.

▼ ◄ ▲ ▼ ◄ ▲ ▼ ◄ ▲ ▼ ◄ ▲ ▼ ◄ ▲ ▼ ◄ ▲ ▼ ◄ ▲

Adrienne took the flashlight over to the water table, and shined the light onto the water. She looked at the way the flashlight was reflecting off of the boats, but mostly looked at the reflection of the flashlight through the water onto a piece of Mylar lying in the water. She then walked over to the teacher's desk and shined the flashlight through the water in a vase of flowers. The crystal in the vase produced a kind of prism, reflecting some colors onto the wall behind the desk. Adrienne shined the light onto the wall, as though she was looking for the color. Then she shined the light through the vase again, but the color didn't appear because the angle wasn't just right.

Jan considered this episode, and the next day brought in some inexpensive prisms for the children to use with the flashlights. She also placed containers of water on the table where the flashlights were. As a precaution, she waterproofed the flashlights by wrapping them in leak-proof plastic bags. As she expected, some of the children began shining the flashlights into the water, but they didn't use the prisms. Wondering why, she tried experimenting with them herself and found that she couldn't make the colors appear in the classroom. In fact, she found that even in the brightest sunlight, it was fairly difficult to make the prisms work as they are "supposed" to.

▼ ◄ ▲ ▼ ◄ ▲ ▼ ◄ ▲ ▼ ◄ ▲

From these initial explorations, Jan concluded that the children were indeed interested in experimenting with light and reflection; that the prisms that she had available to her were not easy enough to use for young children to experiment with them, but that the use of light to produce color was of interest; and that there was some puzzling about where the light is coming from when it is reflected.

▼ ◄ ▲ ▼ ◄ ▲ ▼ ◄ ▲ ▼

Covers on flashlights create interesting patterns to explore.

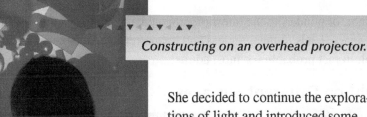

Constructing on an overhead projector.

She decided to continue the explorations of light and introduced some colored translucent paper and some Plexiglas paddles of different colors to the mix of materials available for the children's experimentation. This activity expanded, gradually, into the construction of flashlight "covers" made out of different colors and different cut-out designs that the children used to project onto the wall. The children also began constructing with different plastic and glass objects on the top of the overhead projector.

What Do You Need to Know about Light as a Scientific Concept?

A good starting point for many of the big ideas presented in this book is to examine what we know about the topic from a scientific perspective. Then, we can use this as a springboard to related concepts and curriculum areas.

Here are some basic categories of the concept of light that can help us as we look at this issue and try to determine what are appropriate arenas for children's exploration and experimentation.

Making Light Happen: The Production and Transmission of Light

Producing light—turning lights on and off, shining light on different things, fascinates young children. For younger children, this seems to be largely a question of control, and they may be interested in more prolonged play with turning lights on and off. But for most children, and especially older children, being able to determine when and where light shines is itself an area for experimentation. Given the right place in which to do this, and the right materials available to shine on and through, this can lead to further questions and experimentation.

Questions about the actual transmission of light are inappropriate for young children, since light travels faster than anything we currently know (186,000 miles per second, or 300,000 km per second). Posing questions to children about the speed of light, or pondering the question of what happens to the light when you flash it into space, leads to meaningless and unanswerable questions for children at this level; in fact probably for most adults!

Light on Different Surfaces

A fascinating realm for exploration is shining light through or on different materials: transparent materials such as glass, clear Plexiglas, and water; translucent materials such as paper of different grades of clarity, including cellophane; and opaque materials that light cannot pass through. This form of experimentation often leads to questions and experiments relating to shadows, their changing forms, and their changing nature depending on the object on which the light is shining to create the shadow. What are the different kinds of shadows produced by opaque versus translucent materials, for example? Does color produce colored shadows?

The underlying, and more abstract, scientific concepts here have to do with what happens to the light when it hits the surface—is it reflected, refracted, or absorbed? Many concepts related to reflection, refraction, and absorption are too complex for young children, despite the reference to and focus on these concepts in many elementary science textbooks. However, there are aspects of these concepts that are observable to young children and can be experimented with as long as you as the teacher do not dwell on the underlying explanations that are not accessible to the students. Older children, for example, can experiment with the impact of light on different shades of gray and black and which surfaces get hot. Deeper understanding and explanations need to wait, however.

The Relationship between Light and Vision: How Do We See Light?

Here the issue of experimentation and observability make it difficult to see how children could begin to understand the underlying concepts. Here are a few of these scientific concepts:

- Light is a radiant energy wave and other waves, such as X-rays, radio waves, and ultraviolet rays, are not visible.

- An object is seen by us when light travels from its source to the object and then into the eye, producing an image on the retina.

- This image is interpreted by the brain to create vision.

It is interesting to note that these inaccessible facts (to young children by experimentation) are those areas where children tend to have the most unusual and interesting misconceptions. For example, it is a very common belief of many children that light emanates from objects directly, rather than being reflected off of them, thus permitting us to see them. We can see in their experimentation with shining light, particularly on reflective surfaces, what kinds of questions and misconceptions they may have and can engage children in interesting discussions about their beliefs.

What Is Color and Where Does It Come From?

Despite the fact that color is a major focus in a good deal of early childhood science curriculum, there are limits to what children can understand about color beyond color identification and a few facts about color mixing. This is because color is determined by the wavelength of the light; this can be seen when light passes through a prism, which breaks it up into the seven colors that form the light spectrum. Aside from noticing the beauty of the colors produced by a prism, there is little in creating those colors that helps us understand the science of color. Again, even adults have major misconceptions about the nature of color vision, which is created when an object absorbs all of the colors of the spectrum except the one that we see, which is reflected off of the object to the cones, or sensors, within the eye. Nor does it make a lot of sense that white light is a mixture of all the colors in the spectrum. Children (and adults) have very reasonable questions about that, particularly in terms of the relationship between white and black. Shouldn't white things be hot in the sun? Why not?

And what exactly do children learn about color by mixing colors? What does it mean to a child to learn that blue and yellow makes green? Color mixing, a popular experience in early childhood curriculum, has a very limited relationship to children's understanding of the big ideas of light. Nonetheless, the observation and experimentation with color is intriguing to young children, and there are ways that color can be incorporated into activities as a variable that are appropriate and that maintain and stimulate children's interest about other questions that they are capable of experimenting with.

How Is Light a Big Idea, beyond Science?

Now that we've examined light from a scientific perspective, let's think about light from the child's perspective. Here is where children are capable of the kind of integrative, noncompartmentalized thinking that I am talking about in this book. As we look at what children do, the questions they ask, and the things they are interested in, we can gain ideas about directions in which to go that go beyond science and that connect science with the other curricular domains. I will mention two aspects of light that particularly lend themselves to thinking about connections: reflection and contrast. Both of these have broad and interesting implications for curriculum planning.

Reflection: Repetition, Patterns, and Symmetry

As children explore with light, it is important to introduce highly reflective materials such as mirrors, Mylar, and other shiny surfaces. As children explore mirrors, in particular, they begin to notice the reproduction of images. Children's fascination with kaleidoscopes leads to logical extensions, and older children can spend a good deal of time on the subject of kaleidoscopes, periscopes, telescopes, and other uses for mirrors, actually constructing simple versions of them. Younger children can focus on the use of mirrors to make patterns. Providing younger children with Mylar-covered Plexiglas or other materials that can be duct-taped together to make simple, freestanding mirrors leads to interesting experimentation with the reproduction and repetition of images. The integration of these materials with flashlights and other light-producing objects adds to the fascination.

As children become fascinated with symmetry, connections with patterning and other math concepts are logically integrated. The use of materials such as pattern blocks, unit cubes, and other materials that lend themselves to illustrating symmetry can be used alone or can be directly connected to the study of light through the use of small mirrors. Later, when we look at the big idea of balance, we will explore symmetry in a different way, but with regard to light, the focus on the use of mirrors certainly introduces the ideas of symmetry and repetition that are important aspects of mathematical thinking.

Probably the clearest connection across domains is in the arena of visual arts. Displaying and talking with children about art that illustrates symmetry, reflection, and patterns can make the concept clear. Here is an example of how a teacher could use photographs and pictures to do this.

▼◄ ▲▼◄ ▲▼◄ ▲▼◄ ▲▼◄ ▲▼◄ ▲

Margot, a first grade teacher, has copied and enlarged several pictures and photographs that incorporate reflection in them (see, for example, Miller, 1998). The children talk about what they see, about what reflects, and about where they might look for reflection. They then go on a "reflection walk" around the neighborhood. Margot takes a digital camera and a clipboard, and as the children find reflections, she notes them on the clipboard and has one of the children take a digital picture of the reflection.

Judy, walking with her friend Bobbi, sees a puddle, and excitedly points it out to Margot. "Look, it reflects the tree by the sidewalk!" Bobbi steps in the puddle, and the reflection is disturbed. "Where'd it go?" Judy asks. The two girls have Margot come over and take a picture of the disturbed puddle. They continue walking, and later return the same way to find the puddle calm and reflecting. Judy gets excited again and has Margot take another picture of the puddle reflecting the tree overhead. Then she jumps in it. "Look, I made it go away now!"

When they return to the classroom, Margot has the children write and draw in their journals what they saw that reflected things. While they do that, she prints out the pictures of what they saw, and posts them on the chalkboard. After they've written for a while, she asks if anyone had written about any of the pictures and writes down their comments on the chalkboard under the pictures.

The next day, Margot puts out the materials that had been out the week before—mirrors, flashlights, cellophane paper, and various objects. She asks them if they can see any reflections now that are similar to what they saw on their walk. The children begin exploring the materials, and Judy goes to get some cups of water, trying to reproduce the puddle she saw on the walk.

In this example, Margot has effectively stimulated a good deal of exploration about reflection that began with the provocation of photographs and pictures with reflections. In addition to serving as a provocation, it is an excellent idea to incorporate real art into the classroom for a variety of purposes, particularly as connected to the explorations of the children.

Contrast

Another area in which extensions across the curriculum are clear is the idea of contrast. Experimenting with light and dark, with on and off, leads children to think about the ideas of the absence of light and the absence of dark. In art this is an important concept—that of empty space. And visual art lends itself to contrast in obvious ways. Giving children opportunities to paint with limited options, such as black paper and white paint, or white paper and black paint, makes the contrast evident. Outlines are themselves studies in contrast; children can outline shadows or they can outline projected pictures on the wall. Studying outlines leads to explorations of spaces and shapes, comparisons of size and perspective.

In the domain of language and literacy, contrast can be seen dramatically in the uses of language—studies of opposites or of descriptive language for contrasting emotions. Role-playing, mime, and studying facial expressions can further enhance the experiences of contrast for young children.

And there are many children's books that highlight the ideas of contrast, such as Tana Hoban's books on contrasts, *Over, Under and Through* and *Exactly the Opposite* (Hoban, 1973, 1997). Illustrations themselves can be based on contrast (see *Black on White* and *White on Black*, by Tana Hoban, 1993a, 1993b, for example) that can be studied, posted, and pointed out to children. Then you can provide children with opportunities to do their own illustrations and artwork using outlines and cutouts.

Studying stark differences is an interesting approach to social studies as well. If this is done thoughtfully, one can find examples of extremes in cultural practices and experiences—extremes of climate, radically different styles of dress, or of transportation. Focusing on difference should always be paired with focusing on similarities, because ultimately our goal is for children to see the connections as well as the uniqueness of people of different cultures.

Some of the resources that come to mind to incorporate into a study of contrasts in the area of social studies are Peter Spier's book *People* (1988) and *The Material World* (Menzel, 1994), both of which do a wonderful job of presenting the range of variation across the globe. For young children, you can begin with their own lives, comparing the things that individual children use in their own lives with those of others throughout the world. For example, have all of the children bring into the classroom a common object—a cup they use, their pajamas, chopsticks, or a spoon. Then consider the similarities and differences and compare what you see in your classroom to those of other countries. You can also initiate a conversation between the children in your classroom and a classroom from another country; there are many ways of developing these "pen pal" connections, and they are effective ways of studying variation and similarities across cultures.

Making Connections

One of the important roles of the teacher in this framework is to help children see the connections across the varieties of experiences that relate to the big ideas underlying light. This does not have to be done too forcefully, rather, by subtle reminders of the previous experiences. You could say, "Remember how we explored how different things look when the light is on and when it is off?"

However, it is important to realize that sometimes the experiences in proximity are enough for children to make connections. Listen to what children talk about spontaneously, and you will start to hear the ways they are (or are not) seeing the relationships across the different experiences in different domains. Very often, a teacher who listens well will be able to use those comments to make the connections explicit to the rest of the class. Here is an example.

Angela, a kindergarten teacher, had initiated a number of experiences focusing on contrast. She was attentively observing the children as they read Tana Hoban's (1997) book *Exactly the Opposite*.

Randy, a very verbal and bright five-year-old, says while he looks at the book, "Look, there is a picture of light and dark. We made light and dark in the bathroom with flashlights!"

At the classroom circle later in the day, Angela was leading a discussion about what the children had been doing during activity time. She says, "Randy, I heard you talking about light and dark. Could you share that with us?" Randy happily shares what he had noticed about the relationship between the book and their activities. The other children listen attentively, and Liesl says, "Lots of things are really different!"

Angela says, "Let's make a list of the things we've noticed that are totally different from each other." She starts writing on a piece of chart paper, putting down on one side "light" and on the other "dark." The children start calling out other things that are opposites.

▼◄ ▲▼◄ ▲▼◄ ▲▼◄ ▲▼◄ ▲▼◄ ▲▼◄ ▲

In this way, Angela is able to make explicit some of the underlying connections across activities and across domains, but these connections are instigated by the children. Later in this book, I will talk about the importance of listening to children and how the teacher can pay attention to the children's spontaneous comments. This can be a rich source of information and ideas for the teacher to plan extensions, as well as a way to help children make the connections across the curriculum. Observations and attention to what children are saying is an important resource for the teacher to make things explicit.

Another way to stimulate connections is through the physical environment and documentation. Young children are very visual, and often the presence of something—a poster on the wall, small displays on a shelf, children's work on a bulletin board—can provoke their thinking and connections. Displays in the environment can also be referred to in discussions by the teacher and other children. Returning to Peter and Adrienne's explorations with the flashlight and colored paper, what are some of the things that a teacher could do to provoke thinking in this way?

1. Find photographs and works of art that show reflection. Here are a few examples: *Shadows and Reflections* by Tana Hoban (1990) and photographs in Stephen R. Swinburne's *Guess Whose Shadow?* (1999). Good examples are everywhere, and they are accessible through any library or on the Internet. Copy them, enlarge them if necessary, and put them up on the wall. Putting up a series of pictures that are from different sources is provocative itself.

2. After reading one of the many children's books that have illustrations that incorporate pictures of reflection, make copies of the pictures and post them

on the wall. Leave room on the wall for children to put up the things that they find in books, too. The displays should be dynamic, and children should participate in making them.

3. Take digital pictures of the children as they engage in the activity. In this case, pictures of Peter and Adrienne's flashlight shining. Put the pictures on the wall, and encourage them to talk about what they were doing. You can write down some of the things they say and put them up by the picture. When you do this, be sure to talk with the children about what you are writing down and why. "This is really interesting what you are doing—maybe this picture will give you and other children ideas about what else you can do."

4. As the activities expand and are extended into a range of areas, keep a visual record of all that the class is doing. A large web on the wall showing the connections and how one activity led into another can help the children see the interconnections and can remind them of the things they did previously. Again, it can give them new ideas about what is possible to do next. If you are short on wall space, use large picture books that the children can participate in making (depending on their age) that are available and referred to. You may need to model the use of such reference books.

One of the things that you will find is that if you model this kind of documentation in your classroom, the children will begin to pick up on it and, in a constructivist environment that values children's activity, involvement, and initiative, they will begin to take on the role of documenting their own work. This interest in and willingness to document their own work will be even more likely to happen with older children (kindergarten through second grade); but preschool-age children will certainly participate in the process. The documentation, then, becomes an important part of the curriculum itself. Let's look at how one teacher uses documentation in this way.

Jan has posted on the wall some pictures of the children's flashlight explorations, including Peter's and Adrienne's. Adrienne is looking at the pictures one morning with Mandy, and begins telling Mandy what they were doing. "See, the flashlight was making red!" She is referring to what happens when they were shining the flashlight through red cellophane. Next to those pictures are some of other children putting aluminum foil into which they had poked holes on the end of the flashlight. Mandy says, "Wow! I wonder what would happen if you used the red paper!" Later, during activity time, Mandy and Adrienne try poking holes in the cellophane and shining the

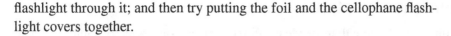

flashlight through it; and then try putting the foil and the cellophane flashlight covers together.

This is an example of how the documentation itself can stimulate extended theory-building in ways that probably would not have occurred without the documentation, and in ways that did not require the teacher to get involved directly. Documentation, and the environment in general, can extend your role as a teacher in important ways that you can use to provoke and facilitate children's engagement and work.

Resources for the Exploration of Light

What are the resources that you can draw on when you don't know what to do next and when you want to generate more ideas around a big idea? I will organize the resources available that I have found useful using the following categories for each chapter: children's literature; ideas from the creative arts; teacher resources; commercial materials, toys, and games; ideas involving technology, including computers, video, and digital cameras; and miscellaneous ideas (e.g., noncommercial materials).

Once I have considered some of the resources available, I will then go through the connecting curriculum domains and realms that make sense for the idea being developed. My hope is that the integration of curriculum domains will make it difficult to pull apart, What is math? What is social studies? Nonetheless, it is a valuable and necessary exercise, given the pressures to "cover" the various curriculum areas. This is also a way to think about what you are expected to cover and to ensure that those topics and subjects are covered in a meaningful way. As an example, let's say that your school district expects children during the first grade year to work on patterning. You can ensure that patterning is dealt with extensively, and, most importantly, in an interesting and meaningful context, through the children's work with mirrors as you work on the big idea of light. You would want to make sure that the materials and ideas that you incorporate in your classroom require children to deal with patterns, and you would also make sure that you document and describe what the children are doing in that realm. As you consider each big idea presented in this book, think about how you could coordinate with the administrative requirements (standards, adoptions, benchmarks) that you are faced with and how the suggestions for assessment and documentation could assist you in meeting them.

I'll start with the resources available to generating curriculum and some of the resulting ideas that you can actually incorporate into your classroom practice around the topic of light.

Children's Literature

It's important to note that the ideas offered here are very selective, intended just to give you an idea of what is possible. Sometimes, searches for relevant children's books do not yield the most relevant books, so it is important to be creative in how you find books. You can start with the obvious, as in the title of the book or the subject matter dealt with. Thus, Margaret Wise Brown's book *Goodnight Moon* (1991) would come to mind quickly because it addresses night and day, dark and light. Other obvious books might include books about shadows (such as *Shadow Play, Night Haiku* by Penny Harter, 1994; Frank Asch's *Moonbear's Shadow*, 1999), books and stories about mirrors (such as McLoughlin Bros., 1980; Zubrowski, 1992), books and stories about color (such as Hoban, 1995; Gold-Dworkin & Ullman, 1999), and illustrations showing the effects of light and color (such as Joanne Ryder's *Night Gliders*, 1996). But sometimes the images in a book or the way the book is constructed might be related. For example, if we start to think about patterns and symmetry, then books such as Ann Jonas's *Round Trip* (1983) and *Reflections* (1987) could be connected and could lead to interesting activities and ideas.

One good example of how to use children's literature is *Water Music*, a book of poems for children by Jane Yolen (1995), with photographs by Jason Stemple. A large and beautiful photograph accompanies each poem, and a number of the photographs show reflections. The most striking is the photograph accompanying the poem fittingly titled "Reflection." The photograph is of a lake by a snow-covered mountain; in the lake the cloud-filled sky is reflected, but the sky is not shown in the photograph. Reading the poem to children, and studying the picture, would be a wonderful project in itself. Older children could pay more attention to the meaning of the poem, trying to connect the lines of the poem to elements of the picture.

Two other books that have illustrations (not photographs) that show aspects of shadows and reflection are Joseph Bruchac and Jonathan London's *Thirteen Moons on Turtle's Back: A Native American Year of Moons*, illustrated by Thomas Locker (1992), and Lynne Cherry's *A River Ran Wild* (1992). In these two books, only some of the illustrations would lead to speculation or interest in light, shadow, or reflection; but by selecting out of each book the pages that are illustrative, and copying them or enlarging them, you can help children see the many ways reflection is portrayed.

All three of these books would be located by searching for the obvious keywords—light, reflection, water. But just by looking through the books that you have on hand, you will undoubtedly find some illustrations of shadows or reflection that can be useful. Older children can engage in that kind of searching themselves.

I have listed some other books that you might find useful in the resource section at the end of this chapter.

Creative Arts

We are at an advantage with this topic, since a great deal of art revolves around the use of light and patterns. You can consult books with collections of fine art for examples of prints that could be copied and enlarged, put on the wall, and used to generate ideas by the children.

Shadow puppets are another logical source for generating questions and activities about light. Consulting a book about the different ways shadow puppets are used and made could give you many interesting ideas for use with children (such as *No Sweat Projects: Shadowy Science*, by Jess Brallier, 2000; *Shadow Theater (Rainy Days)*, by Vanessa Bailey, 1990). For example, children can create shadow puppets, testing them out as they make them, and numerous questions and ideas will come out of the process. Next to the table where they are creating puppets, set up an area in which light is projected. The children are sure to experiment with other aspects of projection, particularly if you make a variety of materials available such as cellophane in different shapes. Follow up on their questions and experimenting and you will have numerous new ideas.

The light table, recently made more common by interest in the work in Reggio Emilia schools, is also a wonderful tool for experimenting with light. Providing many different objects and materials to play with on the light table can result in other questions for experimentation. And light tables do not have to be expensive, cumbersome pieces of furniture. They can easily be constructed out of Plexiglas (or real glass) covered with filmy material, with a lightbulb placed underneath. Nor do light tables have to be positioned horizontally. Think about mounting one on the wall, and see what children might do.

Overhead projectors are another tool for light experimentation and can be used in numerous ways. Try setting up an overhead projector in different parts of the room where children have access to materials to use on it and observe what they do.

Teacher Resources

One book that is a must-read for anyone interested in exploring light with children is *What Children Bring to Light: A Constructivist Perspective on Children's Learning in Science*, by Bonnie Shapiro (1994). In this book, the author explores the ideas about light that children ages six to thirteen hold. Through interviewing them, interacting with them around different activities, and, most importantly, listening to them, she discovered that children's ideas about light are very individualistic and grounded in their different approaches to understanding and learning. This book will give any teacher, including those of you who work with younger children, many ideas about potential questions and explorations of light.

Another book that describes the explorations of light and shadow from the Reggio Emilia schools is *Everything Has a Shadow Except Ants* (Reggio Emilia, 1999), a wonderful compilation of the children's experimentation and representations of their ideas about the topic. Two other books from Reggio Emilia, created by the children of the Diana Municipal Preschool, both called *Light: Children's Thoughts, Images, and Explorations* (Reggio Emilia, 2000a, 2000b), could also be the source of inspiration for activities and provocations related to light and shadow.

Other teacher resources are the many art books that incorporate images of light, shadow, and color. These include *Light and Color*, by Frank Millson (1996); and *Color and Light in Nature*, by David Lynch and William Livingston (2001). Other examples could be found in many of the books documenting the work of Andy Goldsworthy, such as *Time*, (Goldsworthy, 2000) and *Andy Goldsworthy: A Collaboration with Nature* (Goldsworthy & Goldsworthy, 1990). You can also view selected works by him online (best done through a Google search).

Videotapes that might provide ideas and inspiration include Dale Chihuly's *River of Glass* (Chihuly, 1999). In this video, Chihuly, the well-known glass-blowing artist, displays his work throughout Venice in beautiful scenes that highlight the light reflections and color of the glass on the water. The use of clips from such a videotape, which on the surface would not be for young children, could be particularly effective for stimulating thought about reflection and color.

Movement and Music

In the domain of social interaction, children can engage in activities that involve miming, or mirroring, what they see others doing. This exercise, common in music and movement, is an opportunity for exploring how what your own body does may look like what another is doing. To music, children can challenge each other to replicate their movements. This can be done in pairs, or as a follow-the-leader game, or with "Simon says," where one child is creating the movement for others to reproduce. If you have access to wall mirrors the experience is enhanced, because the child can see both himself and the other child in the mirror.

Here is an example of how social mirroring can be done with children.

Nick sets up the large clear piece of Plexiglas so it stands upright using a wooden stand. In his kindergarten classroom the children have been studying mirrors, focusing particularly on making patterns with mirrors and attribute blocks, the focus primarily being on mathematics concepts. He wants to push the children's thinking about mirrors to the level of a "big idea." At group time, he points to the Plexiglas, which is clear, and says that someone gave him this magic mirror. The children are fascinated and listen attentively for him to tell them what its magic is. Nick says that he has to show them how it works.

He stands on one side of the Plexiglas and invites Maddie to stand on the other side. As Maddie moves, he imitates her every movement. She tries to trick him by moving her hand quickly and then stopping it. The children laugh and cheer her on. Nick says that anyone can try it during activity time to see whether the magic will work on him or her.

Several children choose to try the magic mirror, and rowdy games ensue, with children trying to mime each other's actions. Annie gets a marker, and, as it is customary in this classroom to draw on Plexiglas, begins to draw on it while her friend Stephanie draws at the same time on the other side. Another pair of children, David and Nastassia, build identical block structures on either side of the magic mirror. The mirroring activities become so popular that Nick brings out more magic mirrors for the children to use, pieces of Plexiglas of different sizes.

Nick videotapes the children as they engage in this activity and, after a couple of days, shows the group some clips of the magic mirror and the different things that they came up with. They have a discussion about how difficult some of the mirroring was to do. David talks about how it was hard to figure out where to put some of the blocks, particularly when Nastassia placed them on the opposite side of the mirror.

▼◄ ▲ ▼◄ ▲ ▼◄ ▲ ▼◄ ▲ ▼◄ ▲ ▼◄ ▲ ▼◄ ▲

The videotape was a rich source of examples of problem solving and innovative ideas for Nick to take note of in his individual assessments of children. Nick also found himself observing the children as they worked together in dyads, because a number of children had difficulty with the cooperation required for some of the ideas they came up with. Conflicts and interesting conflict resolution strategies became the subject of continuing discussion by the group. Some of the children chose not to participate in this activity, and Nick noted that as well, wondering about the negotiation strategies required to engage in this activity.

Incorporating Technology

We've already referred to the use of a number of technologies to enhance children's exploration of light as a big idea, particularly in the documentation process, but also as an integral part of the curriculum. Among these are the use of digital cameras and

28

videotape recordings. There are some additional resources that deserve mentioning, which could be excellent provocations for children's exploration, or which could be brought in as supplemental resources as their inquiry proceeds.

Some software can give children opportunities to experiment with symmetry in ways not possible with other media. Kid Pix (Learning Company), as an example, has features that give children access to ways of experimenting with reproduction and creating mirror images that raise issues for young children. Playing with a child-accessible painting software program can also add to their experiences.

There are also a large number of websites related to symmetry and patterns. Just to give one example, there are websites relating to Snowflake Bentley (http://snowflakebentley.com), the man who described and discovered some of the patterns of snowflakes and documented them (see also the excellent book of his photographs in Bentley, 2000a). Some of these websites provide further resources for creating snowflakes and experimenting with their symmetry and patterns.

Bringing It All Together: Teachers and Children Explore Reflection

In this section, I'll describe how a teacher could implement a study of light across the curriculum. Let's start with the first grade, and then think about what might be different for four-year-old children.

A First Grade Classroom

Carlos begins by showing his first grade class some clips from the Dale Chihuly videotape *River of Glass* (described earlier) that shows his large-scale art glass being made and then exhibited in natural settings throughout Venice, on the water. Carlos's goal is to provoke the children's interest in and questions about light shining through things, color, and reflection. As he predicted, the children are fascinated by the video clips—some of them ask to see more of the videotape, which he says will be available for them to look at during activity time.

He suggests that those who are interested could construct their own "glass" structures using cellophane, cardboard, Mylar, and other materials available in the construction center, where the children have access to many other materials, including clay, string, wire, and glue. (The children have had some previous experience working with these other materials, and most of them feel comfortable incorporating them into their projects.) He also sets up an area where the resulting structures can be displayed, with an overhead projector, a powerful light source, and a hanging sheet to use as a screen onto which they can project their structures.

As the children create different structures, they begin to expand their ideas. Some create constructions that rest on the ground; some begin to make hanging structures; and others experiment with the materials but don't create any final product. After a number of different structures have been put into the "display area," the children decide that they want to have a show. All the lights are turned off in the room, shades down, and each construction is featured and discussed, using the light source. Then Carlos gives some of the children flashlights to shine on the construction from different angles, creating more reflections and projections throughout the room. Tommy says, "Hey, let's make our own videotape!" Carlos suggests that some of them plan it and that he will get a video camera to use for this purpose.

The next day, Carlos shows the Chihuly video clips again to the class. One of the children suggests that water be brought into the display area, with some of the constructions suspended over the water, and some of them placed on top of blocks set in the water. A group of them work on expanding the display area, hanging a number of other sheets in strategic places, and creating panels of cellophane that could be incorporated into the display.

A small group of the children begin planning the video, and, on Carlos's suggestion, they map it out on a large piece of paper. They also begin testing how the video camera will work to capture the reflections. During this period, other children continue to create structures, and Carlos notices many of the ideas being incorporated into the new constructions.

The process of filming the video is a project in itself, and the children quickly discover the importance of light and how difficult it is to know where to set up the camera in relation to the light sources. Carlos capitalizes on this difficulty, bringing in photography books and art books that show different uses and placement of light. Some of the children explore this further. And, because they've communicated about what they are doing to their parents, they start hearing about different resources that are available to them. Bobbi's aunt, for example, is a collector of antique glass and brings in her collection to show the class. All of the children start to bring in unusual pieces of glassware from home and share the stories of the glass pieces. For example, Lory shares an antique mirror that she got from her grandmother who died. As they look at the mirror, some of them notice that the paint on the mirror has come off in places, which leads them to ask about how mirrors are made. Another parent is an optometrist and brings in lenses of different kinds for the children to look at. While she is sharing the lenses, the children suggest that they be used in the display area to see if different lenses project differently on the screen they've set up. And another parent is able to help Carlos arrange a visit to a glass-blowing studio, to which the children come prepared with a whole set of questions they have generated as a group.

The showing of the videotape doesn't culminate the work on light. The children decide that their work is so good that they want to write a letter to Dale Chihuly about what they have done and send a copy of their videotape to his studio. And other work continues, including the study of lenses and extensive exploration of mirrors.

▼◄ ▲▼◄ ▲▼◄ ▲▼◄ ▲▼◄ ▲▼◄ ▲▼◄ ▲

As you can see, the work in this classroom on light could have taken many different forms, depending on what the children become enthusiastic about. Carlos is flexible enough and resourceful enough to be able to capitalize on this excitement. He is able to facilitate and help to coordinate the work of several different groups of children. But a great deal of the success of such an endeavor depends upon the children's ability to be self-directed and resourceful, qualities that Carlos has engendered from the beginning in his classroom. The children in his classroom are not passive; they are actively inquiring into the world around them; and they know that they are supported in this inquiry in many different ways.

How Would This Be Different for a Class of Four-Year-Olds?

▼◄ ▲▼◄ ▲▼◄ ▲▼◄ ▲▼◄ ▲▼◄ ▲▼◄ ▲

Judith, the teacher of the four-year-olds in a full-day preschool program, uses the videotape as a provocation, just as Carlos had done. She chooses a couple of very short clips to share with the children, which serve as an introduction to a large-scale activity she has set up in the project area, an area that includes a water table, the construction corner, and a shelf full of art materials that can be used in both the water table and the construction zone. In place of the usual materials and props that would be in place, she has chosen materials that could be used in reproducing some of the things that are seen in the clips on the video. This includes small boats in the water table, lots of different colors of cellophane on the materials shelves, and anything she can find that is made of Plexiglas or plastic that is opaque in many different colors—materials that resemble glass. She includes a large quantity of small clear plastic cups.

To partially direct their focus, she introduces one particular activity to serve as a starting point for the children. She holds up one of the plastic cups and says, "We have here lots of cellophane and other paper, paint, and glue. . . . Can anyone think of a way that we could make this cup look like the glass we saw in the video?" Aylin says, "We could paint the cup?" "Put some of the red paper on it [the cellophane]!" says Patrick. Judith says, "These are all great ideas—let's see what you can all come up with."

During activity time a large group of the children work on their creations, and Judith notices that they are talking about whether or not you can see through the glass like you could on the video. She has captured a frame of the video and projects it onto the wall while they are working, and they compare what they are doing with the projection.

Aylin, who suggested painting the cups, begins by putting red paint on a plastic cup and holding it up to the light as she makes each stroke. She notices that when she makes two strokes of paint on top of each other, it is more difficult to see through the cup. "Hey, look at this, sometimes it doesn't work!"

Patrick is busy gluing cellophane on the cup, carefully putting strips of different colors on the same cup, with some of the cellophane overlapping. He too notices that where the cellophane overlaps it is harder to see through the cup. He and Aylin hold their cups up to compare and argue about whose cup is better. Other children are busy trying different combinations of paint, cellophane, and other types of paper. One child glues reflective Mylar to the cup and says, "Look, you can't see through mine but you can see in it!"

Because the "glass making" project is next to a table where there are lots of flashlights and a light table, some of the children shine light into their cups and project them onto a large sheet hung next to the light table. Others set their cups on top of the light table, and look at them closely. Patrick starts building with some of the plastic cups on the light table, putting cellophane in some of the cups and not others, and creates a light sculpture.

Other children take the cups over to the water table, where they quickly discover that if they put the painted cups into the water the paint comes off, as does the glued cellophane. This leads to lots of laughter and excitement, and Jeffrey has the idea to put the cellophane inside the cup and float it on the water. He then gets a flashlight and shines it into the cellophane-filled floating cup and exclaims, "Look, the water is turning color now!" as the light shines into the water. The dissolving paint colors the water as well, and the children begin shining the light into the water, watching it change as more and more paint dissolves.

As you can see, a class of four-year-olds can engage in quite sophisticated, yet qualitatively different, experimentation with light and color provoked by the same videotape used in Carlos's first grade class. The key is to provide appropriate materials and to expect simpler experimentation from the preschoolers. As with Carlos's class, these four-year-olds were accustomed to this kind of experimentation and self-directed play and have come to expect the time and resources that they need. They also know that they can go from space to space, they can use materials that are accessible freely, and they can work together peacefully. The teacher has cultivated this kind of theory-building over a long period of time and the classroom culture continues to facilitate it.

Extending Beyond Science: Language and Literacy

▼◄ ▲ ▼◄ ▲ ▼◄ ▲ ▼◄ ▲ ▼◄ ▲ ▼◄ ▲ ▼◄ ▲

Carlos decides to extend the children's work on reflection to other domains. He begins by having a discussion with the children about it, simply posing the question, "Can you think of other ways that we reflect things besides with light?" Jake right away says, "We can reflect with our voices, like echoes!" The children start talking excitedly about the times they've heard echoes, and the discussion takes off onto different children's experiences.

Carlos then reads to them a poem for two voices, one that involves a lot of repetition and call and response. He involves the children in the poem, and they listen attentively. He then suggests that they might want to try to make their own poems for two voices to describe some of the sculptures they have made and proposes that some children might want to form pairs or groups to do this during project time. He tells the children that there are tape recorders available in the writing area as well as chart paper for writing their poems.

As he expected, some of the children are not interested in this project, but several are, and they go to work during project time. They particularly like the opportunity to use the tape recorders, and they listen to their recordings and rerecord over and over. Two children, Alicia and Lucas, decide to use two tape recorders instead of one, with each of them recording their part on their own tape recorder.

The next day, Alicia and Lucas ask if they can perform their poem to the group, and they set up the "stage" at the sculpture area. Behind curtains, they play their tape recordings, which are simple descriptions of the sculptures "echoed" by the second recording, and then expanded on. The children who have made the sculptures are excited and proclaim that they want to make their own poems!

Judith, with her four-year-olds, is interested in some kind of extension of the experience as well. Since the children seemed to focus a great deal on projecting images onto the screen, she decides to introduce shadow plays as a way of extending into body movement and performance. She begins this by making a cardboard "boat" to use as a shadow puppet and tells the children a story about the boat traveling the canals of Venice, which they had seen on the Chihuly video. The children are thrilled, and she tells them that one of the options during project time is that they too can make their own cardboard boats and can create their own stories to perform.

Several of the children take this project on and begin building elaborate cardboard boats, decorating them with paint and gluing paper onto the boats. When they begin to use them as puppets, they discover that some of the things they decorated them with don't show as shadows, and this leads to more discussion about the nature of shadows and why some things don't show up and some do. At the next morning's group time, Judith asks if anyone wants to share their shadow stories, and one pair does an elaborate, long story. As with Carlos's class, the performance inspires some of the other children to choose the project area in which to make shadow puppets, and the children's stories grow.

▼◄ ▲▼◄ ▲▼◄ ▲▼◄ ▲▼◄ ▲▼◄ ▲▼◄ ▲

In both classrooms, some of the extensions take time and work in order to take off. In many cases, it is a few children's enthusiasm that will be contagious and will inspire other children to work on the project introduced by the teacher. In many other cases, it will be the children's instigation that will lead to extensions such as these. Either way, promoting such extensions into literacy takes planning, and if children instigate, they need to be responded to actively, encouraging such forays into other curriculum domains.

Curriculum Domains: A Summary

Here we'll review each of the curriculum domains and try to summarize a few of the ideas that have surfaced that could provide the basis for activities.

Science	Making light with different sources
	Experimenting with mirrors and reflection
	Shining light through things
	Light in water
Mathematics	Symmetry in patterns, with and without mirrors
	Contrasts, geometric figures

Social studies	Social interaction through miming and mimicry
	Studies of contrast and differences
Language and literacy	Children's literature related to light
	Poems and choral chants involving repetition, mimicry
Creative arts	Light designs and sculptures, light tables, and overhead projectors
	Shadow puppetry
Technology	Graphic design software programs, for children and for adults
	Websites on symmetry, kaleidoscopes, snowflakes, and echoes

Remember that these ideas are just initial suggestions. Obviously there are many more ideas out there, and children can be your best source of inspiration as you watch them engage in whatever initial activities or materials you make available to them. The key is to think flexibly and to think across curriculum domains.

You also want to think about provocations. Here are some of the provocations used in this chapter.

Dale Chihuly video, *River of Glass*
flashlights and cellophane
a book of choral poems
shadow puppets
a large piece of Plexiglas introduced as a "magic mirror"
a children's book, such as *Shadows and Reflections* (Hoban, 1990)

In the next chapter, I will back away from discussing a specific big idea and talk about the role of the teacher in a constructivist classroom where it is possible to explore big ideas with children. I'll then refocus on some specific big ideas, including balance, sound, cause and effect, zooming in and out, the wacky curriculum, and transformation.

Keep in mind that the purpose of doing this is to provide *you* with the inspiration to explore any of these, or other, big ideas in your own classroom. You may be having some hesitations, some reasonable skepticism, about whether and how it is possible in the "real world" of today's highly structured and constrained environments. Suspend your skepticism and allow yourself to imagine what is possible—allow yourself to have a vision of utopia that you strive for in your work with children.

Teacher Resources

Brallier, J. (2000). *No Sweat Projects: Shadowy Science*

Goldsworthy, A. (2000). *Time*

Lynch, D. K., & Livingston, W. (2001). *Color and Light in Nature*

Menzel, P. (1994). *The Material World: A Global Family Portrait*

Miller, J. (1998). *On Reflection*

Millson, F. (1996). *Light and Color*

Reggio Emilia. (1999). *Everything Has a Shadow Except Ants*

Reggio Emilia. (2000a, b). *Light: Children's Thoughts, Images, and Explorations* (2 versions)

Shapiro, B. (1994). *What Children Bring to Light: A Constructivist Perspective on Children's Learning in Science*

Zubrowski, B. (1992). *Mirrors: Finding Out About the Properties of Light*

Children's Literature

Adoff, A. & Steptoe, J. (1982). *All the Colors of the Race: Poem*

Asch, F. (1999). *Moonbear's Shadow*

Bailey, V. (1990). *Shadow Theater (Rainy Days)*

Brown, M. W. (2002). *Goodnight Moon*

Bruchac, J., & London, J. (1992). *Thirteen Moons on Turtle's Back: A Native American Year of Moons*

Bulla, C. R. (1994). *What Makes a Shadow?*

Cherry, L. (1992). *A River Ran Wild: An Environmental History*

Farber, N. (1992). *Return of the Shadows*

Gold-Dworkin, H., and Ullman, R. K. (1999). *Exploring Light and Color*

Harter, P. (1994). *Shadow Play, Night Haiku*

Hoban, T. (1973). *Over, Under and Through*

Hoban, T. (1990). *Shadows and Reflections*

Hoban, T. (1993a). *Black on White*

Hoban, T. (1993b). *White on Black*

Hoban, T. (1995). *Colors Everywhere*

Hoban, T. (1997). *Exactly the Opposite*

Jonas, A. (1983). *Round Trip*

Jonas, A. (1987). *Reflections*

Keats, E. J. (2000). *Dreams*

McLoughlin Bros. (1980). *The Magic Mirror: An Antique Optical Toy*

Paul, A. W. (1992). *Shadows Are About*

Ryan, P.M. (2001). *Hello Ocean*

Ryder, J. (1996). *Night Gliders*

Spier, P. (1998). *People.*

Stevenson, R. L. (2002). *My Shadow*

Swinburne, S. R. (1999). *Guess Whose Shadow?*

Tompert, A. (1988). *Nothing Sticks Like a Shadow*

Wiesner, D. (1991b). *Tuesday*

Yolen, J. & Stemple, J. (1995). *Water Music*

Video

River of Glass, 1999

Websites

Snowflake Bentley: Jericho Historical Society. (2000). http://snowflakebentley.com

Kaleidoscopes and Symmetry: www.adrianbruce.com/Symmetry/14.htm

The Invention of Kaleidoscopes:
http://inventors.about.com/library/inventors/blkaleidoscope.htm

Kaleidoscopes: Light Opera Gallery. www.lightopera.com/gallery.cfm

The Kaleidoscope and How It Works: www.kaleidoscopesusa.com/how.htm

Materials

cardboard

flashlights

kaleidoscopes

light table

mirrors

Mylar

overhead projector

pattern blocks

Plexiglas paddles of different colors

shadow puppets

tape recorders, digital cameras, video cameras

translucent paper

unit cubes

water containers

water table

CHAPTER 3

The Constructivist Teacher: Issues in Implementation

N ow that we've looked at one "big idea" being used in a classroom to develop curriculum, let's step back and talk about some issues in being a constructivist teacher who is inspired by Reggio Emilia. You could find yourself feeling that the overall framework presented in this book and the curriculum ideas put forward here are difficult to implement in your own classroom, given the pressures you are under today related to assessment and accountability. In this chapter I would like to address some of the problems and issues that you could face as you teach in ways consistent with constructivism.

But first I have to address an issue that often comes up for teachers. Many will say that they "can't" do something that it isn't "allowed" in their school or district. While I know that there are some very real constraints on teachers, particularly political constraints in many parts of the United States, I would always ask that you try to be very specific and clear about what constraints you are operating under. When you start to get specific about why you can't do something it is amazing how much those constraints become more manageable.

So the first thing to do is to be sure you are clear about what exactly is difficult for you to implement, and why. Where does the constraint come from? Who is telling you what to do or how to do it? Are you positive about the source of the constraints you have identified? And, next, what happens if you don't do what you think you have to do? What are the sanctions, the punishments, the consequences of doing things differently?

Sometimes a reexamination of these questions will change the issues that you have to deal with and permit you to engage with the real difficulties that you may experience as you move toward constructivist practice. That said, let's consider some of the very real constraints and considerations in attempting to implement constructivist curriculum: time, structure, and planning.

Time

The use of time in a classroom has become increasingly problematic for many of us. In many of today's classrooms, particularly in the public school elementary grades, time is extremely structured and segmented. In the most extreme cases, the daily schedule is at least partly centrally determined, with a block of schoolwide time for literacy that is highly scripted using a teacher-directed literacy program. Sometimes this is true for the mathematics curriculum as well. Often children are pulled out of the classroom for special programs such as English as a second language instruction, special reading programs, talented and gifted programs, counseling, special education, or speech and language intervention. Some schools have specialists who are responsible for music, physical education, or computer technology, and often

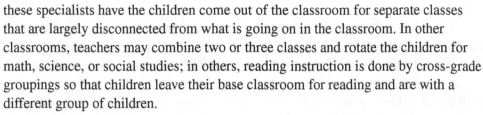

these specialists have the children come out of the classroom for separate classes that are largely disconnected from what is going on in the classroom. In other classrooms, teachers may combine two or three classes and rotate the children for math, science, or social studies; in others, reading instruction is done by cross-grade groupings so that children leave their base classroom for reading and are with a different group of children.

As a result, time is chopped up and segmented by curriculum domains, making it seemingly difficult, if not impossible, to integrate across curriculum areas. There are also fewer long blocks of time when children are together as a cohesive group during which fluid small-group projects could go on with some continuity.

Let's explore approaches to dealing with these difficult issues of time.

To go straight to the core issue, as a teacher you do what you can in the time you have. There are many modifications that can be made in *how* you approach certain explorations and activities that can accommodate restrictions in schedules. At the same time, if you value the principles underlying the need for more time, you can work on the scheduling problems to reduce their impact on the curriculum and on the children, even if you can't solve the scheduling problems. In other words, you do what you can on a day-to-day basis, while still trying to address the larger issues. You "tweak" the schedule as much as you have power to do so to open up larger and larger blocks of time, while participating with colleagues to make that easier within your school. You do the best you can with the time schedules you have to work with, while actively working toward curriculum reform in your school and district that acknowledges the needs children have for connections and curriculum integration that precludes time segregation.

Some of the constraints might be of your own making. Look carefully at the reasons you have for not opening up larger blocks of time in your day. Where do those constraints come from? Are they real? Can you challenge them in appropriate ways? Can you work collaboratively with the English as a second language and reading teachers to come up with a better schedule that will work for your children? Can the PE teacher work with you to incorporate movement into the classroom study of shadows, bringing in her expertise to the classroom and extending the classroom activities into the work she does with the children in the gym?

Even when the constraints are difficult to surmount, though, it is important to realize that constructivism is not an all-or-nothing approach to curriculum. Rather, you can be striving *toward* some of the ideas in this book, doing what you can and seeing how it transpires, then trying a little bit more. Take the hour you have scheduled for science once a week and provide a provocation for some project work related to a big idea that you want to focus on. Then make a connection with the hour you have scheduled for social studies and extend the children's projects over time into that hour. Reenvision the use of those two hours per week. Make a connection with the literature the children are choosing and the writing exercises they are required to do during literacy time. Gradually the lines between those curriculum domains will begin to blur, because the *children* will start to blur them, making connections themselves. This, in turn, will help you to blur them more and more, as it feels comfortable to you.

Your comfort in implementing changes in your curriculum should always be respected. As the teacher responsible for the classroom, your confidence in what you are doing and that you are doing the right thing for the children is the source of your strength as a professional. When you try new things, or change what you have done in the past, you are apt to feel some discomfort. Risk and change involves disequilibrium, some discomfort, and questioning. Am I doing the right thing? Being comfortable is not the issue, but always questioning if what you do is appropriate while being confident that you are on the right path.

The key here is observation and other informal assessment. Paying attention to what the children are doing when they are engaged in the kinds of theory-building across curriculum domains that we are talking about in this book requires systematic and ongoing observation and assessment. Documenting the learning that occurs will provide you with the feedback you need to know if you are doing the right thing. When you start to hear children making connections between what they are doing during "science" time and what they are doing in the gym with the PE teacher, you know you're on the right path. When parents tell you how their children were tracing shadows of the trees in their backyard at different times of the day, after you've been exploring shadows and light in many different ways throughout the week, you know you're on the right path. When a child brings into class a compact disc with sound effects that they discovered in their parent's compact disc collection, excited about sharing the different sounds of rain, you'll know you're on the right path. When you see the children making the connections across all the content areas you teach, and when you see them intrinsically motivated to pursue further exploration of the big ideas you've facilitated them to explore, you'll know you're on the right path.

So here are the things to keep in mind regarding time.

1. Carefully examine your schedule, and think about where you have flexibility.

2. Where you think you don't have flexibility, ask yourself why not. Make sure that the constraints that you perceive are real ones.

3. If you need and/or want to keep your schedule in curriculum segments, begin to see them as interconnected if you don't already. Interconnect just a couple of curriculum areas as a start. Science and social studies are good starting

points, because these are areas where teachers often have the most control over the curriculum.

4. Start as small as you need to; make sure you feel comfortable with the degree of experimentation you take on.

5. Document your explorations. Keep track of what you do and of how children are responding.

6. Collaborate with colleagues in your school if possible but outside your school if necessary. Connect with specialists, other grade level team members, or buddy groups across grade levels.

7. Collaborate with parents. Get parents involved and excited about what you're trying to do. Communicate with parents about what's going on, and connect with their interests and the resources they can provide.

8. Connect with your community. Establish connections with local shops, businesses, cultural groups, and the library. The resources and opportunities for extending the curriculum will multiply the more you connect outside the classroom.

Structure

One of the issues we are faced with in implementing constructivism is how much structure is desirable or necessary for children to be productive and engaged in exploring big ideas.

What is *structure*? Structure is a system of constraints, limits, rules, or guidelines that surround activity. Structure can be implicit or explicit. Structure is provided by you in the form of directions, rules, or tasks. Structure is provided by materials in terms of what possibilities they afford. Structure is provided by the physical environment in terms of what kinds of activities are possible or necessary in the physical space. Structure is also provided by peers in terms of their behaviors, expectations, and desires. And all of these aspects of structure interact. For example, either you could communicate rules for the uses of materials or the behavior of peers in a classroom could make certain activities impossible.

Structure Provided by the Teacher

You set constraints for children's behaviors and activities in a variety of ways. In most classrooms, there is a period of socialization into the classroom culture during which children learn what kinds of things are encouraged and which things are

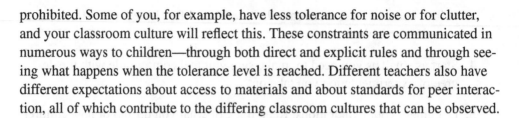

prohibited. Some of you, for example, have less tolerance for noise or for clutter, and your classroom culture will reflect this. These constraints are communicated in numerous ways to children—through both direct and explicit rules and through seeing what happens when the tolerance level is reached. Different teachers also have different expectations about access to materials and about standards for peer interaction, all of which contribute to the differing classroom cultures that can be observed.

Structure Provided by the Materials

Your choices of materials (toys, manipulatives, resources such as books, tools for writing and drawing, art materials, etc.) can provide structure to what children do. Some materials, for example, require adult assistance (a book at a higher level than the child can reach on his or her own; a large block of clay that must be cut with a large knife by an adult before the child can use it). Some materials lend themselves to individual work (puzzles, books); others to social interaction (games, larger-scale building materials). Some materials "suggest" what kinds of things children might explore. Giant LEGOs, for example, encourage building long or high structures and often encourage experimentation with height and length and making comparisons.

Structure Provided by the Physical Environment

The basic design of a room, its furniture, light, ceiling height, all have implications for structure. A large, empty room, for example, will encourage large-scale movement. A room with dividers and clearly delineated spaces for different areas (blocks, reading, projects) will suggest working in one area at a time. A room with furniture and dividers that are moveable and that can serve different purposes will allow for changing the room arrangement, while a room with permanent fixtures and determined furniture will not.

Structure Provided by Peers

Different groups of children can bring different backgrounds, expectations, and experiences to the dynamic mix, and these can have implications for constraints and possibilities for individual children. For example, a group of assertive, self-directed children who have not experienced a lot of constraints can set a tone for the rest of the children in the room who might otherwise have been quieter, more compliant, or less assertive themselves. Even one child who is defiantly oppositional or who exhibits aggressive or violent behaviors can instill a spirit of fear and constraint into an otherwise relaxed and happy group of children. As with the previous categories of structure, these constraints can be subtle or overt.

Let's think about this in terms of children exploring sound in a kindergarten classroom.

Sara has collected a large basketful of materials related to sound, a big idea she would like to explore with the children. This basket contains some different sized pan lids, long plastic tubes, different shaped metal objects, an assortment of bells, some musical instruments, some from other countries, and some different lengths of springs. Sara's plan is to draw on some of these materials when needed as she introduces different ideas about sound and use them selectively based on the children's experimentation and interests.

Sara has a substitute on a day when she's unable to leave extensive lesson plans, and she tells the substitute that she is welcome to use anything she can find in the storage room. The substitute, an inexperienced teacher, takes the basket out of the storage room and dumps the contents out onto the carpet in the middle of the project area, telling the children that they can explore these materials any way they want to.

A number of the children begin exploring the materials, immediately picking up the plastic tubes and banging the pan lids and other metal objects. Because the pan lids are sitting on the carpet, and not hung, they don't make the intriguing ring-like noise that Sara had in mind, and the children lose interest, trying to bang harder and to bang everything in sight with the tubes. Two of the children discover that they can make louder noises by throwing the pan lids down on the carpet, and they begin throwing all the objects, including the musical instruments and the plastic tubes. The substitute, Kerry, has to intervene numerous times, asking the children not to throw the materials because they might hurt someone or the materials. Finally, she tells the children that this is no longer a choice, and she puts the materials back into the basket.

▼◄ ▲▼◄ ▲▼◄ ▲▼◄ ▲▼◄ ▲▼◄ ▲▼◄ ▲

While there is nothing "wrong" with Kerry's effort to have children explore a variety of materials, there was nothing thoughtful about it, and the results were quite predictable. Children will do with the materials what is suggested by the materials. And in this case, there was not a lot of guidance or sense about which materials were available. The resulting random actions on the objects were logical ones. Hitting the different objects was an activity actually suggested by the materials, particularly the plastic tubes. Once one child thought to throw one of the objects down to see what kind of noise it makes and discovered that it makes a louder noise than when it is hit, the other children were likely to follow suit. And without constraints introduced by the teacher ahead of time, there was no reason for them not to do these things.

The question to be asked is what Kerry's purpose was in putting out these materials. What kinds of explorations and experimentations did she have in mind? When

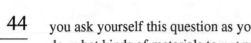

you ask yourself this question as you plan an activity, then it becomes clear what to do, what kinds of materials to *not* put out, and what kinds of direct constraints need to be articulated when introducing the materials.

Too often, we think that materials speak for themselves and that we as teachers don't have to frame their use. But the materials we give children to experience imply multiple activities and actions, and it is our job to think these possibilities through and to plan carefully so that children can have productive and constructive interactions with the materials. We do *not* want to be in a position of constantly controlling children's behavior when they are doing what is logical and suggested by the materials, because when we do that the children are learning more about the need for adult constraint and less about their own self-directed experimentation. Children's own ideas about what to do with the materials are devalued when we have to constrain them. Instead we want to celebrate their own ideas and facilitate them in ways that we feel comfortable with.

Kerry's idea of putting materials out to be explored by the children was not a bad idea. The point to be made here, however, is that it is important to put yourself in the shoes of the child. What will I do in order to explore these materials? What kinds of actions does each suggest individually? What kinds of actions do they suggest given that they are put out together? What makes sense for children to do in this situation? And then the important questions: Are these actions acceptable to the teacher? Are they desirable and productive? Will they lay the groundwork for later experimentation and exploration? What kinds of things can I do to optimize the positive and productive exploration that is desired here? These are the questions that need to be asked whenever you as a teacher create the opportunity for children to explore materials and objects, whenever you present an activity, and whenever you encourage children to play in an area of the room. Your focus should be on trying to look at the possibilities in terms of everything you know about young children, and particularly the children you are working with directly. Your understanding of children of this age with come into play; your understanding of the group dynamics of this class will come into play; and your knowledge of individual children will certainly come into play. For example, if you know that Donna is extremely volatile and emotional today and might be likely to get carried away in such an open-ended exploration of materials, you might have a quiet conversation with her before she begins playing in that area.

Planning

How do we structure the environment and present activities and materials that foster our goals? How can we do this while still responding to children's goals and interests? The issue of structure evolves into a discussion of the role of planning.

In a constructivist classroom, the structure that exists should be purposeful, intentional, carefully thought through to be consistent with the goals you as a teacher, a school, and a community have for children's educational experiences. Planning, the intersection between the teacher's goals and interests and the children's goals and interests, is a key element of the constructivist classroom. Yet planning and structure are both seen by some as antithetical to the constructivist perspective. The myth of constructivism is that you respond to the children's interests and needs, without interjection of your ideas, goals, or needs. But it's important to realize is that the two are not mutually exclusive, and that in a constructivist classroom your ideas, input, and goals *and* children's interests, ideas and goals are interacting. The curriculum is a collaboration among children and teachers, a mutually enriching negotiation and collaboration through which children learn from and with teachers and teachers learn from and with children.

This collaboration is best described by educators grounded in the work of Reggio Emilia, and the concept that captures it the best is the concept of participation. Participation implies the engagement and involvement of those who are connected to children and their education—the parents, the teachers, the community, and, of course, the children. As experienced and knowledgeable teachers, we have a responsibility to plan carefully what we want to see happening in our classroom. Grounded in an understanding of child development, we know what young children are capable of, and we know what directions they will go in as they construct understanding. Experienced in working with children in a variety of different contexts, we have many ideas about what has captured children's attention and engaged them productively in the past, as well as what has not. Being educated people who are continuing to learn and expand our knowledge base, we have knowledge and ideas to share and to be enthusiastic about. Experienced in working with many different adults in different capacities, we know resources to draw on to support young children's struggles and successes. In sum, as teachers we have a great deal to offer.

So when we plan, we draw on all that expertise and experience and offer it to the children with whom we work. But planning must always be paired with its seeming antithesis, which is spontaneity. We cannot plan the magical experiences that happen. We only plan the context in which they occur. Those magical experiences require responses from us that we cannot plan because these experiences cannot be predicted. And so, in addition to the ability to plan carefully, we must also nurture the ability to be flexible, to respond to those things that we cannot predict.

This combination of planning and flexibility is hard to maintain. When we as teachers expend a great deal of time planning and preparing based on what we anticipate and predict will happen, there is the risk of not wanting to let go of what we have predicted. Nor do we want the work we've done to go to waste. Sometimes we will push the anticipated course of events beyond what is warranted given what children do. Sometimes we will continue along the path we have so carefully thought through because we are so excited about it, and we don't realize that the children have been left behind.

This is why observation is the ultimate key to balancing planning and spontaneity. Observing what children actually do, without bias toward what we want to see them doing, is the check on whether we should deviate from what has been planned. This responsiveness to what is really happening—an ability to let go of preconceived ideas—is critical.

The other trap we can fall into when we move forward with what we've planned when children are not on board is to go with children's interests and ideas when they are inappropriate or go in a direction we are not interested in going. It's hard for teachers to acknowledge that children's ideas could be inappropriate, but think about some of the interests that are fueled by commercials, by television shows or movies, or by toys that may be promoting values and interests that are problematic. Some specific examples might be extensive and explicit war play, aggressive violence involving simulated brutality, or hateful and hurtful racism or sexism. All of these examples could be stimulated by children's experiences with videogames, videos, movies, television, books, toys, or comics. While some would argue that if children choose to pursue these interests they should have a safe place in which to explore them, I would argue that exploration of interests of this type is antithetical to the values that are important to model, communicate, and facilitate. Moreover, play along the lines of aggression, violence, and hurtfulness creates an environment of fear, not safety, and a safe environment is one of the most critical contributors to a constructivist classroom setting.

There are a couple of qualifications. First, it is important not to automatically dismiss children's interests without being clear what it is that they want to explore. For example, a child's interest in aircraft carriers may not reflect a desire to engage in aggressive war play, but rather may reflect an interest in the complex community that lives on board a boat. A child's interest in toys that transform from a robot to a vehicle may be piqued by the transformational elements of the materials (quickly moving from a truck to a person) and not related to the story line of the television show that inspired those toys, which may have violent undertones. The scripts that govern children's play with materials and toys, while sometimes stimulated by the toys themselves, may come from many sources. This is why we can see violent and aggressive play happening when children are playing with nonrepresentational materials such as LEGOS or blocks.

Another qualification is that it is important to note when individual children show a tendency toward inappropriate play and to question where those behaviors are coming from. In addition to popular culture and materials, there are times when themes come from children's direct experiences, and it is important to be watchful of these times. The child who is hitting the baby doll and telling her to "shut up" may have observed this on television or she may have observed it at home. Only careful and knowledgeable observation will help the teacher to know whether this is something worthy of further exploration, perhaps by a principal, a counselor, or another teacher.

Once again, observing children's play will illustrate the nature of their interests and will indicate the quality of what they are pursuing and whether or not their interests are ones that the teacher would want to extend and facilitate. By observing children's play we can see what it is they are attempting to figure out and what themes they are exploring. We can then determine whether or not these themes are consistent with the goals of the educational community in which children are working and playing.

Very often, the big ideas described in this book are introduced with a teacher-led provocation designed to intrigue children, stimulate their questions and ideas, and give you the opportunity to see what children already know about the big idea and what they might be interested in. Provocations can initiate study of a big idea and can also be interspersed along the way to see where children might want to go with their explorations. You will plan beyond provocations in order to have ideas about many of the possible directions in which the children might go, think through the possibilities, anticipate interests and problems, and prepare for material needs that might arise. This initial planning will be grounded in your understanding of young children, their interests and needs, and your experiences with previous groups of children exploring similar ideas.

But sometimes you may plan something you have never done before with young children, and you may not even be sure that children will respond positively to the provocation you have come up with. Sometimes you may just have an intriguing idea or interest that you would like to explore with the children to see if the idea resonates, and if it does, what they can do with it. You are a theory-builder too, and it's important to have the courage to try something in order to learn from children.

Constructivist Teaching as a Continuum

To talk about a "constructivist teacher" implies that you are either a constructivist teacher or a non-constructivist teacher. But really there is no such thing as a constructivist teacher. There are teachers who believe that children construct knowledge and who want to teach in ways that facilitate children's knowledge construction. These teachers adapt certain characteristics and aspire to do things in certain ways.

But the fact is that in every teacher there are things that are done that are consistent with constructivism and things that are not. Every teacher displays some characteristics in some contexts and not in others. On a broad continuum, you could see that some teachers are more in tune with constructivism than others.

I would encourage you to see this as something we are constantly striving toward, not something that we achieve. We are also constantly trying to figure it out, since one of the major characteristics of a constructivist-oriented teacher is that they are theory-builders and reflective practitioners. A constructivist-oriented teacher is constantly questioning and learning and is experimenting as he or she goes. A constructivist-oriented teacher is in a constant learning mode. Here I want to underscore the message I spoke of in Chapter 1 that was put forth by Sergio Spaggiari, director of early childhood education in Reggio Emilia. Spaggiari believes that teachers must proclaim a "declaration of ignorance," recognizing that we are profoundly ignorant of what is going on for children and that we are striving to understand. I think this remark captures much of what I am trying to say in describing a constructivist-oriented teacher. Constructivist teachers embrace uncertainty and are open to all possibilities, attentively listening and watching what is going on in order to expand their own understanding and be active participants with children in their construction of knowledge.

The "pedagogy of listening" articulated by the educators in Reggio Emilia (Gedin, 1998), discussed in Chapter 1, means that we are never at rest, never completely confident that we know what to do in any given situation. This uncertainty is difficult for many teachers to hold to, as much of our teacher education, particularly from traditional perspectives, maintains the opposite stance. From a traditional perspective, you are an expert, you understand children, child development, curriculum, and management, and you make decisions based on that understanding. You bring to the situation this expertise that allows you to, in the best-case scenario, predetermine what will be taught, what will happen, and how it will be assessed.

But from a constructivist perspective, while we do not devalue experience and understanding of children, you must maintain the openness to learning that helps you respond to the children you are with in the present. Only by doing that will you be able to really facilitate children's theory-building, because only by being surprised by what children are capable of and by their unpredictability will you be able to go in new directions yourself.

I think it is this lack of certainty in teaching that is both the inspiration and the threat of constructivism. In our traditional teaching paradigms we have been taught to be in control, to know what we are doing and what the outcomes will be, to be able to anticipate every possibility. From a constructivist perspective we lose control in a profound sense. When I tell a group of preschoolers something, each one of them will hear it differently depending on their prior experiences, their developmental capabilities, and their emotional state. And each one of them will, therefore, construct something different from the same "input." Instead of lamenting this fact, the constructivist teacher celebrates it, and willingly lets go of the need to be able to predict what each child will make of the same information.

This uncertainty is also at the root of why assessment for the constructivist teacher is not standardized and is not capable of being standardized. Standardization is antithetical to constructivism. Ohanian (1999) talks quite eloquently, and with humor, about the overvaluing of standardization in our educational systems. The roots of standardization are behaviorist in orientation.

So, nonstandardized assessment is the name of the game for the constructivist teacher, which does not mean *no* assessment, but, rather, meaningful, authentic assessment. That for the most part means that what you do as a teacher is tell a story, describing what you see children doing. You also spend a good deal of time helping children to represent their own learning in as many ways as possible. By helping children tell the stories of their own learning, you are assessing them in ways that are consistent with constructivism, you are seeing what they know. But it is not for the purpose of ensuring that they all know the same thing. Rather, it is so that you can see the richness and diversity of the stories they tell. It is so that you can learn all the possibilities from the experiences that children are having. So that, even when a group of children engage in, seemingly, the same thing, you acknowledge and push for hearing the different ways each individual child is interpreting, making sense of, and going beyond those experiences.

As you can see, being a constructivist teacher, or, rather, striving to be a constructivist teacher, is a complicated business. It requires letting go of the illusion of expertise and of opening up to learning from and about children, and opening up to the possibility of being surprised by what they do and what you see. It requires getting into learning with them, trying to see the world from their eyes in order to capture the same joy that they have as they encounter new things. And it means being satisfied with storytelling, even in an environment that tells us that stories are not enough. It means fighting against the requirements of standardization, even while you may be forced to participate in an environment of testing and standard curriculum goals. It means holding onto those values even when you as a teacher are being told that they aren't valued.

Interestingly, being a constructivist teacher requires exactly the same kind of courage that children exhibit as they engage in theory-building. The uncertainty of teaching is similar to the not-knowing of the learner, the possibility that your ideas may be inaccurate. When a child puts forth their ideas to try them out, they take great risk. They are saying to the world, "I think that I'm right, but hey, if I'm not, isn't that interesting?" Children are the ultimate brave souls, seeing each so-called mistake or error as a learning opportunity. And we, as teachers, need to learn from that bravery; we need to be just as courageous as young children are in facing an unknown world. Theory-building, fraught with risk, takes courage. We cannot be confident, know-it-all, expert teachers. Rather, we must be as the people of Reggio Emilia model—willing to declare our ignorance and profess our interest.

This is what a constructivist teacher is, and it is a moving toward rather than achieving a state of enlightenment. If you embrace constructivism you must be prepared to squirm a little, and you must be prepared to tell lots of stories in the hopes that they will resonate with people who want what's best for children. You must be open to the uncomfortable situation of having to discuss with a parent what you are learning about, with and from their children, even when those parents also want the certainty that the standardization is based on. You must be able to document and describe the efforts you are taking to add to the richness of children's daily experiences, and you do so by making visible what you are doing and what you are learning as a teacher about and with children.

There are many skills that you can acquire to help you to do this, and we will be talking about some of these skills as we move through some of the big ideas in this book. These skills can be roughly put into two categories—skill relating to understanding the world around us and skills relating to understanding and representing what children are doing as they explore their world.

Cultivating the Skills Needed to Be a Constructivist Teacher

Understanding the World around Us

Good teachers are lifelong learners, and this quality is one that needs to be actively nurtured as you embrace constructivism. Learning about the world around us is something that many teachers sometimes put on the back burner, thinking that what they need to study is education, primarily child development and teaching strategies. And while it is important to keep up-to-date in the field of education, it is equally important to learn about things unrelated to the field directly. Teachers need to be active learners in many ways and in many different areas. As teachers of young children, we are responsible for sharing the enthusiasm as well as the knowledge that we acquire as we learn about things outside and inside the classroom.

We often make this learning a lower priority, because if what we are studying isn't immediately connected to the curriculum and interests of the children, we don't always see the implications for our practice. But once you start paying attention to your own needs as a learner, you will see the benefits for children in the classroom over time. For one thing, you will not lose touch with the magic and mystery of not knowing. Having an interest in something that is new and different helps to keep us humble as teachers, and it also helps us to understand the different learning processes that our children are constantly going through. It's much easier to become complacent with what we already know than to strike out into an arena where we are novices.

Again I think that this is one of the lessons learned from the teachers in Reggio Emilia. Cultivating the interests and curiosity about ideas, culture, the natural world in ways that push you into "not knowing" is an underlying value of Reggio Emilia that is communicated in many ways. The excitement about learning is pervasive in Reggio Emilia, and it is actively practiced by the teachers. Teachers not only learn with the children, they are learning outside the classroom as well and bring this new knowledge and learning into the lives of the children they are working with.

How can you do this when you are a busy teacher? There is really no question. There is no alternative but to figure out a way. Resources, knowledge, and new ideas are bombarding us in our technologically tuned in lives, which makes it easier to explore a new area. One way that has worked for many teachers I know is to begin a learning log, a diary in which you keep notes and thoughts about things that you are studying and learning about that are on the surface unrelated to your daily life as a teacher. These learning logs are sources of documentation and self-reflection and help you to see that by doing just a little bit every day you can start to cultivate a hobby, an interest, a new area of expertise that you didn't have when you started. Look around you for ideas of interest areas or cultural experiences that are accessible to you if you have trouble carving out the energy and time necessary for something more ambitious.

Let's look at what happens when Yuji, a kindergarten teacher, makes a commitment to learn something new in order to enhance his professional development.

▼◀ ▲▼◀ ▲▼◀ ▲▼◀ ▲▼◀ ▲▼◀ ▲▼◀ ▲

Yuji has felt "in a rut" and unable to find time to develop outside interests. Although he is active in his local early childhood professional organization, he feels all he does is think about children and teaching, and while he loves his work and finds it stimulating, he wonders if he should expand his interests and knowledge. He has always felt out of touch with his Japanese American heritage and decides to learn the Japanese language.

He begins by taking a weekly class at a local community college, and although he has little time to study, he picks up some conversational Japanese. One of the things he learns is that he is increasingly aware of the difficulty he has when the teacher moves too quickly for him to follow. He realizes that when he is sharing things with his kindergarten children sometimes he moves too quickly for all the children. He becomes more aware of his own pace of communication, which is quick and nonrepetitive. He begins to slow down and to look to his children for cues that they are tuned in, more than he ever has before.

As he learns more, he begins to share with his children some of the words he is learning. They are fascinated that their teacher is also a student, and they learn some of the same words he is learning. Through the class, Yuji makes a connection with a woman who is moving to Japan to teach for a year, and they arrange to establish a connection between their two classrooms.

▼◄▲▼◄▲▼◄▲▼◄▲▼◄▲▼◄▲▼◄▲

Although Yuji took up the study of Japanese in order to do something outside of the classroom, his personal learning had implications for his teaching. We are only good teachers if we are always learners too. It is important to make a concerted effort to incorporate our own learning into our busy lives and to nourish our intellectual curiosity.

Learning to Represent and Document What Children Are Learning

It is often easier for teachers to see the value of documentation skills, but what I would like you to do is think creatively about what these might be. In many of our teacher education institutions, we may learn some skills needed to observe and document—usually in writing—what children are doing when they are engaged in play or tasks in the classroom. These skills can always be improved, and there are many resources that can give us a wider repertoire of these more traditional modes of informal and ongoing assessment that help us to document what children are doing. Different techniques of note taking, different strategies for keeping written records, and different mechanisms for sharing these records with colleagues and with parents are available in the professional literature. Often these are tied to particular curriculum areas. So, for example, Doris (1991) has some wonderful techniques for documenting what children are doing when they conduct scientific explorations. Similarly, Wilde (1992) shares some different ways that teachers might document the spelling strategies that children employ when they use invented spelling. All of these representations of children's thinking and learning are essential for our own reflection and also serve the function of communication with parents and others about the child's experiences in the classroom.

Beyond written notes, which may be more or less informal, there are other techniques for documentation that can be experimented with and incorporated into your classroom practice. One technique used extensively in Reggio Emilia is audiorecording. Placing a tape recorder at a table where children are working, or having one with you when you sit down with a small group of children, can give you a rich source of information that can be overlooked in the moment. Taking the time at a later point to review the tape can give you new insights into what the children are thinking. The key here is to have good, accessible equipment that captures children's talk. If this means investing in a set of wireless microphones, it might be worth the investment. The second key is to make sure you schedule the time to use the tapes that are made. One helpful hint is to have a tape recorder that is capable of fast-forwarding while listening to the children's talk. Otherwise, the time spent listening is at least equal to the time spent recording. Some teachers prefer voice-activated tape recorders, which eliminate the dead space on the tape recording that takes time to go through.

Digital and Polaroid photography is now an indispensable tool for the teacher to use in documentation, allowing for the capture of process through a sequence of photographs, or for the capture of a particular construction or creation that will be taken apart or transformed into something else, such as a large-scale block construction.

Videorecording is another valuable tool for capturing what children are doing. Using videotapes on a regular basis helps prevent children from being affected by the presence of the video camera, as it becomes a natural part of the classroom environment. Regularly capturing on video episodes of children's active work provides a dynamic documentation that cannot be captured with static images. Just as with audiotapes, the important element of the use of videorecording is to review the videotapes soon after they are taken, providing a way to more deeply reflect on an event or an episode. And, as with audiotapes, selecting parts to review more carefully is key to the efficient use of videorecordings.

Once you become adept at using videorecordings and digital photography, the storing of the images becomes an issue. Learning simple means of editing, or relying on parents or colleagues to assist in the process, is important—otherwise you find yourself overwhelmed with photographs and videos with no organization. Creating video and photo libraries is fairly straightforward, but it requires a regular investment of time just as any means of documentation or assessment does. Taking the time early on in your practice to learn these skills will pay off in the long run.

Some teachers are adept at sketching, and may find this a more satisfying way of capturing what children are doing. One way of documenting children's work that was observed in Reggio Emilia was a series of panels on a large piece of paper onto which the teacher was sketching and writing notes, a simple yet effective way of capturing the children's work over time. (An example of this is given in Chapter 8, where the teacher sketches the child's creation of a flower on the ground.)

Regardless of the means of documentation as events occur, deciding what to do with the artifacts is another issue, as we discussed with videotapes. The method for organizing the children's work can take many forms. But the most important thing to keep in mind is that the very process of organization is reflective. When you sit down with notes, audiotapes, videotapes, photos, and sketches you have to decide what it is you want to learn, how you want to look at this information, what questions you have as a teacher. Some teachers have the advantage of being able to work with colleagues, either as teachers together in the same classroom or as teachers who work across classrooms collaboratively. The value of such collaboration is so immense that it is worthwhile to try to figure out a way to make it happen for yourself. In the context of your school, it could be as simple as finding one colleague who shares your interest in learning how to document and reflect on what children are doing, even if that colleague teaches at a very different grade level. It could be as complex as pushing for time and resources for teachers to meet formally in teams during some regular time period. And even if you work in a very isolated way—as many teachers do—and have difficulty finding a like-minded colleague in your school, there are teachers who are interested in networking across schools. Universities or collaborative professional groups can help you link with other interested teachers to create the kind of collaborative relationship that we are talking about.

But let's say that even this is not possible. You can still use the documentation to reflect as an individual teacher on what children are doing. And you can incorporate this reflection into your teaching in as valuable a way as the teacher who has a strong support network.

Another thing to think about with regard to documentation is whether and how the documentation is collected, shared, and used actively with children. Some of the most interesting and informative discussions a teacher can have with children are elicited by the documentation that he or she has collected. Let's look in on one of these encounters to see what might transpire.

Marisa has taken pictures of her first grade children engaged in some active experimentation with gears. Using a large variety of plastic gears that Marisa was able to obtain from a local store that sells recycled and surplus materials, the children were mounting them onto a small pegboard and trying to get them to work. Marisa takes some digital pictures of a series of trials that Ethan makes. It is not clear to Marisa how much Ethan is really thinking

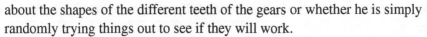

about the shapes of the different teeth of the gears or whether he is simply randomly trying things out to see if they will work.

So she puts the pictures in order on a large board and sits down with a small group of children to talk about it. "I'm curious what you are trying to figure out here, Ethan. Can you talk to me about it?" Ethan looks at the pictures and says, "I was trying to get one gear to move the other." Maria says, "But Ethan, look, the big gear moves the small gear faster!" Ethan and Maria try it out again, then go back to the pictures. Maria says, "Here's how it works," and actually reproduces the picture with the gears.

Marisa introduces an even larger gear and asks Maria and Ethan what they predict this gear will do. Maria thinks it is too large to work, but Ethan says that he thinks it will move it even faster. They try it out, and Ethan's prediction is correct.

▼◄ ▲ ▼◄ ▲ ▼◄ ▲ ▼◄ ▲ ▼◄ ▲ ▼◄ ▲ ▼◄ ▲

Using the pictures has helped Marisa probe further into Ethan's (and Maria's) thinking about gears, and it has stimulated the children to ask questions about what they were actively engaged in. The "slowing down" that this reflection allows is important and can provide the opportunity for deeper thinking and questioning that can't always happen in the moment.

As a teacher, you need to be cautious about how far to carry this kind of deeper reflection. You run the risk of overanalyzing children's active experimentation, and with younger children the effort to discuss and analyze what children are doing can actually backfire and create boredom and disinterest on the part of the children. But the right amount of discussion and questioning can provoke children's thinking as well as help make their thinking visible to the teacher.

In this chapter the focus is on our own professional development—learning to document and represent children's learning. Throughout this book I will be exploring the ways documentation can serve the functions of assessment, reflection, and evaluation. All of these functions of documentation and representation, of course, go hand in hand, and it is difficult to pull them apart. However, it is also important to think about the skills we need to cultivate in order to be good teachers.

The Role of Observation

The importance of documentation and of the representation of what children are learning and thinking is intertwined with your role as a reflective observer. Before you can make sense of what is going on, before you can analyze or look beyond the surface of what children are doing, you need to be able to see what is going on.

Observation is the act of looking closely, carefully, and deeply at what children are engaged in.

Observation is not just a "looking" or an act of visual perception. Observation involves hearing as well, listening carefully and deeply to what children are saying, to the hum and buzz of the classroom, and to the laughter and words that are being interchanged. Observation also involves feeling—getting a sense of what emotions are at play in a given situation. In a sense, observation is an act of compassion, of taking in what is going on at all levels, of sharing experiences.

In order to observe, you have to be able to see, hear, and feel what is going on. The act of observing is not cold and clinical. And yet to some extent it is also important to make sure that you do not impose your own feelings, beliefs, suppositions, and theories on what children are doing. This requires a degree of objectivity, an awareness of what you bring to the observation as an observer, so that you know the difference between what you think and what is going on. The subjectivity will come into your analysis and your decisions about what to do with what you see and hear.

One thing we do know is that, just like with many other skills, teachers become better observers by engaging in observation. Practice and reflection on that practice is what will help you become better at seeing and hearing children.

I will conclude this chapter with a look at the constructivist classroom from two perspectives—the teacher's and the child's.

The Teacher's Perspective of the Constructivist Classroom

What does the classroom of a constructivist teacher look like from the teacher's perspective?

A constructivist teacher comes into the classroom filled with excitement and ideas about what she and the children can do together. Highly motivated and dedicated, the constructivist teacher, because of the view of learning that she has, knows that her role is a complex one and that she has to juggle many roles and has to bring many skills and much energy to her position. And to be a good constructivist teacher, she has to care deeply about children and families and about her relationships with them.

First, she needs to have a great deal of professional development. Grounded in child development and an understanding of the sociology and anthropology of families and culture, she is aware that our knowledge base about children, classrooms, families, and culture is growing and changing. Supported by the context of ongoing professional development, she is highly reflective, looking critically at her own work and that of others.

Second, she needs to communicate to many audiences in addition to relating to the children she is working with. The families and community of her students, her supervisors/principal and colleagues, and the public all have a stake in understanding what she is doing and why. And because of the many misconceptions about constructivism and the focus on high standards and accountability, she is under pressure to communicate even more and differently to the people who care about the education of young children. Because of this, she is actively involved in professional organizations, in the context of which she advocates for young children and quality education, obtains support and resources, and learns the skills of leadership required more and more of teachers.

Third, she must be masterful at obtaining and using resources. In addition to being the typical scavenger and scrounger that most early childhood teachers are, she marshals the help and support of the classroom's parents, community organizations and businesses, and the school and district in which she works. Resources for a constructivist classroom are plentiful but cannot be prescribed because they are often so tailored to the current needs and focus of the classroom and do not follow a specified scope and sequence.

Fourth, she must be planful yet extremely flexible. Thinking (hopefully with others) about the curriculum goals, the needs of individual children, and the needs of the particular group, she must plan activities and environments that allow for multiple possibilities. Because of the multiple possibilities, children can do many different things, and she must anticipate as many as possible but always realize that they will (thankfully) do things we do not or cannot anticipate. So flexibility is necessary so that she can respond appropriately and quickly to what children do, always keeping in mind the overarching goals she began with.

Fifth, she must be engaged in constant observation, both formal and informal, while she is interacting with the children and by stepping back when she can. It is only through observation that she can make decisions about what she should do next and in the future; it is only through observation that she can reflect carefully on the value and meaning of what she has planned and what has transpired. It is this observation that will feed the flexible responses to what children do. Deb Curtis and Margie Carter (2000) have described in great detail the role and techniques of observation that are essential for the constructivist teacher to master.

And finally, just as children learn and play best in collaboration with others, so too does the constructivist teacher benefit from collaboration. Again, the lessons of the work of Reggio Emilia include the essential element of collaborative work for teachers, who reflect on the curriculum and the children with each other, and who learn from talking about and hearing from other teachers. Many teachers who are trying to be constructivist in their practice are isolated and find it difficult to connect with those who share similar goals. It takes extra effort to form a network from which to get the support you need, and it may even need to be a virtual network. Networks and collaborative relationships that are created outside your own work space are often available through professional organizations or universities, and they are well worth the effort needed for participation.

In summary, the constructivist teacher brings to the classroom a spirit and a commitment that is quite intimidating to those who are not familiar with constructivism. But it must be said that many teachers who would not consider themselves "constructivist teachers," may, nevertheless, do many things that are compatible with constructivism. As was suggested in this chapter, think of it as a continuum—most teachers are striving always to be better than they are. And remember that there are many ways to be a good constructivist teacher; no two "good" classrooms look alike!

The Constructivist Classroom from the Perspective of the Child

Now let's consider what the experience of a constructivist classroom would be like for children in that classroom. Remember, as I said in the previous section, there are many different ways that the constructivist classroom can look; nonetheless, there are some things that would cut across those different classrooms from the perspective of the child.

First, children in a constructivist classroom would learn, early on and gradually, clear expectations about reasonable behavior with each other and with materials. There would be a few important rules that would be communicated in ways that would be understandable to the children. For example, taking care of materials and resources and handling things appropriately would be explicitly articulated to the children in ways that would help them understand the reasons for needing to take care of materials and resources. This "reasonableness" test can be applied to almost anything in a constructivist classroom, where the teacher needs to be able to articulate to the children the reasons for a rule that affects the children and the reasons need to be important ones.

Most of the time, those reasons will be comprehensible to the children; occasionally, when younger children are not able to understand the reasons, they need to be explained. As a child, if I didn't already know this from my home, I would learn in school that when I read books I am to handle them with care and shouldn't tear the pages or write in them. I would understand that this is important for myself and for the other children so that we can continue to use the books over time. This makes sense to me, and I treat the books with respect. I also learn, by having this explained to me, that I am not being subjected to a restriction or a rule that is imposed on me for no reason. The expectations for me in the classroom are ones that are necessary for us all to play and work together.

Considering social expectations, I would also understand how I am supposed to treat the other children and the teacher. Depending on the expectations of the teacher and the culture of the classroom that he or she is promoting, I would know what is ok and what is not, and why. I might have come into the classroom not knowing how to express my anger at being kept from doing something I want to do, for example, without hitting or throwing something at a peer. With the clear rule in the classroom that we aren't to hurt each other with words or with hands or objects, I would know why I was not allowed to play in a particular area when I do that. I would also come to understand what it means to "use my words" when I feel like knocking over my friend's block construction when he won't let me play with him. And I would know that the kinds of words I can use are limited to those that are not hurtful. I would come to expect the same treatment from others.

I also know that this classroom is a place where I can have lots of ideas and questions and will have opportunities to explore my ideas and experiment with my questions. This classroom is a place where I am given access to resources and materials, I have choices in what I do and how, and I know I can interact with others in a safe environment. I know there are clear expectations about what is ok and not ok, but I also know that there are many possibilities. My choices are not unlimited, however. Often there are multiple choices, determined by the teacher, of what I can do, and within each activity or area in which I can work I can do a number of different things. In other words, the questions I am asking and the work that I am doing is determined by me within the framework of the teacher's choosing. Sometimes the teacher will ask me to do a particular thing, and she will explain to me why it is important and why she is asking me to do it even if it isn't my first choice. Sometimes she will have all of us do something together. Overall, I have a range of experiences and activities available to me, and, most of the time, I have a great time and I feel like my ideas are important ones, even the ones that I can't act on. And so I have more and more ideas!

As you can see, the child in a constructivist classroom (clearly a prototypical one!) is confident, curious, engaged, and collaborative. It is interesting to think about how the constructivist views these characteristics as being natural to children. The constructivist classroom is one that acknowledges children for who they are and supports them, providing an appropriate and stimulating environment in which they can thrive and in which they can engage in meaningful learning.

CHAPTER 4

Balancing Acts

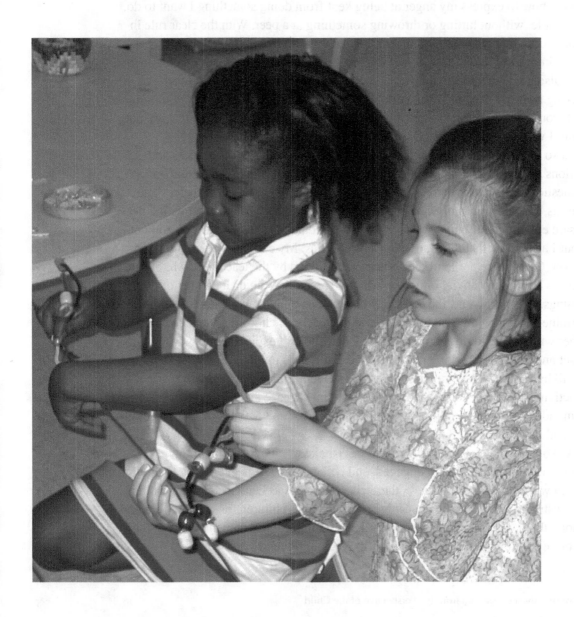

I n this chapter I'll be exploring the big idea of balance, discussing ways that children can explore balance in the areas of mathematics, science, symmetry, and the socioemotional domain. In the process, ways of incorporating documentation into the ongoing explorations of balance will be examined.

▼◄ ▲ ▼◄ ▲ ▼◄ ▲ ▼◄ ▲ ▼◄ ▲ ▼◄ ▲ ▼◄ ▲

Marsha, a teacher of four- and five-year-olds in a full-day preschool, reads the book *Mirette on the High Wire* (McCully, 1992) to her class. She has chosen this book on purpose, as a way to provoke the children's thinking about balance through focusing on the different strategies for balancing on the high wire in the circus. She is not sure what aspect of balance the children will be interested in, but she has been thinking about it herself after a trip to the circus. She has decided that balance would make a good focus for her curriculum for a while, a big idea with which she can integrate the curriculum across different domains.

▼◄ ▲ ▼◄ ▲ ▼◄ ▲ ▼◄ ▲ ▼◄ ▲ ▼◄ ▲ ▼◄ ▲

Marsha is embarking on work revolving around a big idea, the idea of balance. Her beginning provocation, the reading of a children's book, and her initial interest in the subject, are good entry points for our introduction of the study of balance. Balance is a big idea that underlies many concepts in many curriculum domains, and in this chapter I will be exploring the idea and thinking about the ways that it can be incorporated into the curriculum. Let's look at how Marsha can expand her initial thoughts and interest.

First, she sought materials that incorporate the idea of balance. There are many materials and games, some very focused on balance. Here are several commercial games that she started with:

Don't Spill the Beans (Milton Bradley). Children take turns putting beans on top of a tippy container until it tips over.

Stacrobats (Ravensburger). Children connect plastic figures onto a base; they take turns and need to keep it balanced to win.

Topple (Pressman Toy Corporation). Children take turns placing objects on top of a precarious base.

Chairs Game (Fundex Games, Ltd.). Children take turns balancing plastic chairs on top of each other to make a tower, until it falls over.

Jenga (Hasbro). A game for older children, who take turns taking a stick out of a stack of sticks and placing the stick on the top of the tower, until the tower collapses.

62

She also found some folk toys, including a balancing bear on a unicycle that travels across the room on a string holding a weighted bar. Having these balancing toys in the room can serve as a provocation just by their presence.

As children play with these games, they may become curious or interested in a number of things related to balance. One of these is the issue of distribution—it matters where you put a bean, or where you put a stick, for the stability of the structure. Another is the issue of symmetry —balance occurs when there is some kind of symmetry between one side of the structure and the other. These two issues—distribution and symmetry—will be woven throughout this discussion of balance as organizing ideas.

Underlying Ideas

Let's back up and look some of the underlying concepts involved in balance. A good way to start is to think about what children do when they engage in balancing activities in their everyday world. Riding bicycles, going on seesaws, riding a skateboard, walking on a balance beam on the playground—all of these activities involve balancing their own bodies. Similarly, they balance pencils on their fingers, books on their heads—and in the process have to experiment with where to put objects so that they will balance. In lots of children's play, particularly with blocks and manipulatives, balance is a focus—as when children try to build a tower of blocks. In all of these cases, you end up putting weight on one side, then the other, to try to estimate what will equalize the weight on both sides. So, one of the major concepts underlying balance is *estimation*, or guesswork, which children love to do in many areas of their lives. Another concept that is involved is *comparison*, another everyday activity of children—how big or little things are in comparison to each other, how heavy or light, how tall or short. *Measurement* is an important aspect of both comparison and estimation. Although estimation, comparison, and measurement underlie many other big ideas, these concepts and activities are central to balance.

Yet another concept involved is *symmetry*, important particularly for mathematical thinking. Patterns, correspondences, and symmetry are natural elements of considering balance. Symmetry involves the idea that there are equalities across a midpoint. Symmetry is also important aesthetically and musically, it is an important design concept, and it underlies many ideas of architecture and engineering.

Returning to Marsha, what happens when she introduces the book, *Mirette on the High Wire*, to the children? In this case, they were intrigued by how Mirette put her arms out to balance on the high wire, but the children did not get far beyond this interest after just reading the book. So Marsha decided to surround the children with balance in the classroom. She introduced three games, Don't Spill the Beans, Topple, and Stacrobats. She also created several handmade games that involve the same ideas of balance as these games, but that make them more explicit. For example, she took a pan balance, and, using cardboard, created a large flat surface resting on top of each pan, marked off with lines, so that individual beans can be distributed in a more visible way.

Marsha also began thinking about the children's interest in how Mirette, the high wire walker, balanced with her hands out or with a stick, and thought that this might be extended by creating their own "high wire," creating performers with pipe cleaners. Using beads as weights, the children had opportunities to experiment with making their performers balance. The combination of these games and activities ended up capturing the children's interest, and soon they were asking numerous questions about balance as they tried to put different types of objects and weights on the performer's balancing sticks.

After the children had spent quite a bit of time creating their performers experimenting with different weights, Marsha observed that as they explored the different configurations, they would replicate the stance of the tightrope walker with their own bodies, holding their arms out and standing on one foot. She and several of the children decided to set up their own "high wire," creating a balance beam with wooden boards (only a few inches from the ground), long plastic poles to balance with, and weights to hang on the poles made out of sand-filled plastic bottles.

▼◄ ▲ ▼◄ ▲ ▼ ◄ ▲ ▼◄ ▲ ▼

Despite the children's initial unenthusiastic response to the idea of balance, Marsha persisted by surrounding the children with opportunities to explore balance, activities and materials interesting enough to spark their interest. This is the meaning of *provocation*—an intentional sparking of interest.

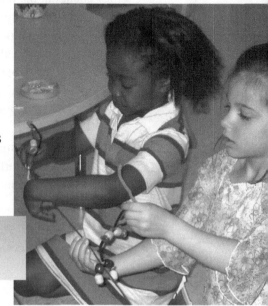

▼◄ ▲▼ ▲ ▼ ◄ ▲ ▼

These girls are working hard to make their pipe cleaner figures balance on the wire.

The Mathematics of Balance

As stated earlier, the study of balance incorporates many important mathematical concepts, mostly focused on the distribution of weight and mass around the balance point. The resulting study of balance thus includes comparisons and measurements that can vary from simple to complex. On the simplest level, we can look at a child trying to contribute to a mobile made out of coat hangers by placing the second coat hanger at one place, then moving it over so that it hangs equidistant from the other one and balances. On the more complex level, we can see a child trying to contribute to the same mobile by hanging sand-filled beanbags of different weights at different points on the coat hanger.

Here is an attempt to focus on the mathematics of balance with kindergarten-age children.

Amy takes a large wooden disk, and attaches it to a large spring attached to a base (Figure 4.1). This constructed game is modeled after a smaller-scale toy that she has seen in a toy store (one that was very expensive!). She puts next to the disk a basket with beanbags. As children start to play with it, they place beanbags on top of the disk until it tips over and the beanbags fall off. After much laughter and excitement at making them tip over and fall off, Amy suggests that they play a game, taking turns putting the beanbags on the disk and counting as they do it. Amy has used masking tape to put a mark down the middle of the disk. As the children place the beanbags, they count out the numbers on each side of the disk.

After the children have mastered this game, Amy decides to make it more complex. She has beanbags of three sizes—small, medium, and large—and these sizes are clearly recognizable because they are of different colors. Amy tells the children that the game is different now, and they are to figure out how.

As the children play, they realize that it is not just the number of beanbags that matter, but the size as well. They start to figure out the different combinations of bags that equal other bags. The game becomes more complicated,

Even simple coat hangers pose a balance problem.

and they have a renewed interest in figuring it out. In the process, they are dealing with some more advanced mathematics that Amy is able to talk about with them in other contexts.

▼◄ ▲ ▼◄ ▲ ▼◄ ▲ ▼◄ ▲

Similarly, Marsha is able to make the mathematics involved in the children's balance game more explicit by encouraging the children to keep track of how many weights they need on each side to make the tightrope walker balance. And, when the children are tightrope walking on the balance beam, she is able to have them keep track of the weights they are using on their poles. The children quickly realize after some experimentation that the weights on each side must be equal in number and equidistant in order for them to balance.

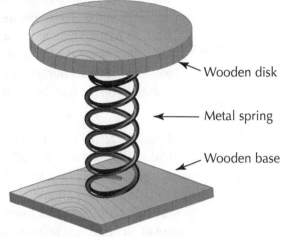

Wooden disk

Metal spring

Wooden base

Figure 4.1 *Homemade Balance Game*

Making Balance a "Bigger" Idea

▼◄ ▲ ▼◄ ▲ ▼◄ ▲ ▼◄ ▲ ▼◄ ▲ ▼◄ ▲ ▼◄ ▲ ▼◄ ▲

One of Marsha's goals is to expand the children's exploration of balance beyond the science and mathematics that they have been focusing on to this point. In order to do that, she begins introducing another curricular focus, the study of ecology and the interdependence of living things. Her explicit intention is for children to make the connection between what they have been doing with the physics of balance and ecological balance. She is curious as to whether or not they will be able to see this connection, and does not want it to be artificial or contrived. So, while continuing the experimentation and exploration of the physics of balance, she introduces some children's books related to ecology. One of these, Lynne Cherry's *The Great Kapok Tree: A Tale of the Amazon Rain Forest* (1990) has been popular with many of the children. Marsha decides to highlight it through a group read-aloud.

After the reading, the group has a discussion about the impact the chopping down of a tree can have, and the children begin talking about the wetlands that borders their school. They decide to go for a walk through the wetlands and take pictures (using the classroom's digital camera) of what they see. On their walk, they see live trees, they see a recently felled tree, they see a decomposing tree, and they see an area next to the wetlands where some bulldozers are preparing for some home construction.

Back in the classroom, the pictures are printed out and posted on the wall. As Marsha had hoped, a couple of the older children begin to talk about the impact the bulldozing might have on the animals and trees in the wetlands. She encourages them to dictate their questions and posts their questions on the wall by the pictures.

Is this a stretch? If you are interested in encouraging the connections across the curriculum, if you want the really big ideas to be meaningful to the children, you need to be creative in how the connections can be made, and sometimes you'll need to take risks. It is important to keep in mind that the goal is for the children to see or make the connection, not to have the connection made for them. Because of this, careful observation and attentiveness to what children say and the questions they ask can guide you in deciding whether or not children are making the connections.

That's not to say that you shouldn't draw out the connection by making it explicit when appropriate. This "making explicit" can be done in several different ways. Here are some ideas relating to the previous example.

First, Marsha could lead a class discussion during which she might pose the question directly to the children: "Does anyone see any connection between what we have been doing with tightrope walkers and what we are doing with the forest?" This might open up a discussion that makes the connection more explicit. If it doesn't, it is important that the teacher not answer that question directly, but might instead say, "Let's just keep thinking about that one and come back to it later."

Second, Marsha could use documentation and display of the class work to make the connection explicit. On the same wall where the children have drawn pictures of what balances the tightrope walkers, there could be a display of pictures from the wetlands that children have put in some relationship to each other. The first set of documentation might say: "What happens if you take away the balance on one side?" with pictures the children have drawn depicting off-balance tightrope walkers. And the second, next to the first, might say: "What happens if you take away the trees?" with photos of the wetlands, and with the children's written predictions of what would happen to each element of the wetlands they observed, such as a photograph of ferns proliferating in the shade of large trees.

Third, Marsha could incorporate some of the same vocabulary and language across the different arenas of study. Using the words *balance* and *distribution* in both contexts could help children make the connection. And talking about the same processes across domains can help too—discussion about estimation, prediction, and comparisons when talking about tightrope walking as well as ecological issues.

Let's look at what happens when a teacher of older children decides to use the big idea of balance to integrate curriculum. In this case, the teacher has decided to focus on mobiles as a way to introduce balance.

Barbara and Angie are teaching partners—each has a self-contained second grade classroom. They decide together to embark on a study of balance using mobiles as the provocation and focus of activity.

Barbara has recently returned from a visit to a museum in another city where the work of Alexander Calder has been featured, and she is very excited about sharing the pictures of mobiles with the children. In preparation, she enlarges the pictures from a book and puts them on overheads so that the class can see them clearly. She also has a small mobile in her house that she carefully packs up and brings into the classroom. Before the children of both classes come into her classroom, she hangs the mobile from the ceiling. She and Angie have discussed whether they should start with children building mobiles or by showing them what an artist does, but they decide on the latter, thinking that seeing what is possible will be inspirational rather than intimidating.

Barbara shares a number of pictures of the mobiles, and, as she does, Angie watches the children carefully. They seem attentive and focused on the pictures and ask a number of questions. But the pictures are static, and the children want to see how the mobiles move. So, as anticipated, Angie and Barbara tell the children that they will be making their own mobiles. They provide wire, string, and a variety of objects of different weights that can be hung on the mobiles. They also tell the children that there are "many other things" that they could incorporate into their mobiles so that they do not feel restricted by what the teachers have put out. In these classrooms, the children are used to having access to materials in the cupboards, and so they are not hesitant to get materials as they need them.

Half of the children go to work in the other classroom, where the same kinds of materials are available. After only a half hour of work, the teachers tell them that they can continue work on their mobiles tomorrow and also suggest that they bring in objects and materials from home that could be used. In the last fifteen minutes, they all take out their project journals and draw a picture of the mobile they are making, what they have planned, and the questions and problems that they have encountered.

After school, Angie and Barbara look at the children's journals and jot down some of the questions that seem to be coming up for the children. As they talk about what they have read and what they observed, they notice that most of the work the children are doing is trial and error. They decide that they want to encourage, indirectly, more of a focus on the weight of the objects that the children are putting on the mobile. To do that, they get pan balances out of the storage room and put them at each table. Over the next few days, some of the children incorporate the balances into their predictions of what will work, and there is quite a bit of discussion about how some things that are bigger weigh less. Angie and Barbara notice more specific questions recorded in the journals and attribute that in part to the use of pan balances.

▼◄ ▲▼◄ ▲▼◄ ▲▼◄ ▲▼◄ ▲▼◄ ▲▼◄ ▲

The Socioemotional Realm

The big idea of balance has particular relevance for children in the socioemotional domain. Think about equity, fairness, justice, and sharing—all issues of significance for young children and issues that children are wrestling with in many ways. Seeing these issues as an important part of the goals of education and spending time addressing them as part of the curriculum is an important and logical extension of the study of balance as a big idea. DeVries and Zan (1994) have articulated a framework for looking at the culture of the early childhood classroom that has, as a major focus of the curriculum, the socioemotional development of children. They discuss a number of ways that teachers can explicitly address these significant issues.

Will children be able to see the connection between the things they are exploring in the physical realm related to balance and the socioemotional issues of balance? This is a question without a simple answer. And does it matter if they do? There are a couple of things to think about. First, there are certainly qualitative differences between children's thinking in the two domains. Concerns about fairness and equity for young children elicit emotional responses and are not grounded only in logical thinking. Learning about issues of physical balance, while colored by the children's interests and beliefs, does not have the emotional tension. Because of these qualitative differences, in some regards there will not be a natural connection. Second, however, there can be some value in articulating the relationships, if only to give children some tools—language and conceptual—for thinking about and talking about the more emotionally charged arena of socioemotional development.

Here is an example of how the language of the physical realm can help children to talk about a social issue.

Abby and Alex, two four-year-olds, are each involved in creating a collage using some materials that are available on the art shelves. A small container of feathers is almost empty, and Abby dumps the three remaining feathers onto her paper. Alex gets very upset and says to the teacher, "It's not fair! She got all the feathers!" Abby says, "But you have all the buttons, and I wanted the buttons too." Katrice, the teacher, decides to make the issue explicit. She says, "You know how when we were building mobiles some things that look different balanced? You could think of this in the same way. Maybe since you got the buttons that Abby wanted it is ok that Abby gets the feathers." Alex says, "Sort of like the feathers balance out the buttons?"

Symmetry

Symmetry is another important component of the big idea of balance. When something is in balance, there is something equal about each side. This equality can be physical, as when the two sides of the pan balance with weights; it can also be visual or aesthetic, as in symmetrical patterns.

Looking for patterns is a traditional element of early childhood curriculum, often discussed as an early mathematical skill that we can promote in our classrooms. Many materials and games are focused on symmetrical patterns. Think about activities that involve mirrors. *The Magic Mirror: An Antique Optical Toy* (McLoughlin Bros., 1980), for example, presents a series of pictures to be viewed with a mirror, and mirrors can be used to find or make symmetrical patterns. And although things like pattern blocks, attribute blocks, and beads do not have to be used to create symmetry, children often use these materials for that purpose.

Many things in the natural world are symmetrical—rainbows, butterflies, snowflakes, many flowers and plants—and children can search for symmetry in the world around them. They will also find many man-made things to be symmetrical—wheels and vehicles, machines, constructions such as buildings and bridges—and, once symmetry is a focus, many more things can be seen and found.

Technology and Symmetry

Technology can provide support for these explorations. Here are some interesting tools that you can obtain through the Internet. Although some of these sites and programs are designed for middle school students and up, there are resources for teachers here as well as some elements that are appropriate for younger children.

Symmetry (www.adrianbruce.com/Symmetry/). A particularly interesting site created by students in a sixth grade class from St. Kieran's Manly Vale in Sydney, Australia. The site is designed to bring together resources for students on symmetry. They have included examples from nature, the human body, architecture, kaleidoscopes, hubcaps, and more.

Virtual Manipulatives—Reflection (www.teachers.ash.org.au/mikemath/movies/symmetry1.html). This site offers an interactive program that creates reflections of objects.

The Butterfly WebSite (http://butterflywebsite.com). This site, in addition to lots of information on butterflies, has a photo gallery with butterfly and moth images.

SymmeToy—Symmetric Art Program (www.hufsoft.com/software/ page4.html). This site permits the downloading of a trial version of a Windows program for creating paint patterns, symmetry roses, and tessellating art.

Wilson Snowflake Bentley—Photographer of Snowflakes (http://snowflakebentley .com). In addition to lots of other resources on the famous photographer (also see the children's book, *Snowflake Bentley*), there is a link to Original Wilson Bentley Images, which has twenty-one of his original photographs.

Exploring Symmetry in a First Grade Classroom

Jacob's first grade class has been exploring symmetry ever since one of his students shared his grandmother's butterfly collection, a set of twelve beautifully mounted butterflies in a case. The children explored the Butterfly WebSite and looked at a number of resource books that Jacob found at the library. The study of butterflies led quite naturally to a study of symmetry, and Jacob had them design their own butterflies by making one side of a butterfly and then reproducing it as a mirror image with a copy machine.

Jacob decided that he wanted them to explore this idea further, beyond butterflies, and so they went for a "symmetry search" in their urban neighborhood. On their walk, they took the class's two digital cameras, and each child brought a clipboard with paper and pencils for sketching what they found and for making notes.

On their return to the classroom, the children organized their notes and sketches, and the group in charge of the digital pictures printed out what they had taken. Then they all sat in a group and shared the many examples of symmetry they found. These included doors, windows, buildings, bridges, trees, hedges, signs, streets, and so on. The children were surprised at how many things they saw that were symmetrical. They decided to create an exhibit to display what they had seen. One idea was to put the symmetrical items on the board on folded paper, so that as you opened it up you saw the symmetry from one side to the other. Another idea was to put a half picture of the item on the wall, with a plastic mirror that could be used to reflect it. The children decided to do both, and the butterflies they had created bordered the resulting display.

One of the children's mothers was so amazed and delighted by the resulting display that she volunteered to capture their pictures and put them together into a book so that they could share it with others. She and several of the children worked together during their project time.

This study of symmetry, stimulated by sharing of a butterfly collection, was facilitated by Jacob's encouragement to go beyond butterflies. The resources and opportunities provided fed the children's already high interest. And the involvement of a parent ensured that the experience would be documented and recorded for the future and also showed the children that their work is of interest and value to others.

Creative Arts and Balance

There are numerous activities that can be done using art materials that focus on balance, particularly in patterns and symmetry. Creating "ink-blot" paintings, where paint is put on one side of a piece of paper and the paper is folded over, can serve as a template for symmetry activities using other kinds of materials, such as folding a magazine photo in half and mounting it on a large piece of paper for a child to draw in the missing half. Paper cutting, the kind used to make snowflakes and paper dolls, can also provoke lots of thinking about symmetry.

Another medium through which children can explore balance is sculpting with various materials, as shown in the following scenario.

In a first grade class they have been exploring ideas of balance, and Lua, the teacher, has in the past provided the children with the opportunity to work with clay, so they are familiar with working with clay and the tools used. She gathers the children together and tells them that today they will be working with clay in a new way. She pulls out a piece of clay that she has formed into a T shape, places it on a narrow block sitting on the table, and asks, "What do you think will happen if I add some clay to one side of the T?" Paul raises his hand and says, "I think it will fall over." "Let's see what happens." Lua puts the clay on the side of the T-shaped structure, and, as predicted, it topples over. The class applauds, and Lua says, "Can anyone think of a way to get it to balance again?" Shelley suggests adding some clay to the other side. Lua takes a piece of clay clearly larger than the piece she had already put on and says, "Like this?" "No! It needs to be smaller—more like the other side." So Lua adjusts the ball of clay and puts it on the other side of the T, sets it upright, and the children applaud again as it balances. Lua suggests that they might want to try to create other "balancing sculptures" during their project and activity time.

▼ ◄ ▲ ▼ ◄ ▲ ▼ ◄ ▲ ▼ ◄ ▲ ▼ ◄ ▲ ▼ ◄ ▲ ▼ ◄ ▲

Lua's presentation of the balancing sculptures focuses on the science of it—the balancing of weight on two sides. But, as you can see in what followed, it led to some explorations around aesthetics.

▼ ◄ ▲ ▼ ◄ ▲ ▼ ◄ ▲ ▼ ◄ ▲ ▼ ◄ ▲ ▼ ◄ ▲ ▼ ◄ ▲

Paul and Sharon are at the project table working with clay, and they have created together a T-shaped structure similar to Lua's, but have put a round ball of clay on the top and have added hands to the ends of each T. Sharon brings a tub of collage materials over to the table where they are working and begins to stick feathers and beads onto the structure, systematically placing the feathers and beads equally on each side. Paul begins to put one feather in one "hand" of the creation, and Sharon says, "No, no, it has to be the same!" Paul proceeds to put a feather in the other hand. The two children work intensively to cover the clay creation with decorations so that the two sides are the same.

The next morning, Lua asks Paul and Sharon to share what they've done with the class and to talk about it. They point out how the decorations on each side are the same, and Justine says, "Hey, you could use a mirror!" She runs and gets a mirror, which the children have been using in the construction area, and holds it up to one side of the clay figure. "See, it's the same in the mirror too!"

▼ ◄ ▲ ▼ ◄ ▲ ▼ ◄ ▲ ▼ ◄ ▲ ▼ ◄ ▲ ▼ ◄ ▲ ▼ ◄ ▲

This is a good example of how the children can make connections across the different activities and curriculum areas when they have the opportunity to come up with their own ideas and have access to materials and resources to share them with others. The impact of having that connection made by another child rather than by the teacher is powerful. While Lua, the teacher in this example, created the environment and presented activities and materials that foster thinking about balance and symmetry, it is the children's immersion in these ideas that helps them come up with new ideas, and it is their own deep thinking that helps them make the connections themselves. This is a connection that Lua might not have even thought about. But if she had, and if a child hadn't thought of it herself, she could have had mirrors handy and asked it they could think of another way to look at the figure as symmetrical. As it was, she didn't need to!

Documentation can provide these children with another way to explore symmetry. Lua could ask Paul and Sharon how they could capture what they've done. She could suggest that it be something to put on the wall, or in a newsletter to parents, or into a class book where records are kept of what the children are doing. Paul and Sharon could come up with a number of different possibilities, including taking a digital picture of the creation or drawing the creation. By encouraging them to do both the photograph and the drawing, Lua could use the drawing activity as an opportunity for them to explore symmetry more deeply. In the process of drawing the figure, Paul and Sharon would have to think about the issue of symmetry all over again as they decide what to draw where.

Documentation is serving a number of different goals in this case. First, it is a method of capturing the work that is done in the classroom, and it also could be an individual record of what children engage in that could be helpful for assessment purposes. Second, it is a good way to share with others what is being done, particularly if the documentation includes some description of how this creation came about, a description that can also be captured in a number of different ways. And third, it is an opportunity for children to reflect at a different level on the work they are doing and to express their thinking in another medium. Documentation that is appropriate for the age of the children with whom you work is an important component of the work that the children do, serving as yet another extension of the activity itself.

Think about the impact of a number of pictures on one wall, all pictures reflecting the children's work on symmetry. Such a display would itself encourage further thinking about symmetry. Such a display could even be the stimulus for Justine's idea of using a mirror to look at Paul and Sharon's figure a different way. Documentation can provide much of that stimulus by making the work of children more visible and present for them to think about. And it is that thinking about what they've done previously that helps children understand more deeply what it is they've been engaged in, since concepts in action that are unarticulated, while the first step, are only part of the process of understanding.

Language and Literacy

We've seen how one good children's book can help provoke an interest in balance. Here are some other books that could be used:

Gerstein, M. (2003). *The Man Who Walked Between the Towers*

Glanz, J., & Lipton, E. (2003). *City in the Sky: The Rise and Fall of the World Trade Center*

Mooney, M. (1994). *A Matter of Balance*

Wells, R. E. (1996). *How Do You Lift a Lion?*

Another way of extending the study of balance into the literacy and language realm is to look at the symmetry in language, both written and spoken. There are many illustrations of symmetry and patterns, particularly in poetry and song, and there are ways of focusing on the symmetry. Reading and writing poems, singing and writing songs, are ways of having children listen for patterns and create their own.

Physical Balance

Constance Kamii and Rheta DeVries (1978), in their early work on constructivism and the construction of physical knowledge, describe children in a preschool playing with boards and rollers, an activity that is documented in a videotape (no longer available) called *Playing with Rollers*. Children are given large boards and wooden rollers in a large empty room and experiment by standing on the boards on top of rollers, by making the rollers into catapults, and by moving boards across the room on top of the rollers. This experimentation involves a great deal of balance, coordinating one's body movements with the actions of the objects. It's a model for some wonderful experimentation that children could engage in through which they could explore balance. This could occur on a large scale, as Kamii and DeVries describe, or it could be done on a smaller scale, with smaller wooden boards and smaller rollers, if space is a concern.

Here's an example of how one teacher created opportunities for experimenting with physical balance.

Ruth brings into her classroom a heavy large sealed box filled with books, and places it in a corner of the second grade classroom. She tells the children that their challenge is to figure out all the different ways that they can move the box to the other side of the room without lifting it, using dowels, balls, and boards. She has them form teams of three or four children and tells them that they must sketch out several ideas before they can try one.

The children start work in their teams, and each group comes up with a couple of different ideas. Group one's ideas include putting four balls under a large board, and sliding the box onto the board gradually. Group two comes up with the idea of sliding it across the floor on a piece of cardboard, shifting the cardboard from one side to the other as it moves.

As each group finishes, they show Ruth their ideas, and they take turns trying the different ideas. Some of them work better than others. The balls move the box a short distance, but it immediately falls off, and so the children decide this works but not very well. The box on the board doesn't slide any better than the box on the floor. The third idea—to put dowels under the box—works the best. They initially put a whole row of dowels under the box close together. The children proceed to argue about how many dowels are needed, and they end up experimenting to see how few dowels will move the box across the floor.

Some of the other groups have similar plans and have an opportunity to experiment with the box to see for themselves. Ruth is observing carefully, sketching each idea in her notes. Finally, Diandra and her group, who have been trying to put the box on a large cardboard tube on which they've balanced a board, discover that the box flips over and the books spill out. "Hey, I have a different idea," Diandra says, "let's tape the box shut so that it can flip over!" Using duct tape, they tape the box shut and with great noise and excitement the box is flipped over end on end using the board and the tube. By the time the box reaches the other side of the room it is a little damaged, but the children are so excited at their unique solution to the problem that Ruth is delighted by their creativity.

The children start experimenting with moving other smaller objects in similar ways, such as single books, individual blocks, backpacks, and rulers.

Ruth finds a book called *Moving Heavy Things* (Adkins, 1980) and shares with the children the different methods and tools that have been used to move things. The children become interested in the pyramids, because of the different ways that the large blocks were moved without machinery, and several of them begin to study this independently during their project time.

Other ways children can be given opportunities to experiment with balance occurs on the playground, where some equipment still allows for experimentation with balancing their bodies. Climbing structures, large round concrete tubes, and other outdoor play equipment can provide the challenges for balance. If school playgrounds don't have such equipment, explore a neighborhood playground or a gymnasium where there may be equipment available for children to play with. Or create opportunities in the hallway, the cafeteria, or whatever indoor or outdoor space you have available to you.

▼ ◄ ▲ ▼ ◄ ▲ ▼ ◄ ▲ ▼ ◄ ▲ ▼ ◄ ▲ ▼ ◄ ▲ ▼ ◄ ▲

Sun is a preschool teacher from Korea, who is in the United States to study early childhood education. She is working with a group of children on the big idea of balance and is amazed at how little experience children have with balance compared to Korean children. In Korea, there are many historical games that are still played today related to balance, including teeter-totter-like structures that children jump on to make the other child go up into the air. Sun decides to re-create this structure in the carpeted project area in order to show children safely what is involved. She makes a model of the structure to show them before they experiment with the real thing and shows the children pictures from the Korean historical village of the large ones that were used by adult women. Today, modified versions of these are seen on some playgrounds in Korea.

The children are interested in the idea that Korean children might play different games and have different equipment than they do, but they are most interested in trying it out. Because it is a lively and potentially dangerous activity, Sun has them try it out under close supervision. As she expected, they spend a lot of time trying to just balance each other on the apparatus and less time trying to get the other person to "fly" into the air.

▼ ◄ ▲ ▼ ◄ ▲ ▼ ◄ ▲ ▼ ◄ ▲ ▼ ◄ ▲ ▼ ◄ ▲ ▼ ◄ ▲

Exploration of other culture's games and activities is another way you can integrate cultural understanding into children's everyday activities. Taking time to research how other country's children engage in play and with what materials can provide children with rich connections, both in terms of the specifics of the big idea and in terms of the more general issue of the similarities and differences across cultures and countries.

▼ ◄ ▲ ▼ ◄ ▲ ▼ ◄ ▲ ▼ ◄ ▲ ▼ ◄ ▲ ▼ ◄ ▲ ▼ ◄ ▲

Jennifer, a first grade teacher, has studied Japanese educational practices and has seen pictures of children in the elementary school on high stilts, up to six feet high. This intrigues and puzzles her, as stilts are not something commonly explored among her children. Although Jennifer recalls stilts from her own youth, she hasn't seen them used at all by children in the past couple of decades. The Japanese children's ability to balance, which is needed to walk on stilts, seems quite advanced to Jennifer, and she decides to experiment with this idea with her children. She has been connecting her classroom with a first grade classroom in Japan, and they have had some e-mail communication between the children of this classroom and her children about a variety of issues and questions.

She decides to let the idea of stilts come from this communication, if possible, and suggests that they ask about what kinds of things they do in their physical education program. After sharing many of their common experiences, some of the Japanese children mention walking on stilts. Later, when the children start to discuss what they are finding out, the use of stilts comes up—something most of the children have only seen at the circus, if they've seen it at all. Jennifer shares her pictures of the Japanese children on stilts with the class, and they engage in a discussion over e-mail with their Japanese friends about how they learned to walk on stilts.

Jennifer's classroom decides they want to try to walk on stilts, and so they start the way the Japanese children started when they were in preschool. Japanese children begin with blocks of wood strapped to their shoes and gradually use thicker and thicker blocks, eventually graduating to real stilts.

Jennifer's children, after trying the blocks and seeing how difficult it is, find that their admiration for the Japanese children increases. The time needed to become accustomed to even short stilts challenges many of Jennifer's first graders. Although they never graduate to real stilts, they do a lot of experimenting with balancing their bodies on the short stilts and of trying to walk and look natural. The class has some good discussions about how some things like stilt-walking take a lot of early experience in order to become as skilled as the Japanese children. Some of the children talk about the gymnastics classes they are taking and how hard some of the things are that look so easy when you see the Olympic stars do them. This leads to a study of gymnastics, much of which incorporates what they have learned and studied about balance.

▼◄ ▲ ▼◄ ▲ ▼◄ ▲ ▼◄ ▲ ▼◄ ▲ ▼◄ ▲ ▼◄ ▲ ▼◄ ▲

Jennifer has capitalized on a cultural difference related to early experiences, and in the process she is able to provide her children with some opportunities to experiment with balance as well as learn something about those cultural differences.

As you can see, the big idea of balance is complex and far-reaching and effectively integrates many curriculum domains, including mathematics, science, language arts, creative arts, and social studies. And it is one that is inherently fascinating to children at different ages, making it easy to provoke and retain interest in extensions and deeper exploration.

Resources

Children's Literature

Adkins, J. (1980). *Moving Heavy Things*

Cherry, L. (1990). *The Great Kapok Tree: A Tale of the Amazon Rain Forest*

Gerstein, M. (2003). *The Man Who Walked Between the Towers*

Glanz J., & Lipton, E. (2003). *City in the Sky: The Rise and Fall of the World Trade Center*

McLoughlin Bros. (1980). *The Magic Mirror: An Antique Optical Toy*

Martin, J. (1998). *Snowflake Bentley*

McCully, E. A. (1992). *Mirette on the High Wire*

McCully, E. A. (1997). *Starring Mirette & Bellini*

McCully, E. A. (2000). *Mirette & Bellini Cross Niagara Falls*

Mooney, M. (1994). *A Matter of Balance*

Wells, R. E. (1996). *How Do You Lift a Lion?*

Videos

Cirque du Soleil—Anniversary Collection, 1984–2005. (2005). (Also see website: www.cirquedusoleil.com/CirqueDuSoleil/en/default.htm)

Calder's Circus (2001)

Websites

Symmetry: www.adrianruth.com/Symmetry/

Virtual Manipulatives—Reflection: www.teachers.ash.org.au/mikemath/movies/symmetry1.html

Paint Shop Pro: http://simsub.digitalriver.com/cgi-bin/se/jasc/psp91117/0/keyword/paint_shop_pro_exa

The Butterfly WebSite: http://butterflywebsite.com

SymmeToy—Symmetric Art Program: www.hufsoft.com/software/page4.html:

Kids Snow Page: http://ccins.camosun.bc.ca/~jbritton/snow/snow.html

Snowflakes: www.its.caltech.edu/~atomic/snowcrystals

Wilson Snowflake Bentley—Photographer of Snowflakes: http://snowflakebentley.com

Games

Stacrobats (Ravensburger)

Topple (Pressman Toy Corporation)

Chairs Game (Fundex Games, Ltd.)

Jenga (Hasbro)

Don't Spill the Beans (Milton Bradley)

Materials

all kinds of balances for weighing things, including pan balances

plastic coat hangers (for mobiles)

In the construction/art areas:

balance beams

beads

boards and rollers

clay

mirrors

pipe cleaners

pulleys

stilts

wire

CHAPTER 5

Zooming In and Out

This big idea is one that capitalizes on something that children find fascinating—changing perspective. At the end of the movie *Men in Black* (Sonnenfeld, 1997), there is a fast zoom out that shows the earth as a marble in a game being played by aliens. Similarly, in the movie *Osmosis Jones* (Farrelly & Farrelly, 2001) we zoom into a man's body in which we find a microcosm of society, with germs battling white blood cells. Zooming in, zooming out—an interesting way to look at changing perspectives and one that gets at some important concepts for children to ponder, concepts relating to the very small and the very large, looking closely and magnification, geography and culture, and physical and social perspective-taking. In this chapter, I'll be exploring how children's explorations of zooming in and out can be woven through the curriculum domains of mathematics (through measurement, scale, and proportion), social studies (explorations of other cultures), and literacy (through dramatic play and children's literature). Technology is a particularly useful tool to use in the exploration of the big idea of zooming in and out.

A good way to start thinking about this big idea is to look at the *Powers of Ten*, documented on a videotape about the work of Ray and Charles Eames (1968) and also available in book form (Morrison & Morrison, 1994). As the video opens, you are looking at a man lying on a beach. Each subsequent view is one power of ten farther away from the man, resulting in our fairly quickly seeing the earth, and then beyond into the galaxies. Zooming back in, we return to the man on the beach, and then proceed to zoom into his hand, again by powers of ten, until we are looking at atoms.

Another inspiration for thinking about this big idea is to read the books *Zoom* and *Re-Zoom* by Istvan Banyai (1995a, 1995b). Each of them, without words, takes the reader out or into the scene by focusing on one part. These two books are the very best around for considering the issues of zooming in and out. In *Zoom*, for example, the full page rooster gradually, through a series of wonderful pictures that zoom progressively out, occupies a smaller and smaller place in a scene.

While both of these sources can be used with young children, for now let's just use them to stimulate our thinking as teachers. What can we do with this big idea? In the following, we'll sort through the different issues that are raised by zooming in and zooming out.

Micro, Macro—The Very Small and the Very Large

There are so many ways that children can look at the issues of size, ways that are typical in early childhood education—magnification and enlargement are two ways. Children's fascination and interest in the very small can be seen in age-old interests in "invisible worlds," such as the fairy world, where small creatures have mushrooms as umbrellas, and in the intense desire children have in toys coming to life, as animated in the movie *Toy Story* (Lasseter, 1995). And once you create worlds in which there are "little people," those little people inhabit a large world. Imagining the world from the perspective of the small is another theme of much children's literature (such as *George Shrinks*, by William Joyce, 2000). What is it like to be walking in the garden from the fairy's perspective? What is it like to be face to face with a human shoe, as in the movie *Honey, I Shrunk the Kids* (Johnston, 1989)? Ordinary objects in large scale are popular in children's museums and theme parks, as in a popular museum exhibit where a desktop is large scale and children can try to lift a huge pencil or climb on a huge telephone.

Focusing on magnification alone, however, will not fully inform our big idea. We need to consider the use of magnification in the context of perspective-taking. What kind of a world does a bug live in? What is it like to swim in a pond if you are a small aquatic frog? Examining the pond water through a projecting microscope and creating large-scale drawings of the small creatures found, then creating a mural or an environment in a dramatic play area that replicates the pond, are very effective ways that children can consider the perspective of others that are smaller than they are.

It is also possible to consider what it would be like to be larger or to see things from the perspective of zooming out. Consider the "bird's-eye view" that children find fascinating. Creating an overview of the classroom and trying to see it from the perspective of a giant, perhaps by making a scale model, is an exercise that can stimulate such perspective-taking. Taking photographs with a digital camera of familiar sights or places from distant perspective can lead to discussions of scale and size, such as if you take a photograph of the school playground from a balcony of a home across the street from the school and consider what others see (and don't see) from a distance.

Children's Literature Relating to Zooming In and Out

Some wonderful children's literature can serve as the core for the exploration of zooming in and out. At the end of this chapter is a list of some possible resources, with brief descriptions of how each one relates to zooming in and out and perspective-taking. Here's an example of how a teacher used a children's book, Chris Van Allsburg's *Two Bad Ants* (1988), to extend her children's exploration of perspective-taking.

As she is getting her coat on to leave, Anita, a four-year-old, notices that there is a chain of ants walking across the counter near the sink. She calls out to the teacher, "Ant alert! Ant alert! Someone get the poison!" Donna says, "Kill the ants, kill the ants!" Cheryl, the teacher, thanks Anita for pointing it out, and says she'll take care of it. After the children leave, Cheryl thinks that this would be a great opportunity for the children to explore perspective-taking, using the ant's perspective as a starting point. While she does not think Donna is a "killer," she is concerned about the tone in her voice, and wants to capitalize on this teachable moment. She first checks out the ant situation and finds that they are coming in from the window and ending up in a small container of sugar that is sitting on the counter. She leaves the ants and their trail where they are.

In the school library, she gets the book *Two Bad Ants* and decides to use this the next day.

When the children come in the next morning, Anita and Donna seem to have forgotten about the ants. When they all come together for a story, Cheryl reads the book to them. Anita says, "You picked that book because of the ants I found yesterday! Where did they go?" Cheryl suggests that they all go and look. As they gather around the counter, Brian says, "Watch out where you step." Only one ant is walking across the counter, and the children get very excited. "Where is it going? What is it doing?" Donna and Anita decide to stay in during recess and watch where it goes, seeing that it is headed for the sugar container. Cheryl listens closely to their discussion, noticing that they are personifying the ant, probably as a result of the story.

The next day, she notices that a group of the children are pretending to be ants in the dramatic play area. At group time, she asks if anyone has any ideas about what the ants are doing on the counter. "Maybe they are thirsty," says Demarcus. "I think they are lost and trying to get out," suggests Julia. "No," says Anita, "they are eating the sugar." "I like sugar," says Bobbi, "but my Mom says I can't eat it very much." The children launch into a discussion about what ants eat. "Does anyone have any questions about how the ants live?" Cheryl asks the group, with a marker and chart paper ready to write the questions down. "Where do they sleep?" one of the children asks, and Cheryl writes it down. "What kind of house do they live in?" "Do they have babies? I've never seen a baby ant." More questions ensue until the paper is filled up. Cheryl then asks what they could do to find out the answers to some of these questions. "We could build a house for the ants!"

A lively discussion about the ants' houses leads into activity time, during which Cheryl and several of the children gather the materials the children decide they need for the ant house building. As they build the ant houses, much discussion and work relates to the size of the house that an ant would need, and the children begin to consider the issue of scale—what size house would work for something an ant's size?

That afternoon, Cheryl visits the district library and finds a number of trade books about ants, as well as some more fiction that includes ants and other bugs. She brings them into the class the next day, and the children use them as they build the ant houses.

Cheryl is appropriately responding to the children's interests, and the resulting project work is engaging. She continues to wonder how she could extend it so that the children will think about the big idea. What could she do?

▼◄ ▲ ▼◄ ▲ ▼◄ ▲ ▼◄ ▲ ▼◄ ▲ ▼◄ ▲ ▼◄ ▲

One possibility comes from the early work of George Forman (Forman & Kuschner, 1983; Forman & Hill, 1984) in which he and his colleagues describe children making scale models of their own classroom. Because the children in Cheryl's classroom are so engaged in house building, and are already having discussions about relative size, it would be a logical extension to encourage scale models of environments they are familiar with—the classroom, the playground, the neighborhood.

Cheryl could do one of two things to introduce such an extension. First, she could just be explicit and say, "I noticed how great you all were doing building the ant houses, and thought we could build a replica of our classroom," and then begin the process of scaling down the classroom environment. Or, she could introduce another book, such as *Me on the Map* (Sweeney, 1996), as a provocation and encourage a discussion afterward about what they could do to make a map of their own classroom, which could lead into the children creating a model of the classroom or, which playground. Either way, Cheryl is basing her extension on her observations of what at least some of the children were focused on and interested in. It is likely that the group would respond to such an extension because of that initial interest and that they could see the connection between their work with the ant houses and the work developing a scale model.

The extensions into map making and looking at maps and other scale models could follow, again depending on the interests and discussions of the children in the classroom. Cheryl could also be introducing the literature described earlier, with the intent of encouraging such connections and further interest in perspective-taking.

What could a teacher of older children (say, first or second grade) do that would be appropriate, beyond what was done by the children in Cheryl's class? It is important to think about issues of developmental appropriateness and the incredible range of ability and interest in any early childhood classroom. Because of this variation, it is likely that some children in a second grade classroom could engage in, and learn a great deal from, the same activities that Cheryl did in her preschool classroom, just as some of the children in Cheryl's classroom would interact with the activities without understanding some of the principles of, say, proportion and scale that could be a part of the activity. Side by side, these children of many different interests and abilities will learn from and interest each other. As early educators, we must always keep in mind the incredible range of possibilities in any class of young children and accept the needs of all children.

That said, older children are more likely to be able to engage in more extensive reflection on the work, are more capable of reading and writing related to the work, and are able to engage in more sustained work than younger children. In addition to classroom documentation that is done by groups of children, older children can document in journals and through other means in ways that can be shared and reflected on in small groups. If you are a teacher of older children you will also be more concerned with the pressures to teach to prescribed standards and may need to incorporate specific skills and content into the curriculum. This is the place to do so rather than trying to meet those standards through disembodied teaching without a meaningful context. Because of this, the teacher of older children will need to have resources for more complex reflection and opportunities for sharing and reflection to a greater extent than teachers of younger children.

How can you incorporate these "mandated" skills and concepts into such work? Measurement, one content area addressed in the primary grades in different ways in different states, can serve as an example. Because developing a scale model raises issues involving measurement, it is a logical place for measurement to come into play, and it probably will naturally. If it doesn't, however, there are ways that you can facilitate and stimulate measurement work on the part of the children. Here are a few of these ways:

1. Pose a question—verbally or with a big chart on the wall. "How big would a chair need to be in our model?"

2. Introduce some tools. Measuring tools— tape measures, rolling measurement devices, ropes and string, masking tape—are fascinating to children. Model the use of these tools in addressing children's questions.

3. Encourage different ways of coming up with the same answer. "Can anyone think of another way we could measure this?"

4. Introduce vocabulary in meaningful context. This is the best way for children to learn and also remember the words that will tap their knowledge on tests. *Proportion, scale, estimation*—all are words that can be easily incorporated into your language as you discuss the scale models.

5. Document and highlight the children's work related to measurement. Take digital pictures, write down what children are doing, and encourage them to share with each other and with the class what they are learning with regard to measurement.

The focus on measurement can take on a life of its own, and can lead to related projects. Older children who are interested in and have opportunities to engage in measurement and comparisons will want the opportunity to explore further all the different ways that things can be recorded and compared. You will need to be able to capitalize on that interest when it is appropriate.

Technology as a Tool for Perspective-Taking

There are numerous ways that technology can be used to focus on zooming in and zooming out. These can vary considerably depending on your access to equipment, materials, and resources.

Some simpler uses of technology include the use of overhead projectors and copiers. In addition to being a great source of light (see Chapter 2), an overhead projector can be used to enlarge many things and project the images onto the wall, where paper can be hung so that objects or pictures can be outlined. Copiers can be used to reduce and enlarge pictures.

More complex but increasingly accessible uses of technology incorporate digital imagery. Digital cameras are, in my opinion, an essential part of a teacher's resource kit for capturing and quickly displaying things that children do and events that they participate in (a walk, a field trip, a celebration). Digital images on the computer can be played with in numerous ways, including enhancement, enlargement, reduction, mirror images, negative images, and multiple duplication. With younger children, such use of technology will be done primarily by you as part of the curriculum; with older children, the use of technology itself can be the focus of activity and learning.

In the work of Reggio Emilia you can see a rich use of technology. The reproduction of children's drawings and other artistic creations is used extensively throughout the documentation of their work. Photographs are used in many aspects of their project work. Projection in large scale on walls and on screens is incorporated into much of their work. A good example of the use of projection is seen in the video *To Make a Portrait of a Lion* (Reggio Children USA, 1980), in which a picture of the lion statue in the town square is projected onto a wall for children to interact with. Let's look into a first grade classroom that is exploring this big idea.

▼◄ ▲ ▼◄ ▲ ▼◄ ▲ ▼◄ ▲ ▼◄ ▲ ▼◄ ▲ ▼◄ ▲

Lucy, the teacher in this public school classroom, knows that she is to "cover" measurement and fractions, and there is a good deal of pressure on the teachers in her school to be accountable for addressing the standards the district has delineated. While she concurs that these are important things for young children to learn, she does not want the need to address them to change her focus on project work and integrated curriculum. She also is planning on doing a social studies unit on their city and decides that she can address all of these curriculum areas through an integrated project focusing on maps and scale models.

With the help of several parents, she decides to go on a field trip using public transportation. She presents the plan to the class by putting a bus map of the city on the overhead projector. She then gives the class the task of figuring out how to keep track of planning and recording where they will go. In her planning, she anticipates that they will culminate this trip by creating a large mural of the city with their route on it, but she is interested in seeing what ideas the children have and hopes they will generate that as one of the ideas.

The class, which is accustomed to working in small groups on tasks, spends some time deciding what "jobs" need to be done and forming groups to accomplish them. Once they get into their groups, they begin working during their class project time. Some of the children are planning the route; others are deciding how they will track and record where they go; still others are talking about creating a large-scale map of the city on which they can record where they went when they return.

When they come back to report on what they have done to plan the trip, one of the children says that his father works at the historical society and that they have a three-dimensional model of the city there. The children decide that one of their destinations will be the historical society and that they want to create their own three-dimensional model instead of the two-dimensional map that the children originally planned.

▼◄ ▲ ▼◄ ▲ ▼◄ ▲ ▼◄ ▲ ▼◄ ▲ ▼◄ ▲ ▼◄ ▲

Lucy is pleased with the progress the children are making and the directions the project is taking. She can see how the three-dimensional model-making will lead to issues of scale and proportion, and begins to gather and prepare resources that can help the children think about those issues, resources that will direct their attention to the math and problem solving that they will be expected to know later. These resources include books, such as David Macaulay's books on buildings and structures (*Castle*, 1982a; *Cathedral: The Story of Its Construction*, 1981; *Pyramid*, 1982b), and some Internet sites, including Google Earth, which allows you to zoom in on any part of the world, or other sites that display maps with which you can zoom into neighborhoods or zoom out and see the entire city. She also plans for another child's mother, an architect, to visit the class and talk about scale and planning. She feels confident that the standards she is expected to cover will be addressed as the project unfolds.

The Role of Symbolic Play and Role-Playing in Perspective-Taking

Engaging in symbolic play and role-playing is an essential part of exploration of the big idea of zooming in and out and perspective-taking. Young children's pretend play serves as an important way that children make sense out of the world and construct a great deal of understanding. From the perspective of Piagetian theory, pretend play is a way that children assimilate concepts and ideas, practicing and expanding on their ideas about how things are "supposed" to work, putting themselves into another's shoes through role-playing. Katz and Chard (2000) discuss the role of dramatic play in supporting project work, in which the teacher creates imaginative play environments where children can engage in symbolic play related to the project at hand. Thus, for example, a project involving a school bus could incorporate the construction of a school bus out of cardboard, which then occupies the dramatic play area. As the children play in that area, they will practice and implement their scripts about riding in and driving a school bus, scripts that are evolving through their project work. Using the dramatic play area as a context for supporting project work is one arena in which teachers can facilitate and stimulate children's ideas around the project work.

Dramatic play is particularly amenable to your indirect facilitation. The reason for this is that children's pretend play is largely dependent upon the props and materials available for them to play with (see Chaillé & Young, 1982). Without props related to doctor play, for example, children are unlikely to play doctor. Unfortunately, many teachers who have dramatic play areas in their room are satisfied with a set of standard and unchanging props, often associated with "house"—toy food, play dishes, baby dolls. As a result, the play of children in the dramatic play area is often focused around traditional "house" play. While such play may be rich and valuable, there are many other possibilities for the use of the dramatic play area that are being missed.

Because of the impact teachers can have on the focus of children's symbolic play, the dramatic play area is full of possibility for extending the work on perspective-taking that is going on throughout the curriculum. Depending on the focus of children's interest, the dramatic play area can be turned into a habitat for an animal or any environment different than their own, such as a shoe store, which may come out of children's explorations of feet and shoes. Here is a good example of how a preschool teacher transformed the dramatic play area to facilitate the children's interest in horses.

▼◄ ▲ ▼◄ ▲ ▼◄ ▲ ▼◄ ▲ ▼◄ ▲ ▼◄ ▲ ▼◄ ▲

Brandeis, a teacher of three- to five-year-olds, decides to turn the dramatic play area into a barn to support the children's exploration of what it's like to be a farmer. Since some of the children have been particularly interested in horses after a visit to a local farm, she wants to incorporate objects and materials that would encourage role-playing around that theme. She got some hay to put into a part of the dramatic play area (after checking with the fire department for its safety) and borrowed a real saddle from a friend. The children wrote a letter to their parents asking for other props, and parents donated plastic toy horses and other farm animals, a game of horse-shoes, some dress-up cowboy clothes, boots, and hats, and posters of horses and cowboys. With the children's help, they transformed what had been a "house" area into a setting for horse play.

▼◄ ▲ ▼◄ ▲

▼◄▲▼ ◄▲▼ ◄▲▼

Children playing in a "shoe store" dramatic play area.

The Role of Symbolic Play and Role-Playing in Perspective-Taking

Symbolic Play for Older Children

It is rare to find time or space dedicated to symbolic play in classrooms for children older than kindergarten. So what can a teacher in the primary grades do to incorporate children's dramatic play into the curriculum? Here, literacy is the key. There are many ways that primary-age children turn their symbolic play into creative writing and storytelling, and this is a prime way for encouraging perspective-taking. Writing letters or describing something from the perspective of someone else is a common practice that can enhance perspective-taking. Here is an example.

Emily reads the book *Diary of a Worm* (Cronin, 2003) to her third grade class. In this book, a worm is keeping a journal of his life, and it is full of artwork and writing that captures a lot of information about a worm, but, more important for our purposes, is in the worm's voice. The children respond very positively to the story, and later when they are writing in their writer's notebooks, Jonathan shares with Emily that he has decided to write a "journal entry" from the perspective of his new kitten. At the group sharing time, at Emily's request, he shares his story with the class, and many of them decide to do the same thing. The series of stories that results is put together by the teacher into a class book.

Another avenue that you can take if you are a primary grade teacher is drama. Many small vignettes can be written and acted out by children, who are quite capable of scripting and creating stories in which they take on different characters. Additions of costumes and stage decorations can become projects in themselves and also involve thinking about the roles that they are to play, which requires perspective-taking. With some planning and preparation of the children for the process, such playacting can become a common occurrence in your classroom.

In both journaling and the use of drama, technology can enhance and encourage the experience. Videotaping the performance is a great way for children to replay and reflect on what they have created. Even more motivating is teaching children how to use the video camera or the digital camera for creating a story or video production of their own. Creating stories and adding pictures and artwork to digital creations is also highly motivating for young children who have often developed those skills in other contexts. If they haven't, incorporating the technology instruction needed to produce electronic stories can enhance the children's writing experience. If you or your students are lacking in those skills and resources, teaming with a classroom of older children can provide the mentors needed—a great experience for the older children as well.

As stated earlier, the concepts of micro and macro, and issues of size and comparison, come up naturally as we explore the ideas of zooming in and out. Concepts of proportion, fractions, part/whole, and inclusion are all relevant here.

Young children are interested in looking at the "pieces" of things, and this lends itself to exploring some of these mathematical concepts. Trying to identify something from its parts is a good exercise in perspective-taking. Games in which the object is slowly uncovered, as in a puzzle, accomplish this. Puzzles are not necessarily a material that a constructivist would appreciate, largely because most puzzles can only be put together in one way. Usually, putting a puzzle together begins through a process of trial and error. Once the puzzle is mastered, putting it together is a matter of repetition. While satisfying and enjoyable to some children, this is not inherently a constructivist activity. Another way of looking at puzzles is to see them as exercises in part/whole relations. Think about ways of creating puzzles that would focus on that concept.

▼◄ ▲ ▼◄ ▲ ▼◄ ▲ ▼◄ ▲ ▼◄ ▲ ▼◄ ▲ ▼◄ ▲

Terri, a second grade teacher, takes a digital photograph of the playground and makes it into an overhead. She then cuts it up so that the parts of the playground are not clearly identifiable. Putting a piece of it on the overhead, she has the children call out what they think the piece represents, until gradually the entire playground is reconstructed. She then challenges the children to come up with their own ideas for puzzle making, suggesting that they try to challenge each other with the pictures they decide to take.

▼◄ ▲ ▼◄ ▲ ▼◄ ▲ ▼◄ ▲ ▼◄ ▲ ▼◄ ▲ ▼◄ ▲ ▼◄ ▲

You can also think about the ways children can put things in order by size as a way to generate explorations. Begin by reading one of the many variations of *Goldilocks and the Three Bears*. Then have the children explore the environment for other things that are in order of size. In most classrooms, there are a number of items that can be found in different sizes—DUPLOs and LEGOs, marbles and balls of different sizes, cups—which can be used as starting points. One of the most intriguing types of toys is the nesting toy, which comes in many configurations. There are the elaborate Russian nesting dolls, and there are many variations of them, from simple to complex. There are very simple baby toys that nest and that can be used even with older children to talk about proportion and seriation. There are nesting blocks, nesting eggs, nesting balls, and many other things that nest in a similar way (e.g., measuring spoons and cups). You may find that a parent or someone in the community has a collection of nesting dolls that they could bring into the classroom. Keep in mind the real goal, which is for the children to start to look for and see series in the world as a way to focus on increasing and decreasing size.

Here is another way you can focus on size variation.

Pam, the teacher of a group of three- to five-year-old children, took pictures of each child in the class and then duplicated them in three different sizes, mounting the pictures on cardboard rectangles. These pictures were available on the resource table, and the children began to use them in a number of ways, putting them into groups, mixing them up and then sorting them. Josiane took the three pictures of her best friend Diana and began to draw a picture of Diana's dog, one for each size picture—the pictures of the dogs were graduated in size too. After cutting each one out, she glued it on a piece of cardboard and paired each one with the corresponding picture of Diana. Other children started to create "companion" pictures like Josiane had done. After a few days of this work, Pam asked the children if they would like to put some of these series pictures on the wall, and the children dictated their stories about the "little one, the middle one, and the big one."

Another way of exploring zooming in and zooming out and incorporating mathematics (as well as other curriculum areas) is to use as a provocation the movie *Honey, I Shrunk the Kids* (Johnston, 1989). In this movie, the scientist father develops a device for shrinking things and accidentally shrinks his two children. Some of the escapades that result could serve as excellent launching points for exploration of perspective-taking and trying to understand what it is like to be small or large.

Sierra shows her kindergarten children one of the excerpts from the movie *Honey, I Shrunk the Kids*, in which the shrunken children are in the grass of the backyard, encountering large bugs and huge blades of grass. She asks the children to think about any part of the classroom and to try to imagine what it would be like to be shrunk and trapped there. They form into their buddy pairs, and she hands out jeweler's loupes and asks them to find a very small area, one square inch, that will become their inch. She also hands out little square frames for them to use and suggests that they tape the frames onto their square inch.

The children spend quite a bit of time running around the room, trying to find just the right area to choose. There is some squabbling over some of the popular places, such as the ant farm. Sierra reminds the children that it doesn't really matter what square inch they find.

Once they have their square inches, they are to "map" them, study them closely with their loupes, draw them, re-create them in clay on a larger scale. They are given a number of options of how they can represent their square inches, and many of the children choose to use multiple media.

To the children's surprise, some of the square inches that appeared empty are really not, with little pieces of lint, dust, and other such things to include in their descriptions of their inches. As Sierra had hoped, some of the children spontaneously start to talk about what if the square inch was the room, which she would have suggested if they had not. Some of the children ask if they can have a larger area instead of a square inch, and Sierra suggests that they do both and then compare them—how is it different if you have a larger area?

Grant decides to introduce a family to his square inch, making tiny clay pieces that represent the people who inhabit his square inch. He and his partner Rebecca have two squares, one a square inch and the other larger, a six-inch square. They make similar clay family members for the larger one, and the exercise in relative size is a difficult and an interesting one. Sierra takes digital pictures of their work and spends some time discussing it with the whole group at their meeting time. This gives many of the children ideas of what they can add to their areas, and many other "families" begin to appear, all of different sizes. Grant and Rebecca make true-to-size representations of their square inches, which proves to be quite difficult.

Sierra, seeing this struggle, decides to indirectly help them. She takes a picture of one of the larger representations and then reduces it on her computer to a smaller size. The resulting prints are left out to show all the children, and Grant and Rebecca immediately make the connection. They take their larger representation and ask Sierra to make a photograph of it and then reduce it for them.

The children's resulting maps, diagrams, and clay models are displayed around the room. Many more photographs are taken, and the resulting photographs are, on the children's insistence, blown up and reduced down to show the different sizes that are possible.

This interest in reducing and enlarging photographs gives the children many other ideas. Toni and Rachel decide to take a photograph of each other and then experiment with reducing it and enlarging it. Sierra facilitates the exploration of size changes by having prints of graduated size made of many of the photographs the children are experimenting with.

By following the children's lead, and by introducing appropriate tools for the children to use as their interests develop and change, Sierra is facilitating some interesting and important studies of comparisons, seriation, and scale.

As another focus, consider using a bird's-eye view as a way of thinking about zooming. The book *Earth from Above* (Arthus-Bertrand, 2002) could be used as a provocation for this focus. In this book pictures of different parts of the earth from above are stunningly presented. Taking samples from this book and projecting them onto a screen, would probably be sufficient to intrigue children.

▼◄ ▲▼◄ ▲▼◄ ▲▼◄ ▲▼◄ ▲▼◄ ▲▼◄ ▲

Kendra shows her second graders the book *Earth from Above* and has some excerpts that she projects for them to start to talk about. The discussion that the children have leads to the question: What would their school look like from above? What would their town look like? The children generate a whole list of things they would like to see from space, and they start to explore the idea of getting a bird's-eye view of familiar places and buildings.

This list gets posted, and they begin by trying to predict what some of the things would look like. Different groups form to look into different places. One group is interested in the school buildings, another in the playground, another in the store across the street from the school, another in the parking lot. Each group begins by talking about and sketching what they think the photograph would look like. For some of them, this requires some investigation. The building group can't remember what the roof looks like or might be made out of, so they go outside to explore this. The playground and parking lot group go to the second floor of the school building, where they can look out onto them.

As the children continue their work, many questions arise about what kinds of things they would see from above. A delegation of the building group goes to the principal and asks permission to go to the roof with the custodian, where they take their clipboards and make notes about what is up there. There is a great deal of discussion about how they might actually see the area from above, including suggestions that are not feasible, such as renting a helicopter. Then one of the children, Rick, comes to school on a Monday morning after having gone to the science museum, where he has found a kit in the museum store that allows you to send a camera up with a rocket and take a picture. With the help of several of the fifth graders and Rick's father, they successfully launch the rocket and the picture is parachuted back to the ground. The day of the launch the children are very excited, having made lots of predictions about exactly what will be seen in the picture. The class stands out on the playground, looking up as the rocket is launched and takes a picture.

The resulting picture is enlarged and multiple copies are made. The children spend a good deal of time making comparisons with their own predictions. And the part of the photograph that captures the children looking up is isolated and enlarged, and Kendra mounts it on the wall as the "best picture of this class ever!"

The children have been sharing their work on this project with their families through their class newsletter that goes home every week. Julia's mother works for an insurance company, and in her work she uses maps of the city in which they live that are made from photographs taken from above. She locates the maps of the school and gets copies of them for the class. She comes into the class and shares the maps, talking about how they are used in her work and by other people.

▼◄ ▲▼◄ ▲▼◄ ▲▼◄ ▲▼◄ ▲▼◄ ▲▼◄ ▲

Kendra has facilitated this exploration, but it is the children's interest and initiative that has made it a successful project, and that has allowed the children to explore perspective-taking in a way that is truly memorable. This example also shows how the cooperation and involvement of the whole school can enhance the experience of children within one classroom. In addition, it was important that Rick's parents were aware of the project, and supportive of it, in their visit to the science museum store and the subsequent rocket launching. Keeping parents informed, up-to-date, and involved really pays off not only for individual children like Rick, but for all the children who can benefit from what parents can contribute to the classroom.

Here is a simpler version of this kind of perspective-taking experience involving the bird's-eye view.

▼◄ ▲▼◄ ▲▼◄ ▲▼◄ ▲▼◄ ▲▼◄ ▲▼◄ ▲

Sandra's fellow preschoolers have been spending a lot of time playing with kites and parachutes, since it's been a warm and windy September. Their class has been designing and making different types of kites and then trying them out in the field next to their school. Sandra decides to make a kite that will carry her miniature troll doll up into the sky, and she carefully attaches the troll with pipe cleaners to the kite that she has made out of paper and string. After she successfully flies her kite, she takes the troll off, and it rejoins the other little trolls that she is playing with. Sandra has the troll tell his friends about what it was like to be flying up there, and she has the idea that the troll could take a picture when he flies the kite!

She enthusiastically shares her idea with the teacher, Polly, who exclaims, "What a wonderful idea! I wonder how we could help your troll to do that?" The children put forth a number of different ideas, and they write down all the possibilities. Although the ideas the children have are not possible, Polly suggests that they take a very large ladder out to the field and take a picture looking down from it as though it was attached to a kite. This satisfies the children, and they help Polly and the custodian carry the school's ladder out. Polly and the children hold the ladder while the custodian climbs to the top and takes a picture looking down on the children. Sandra makes him take her troll up with him.

The picture is the subject of much discussion by the children. Polly, seeing the children's interest in this, decides to use the stepladder to take some pictures from other vantage points inside the room as well, so that the children can look at their room from above. This leads to even further discussion and interest in the perspective from above. Some of the children begin sketching their playground from an upstairs vantage point. Polly, wanting to enhance their engagement in their explorations, shows the children a clip from the video of Peter Pan where he and Wendy are flying over London. As a result, many of the children, including Sandra, begin telling stories and

drawing pictures about the flying trolls and what they see when they fly, both inside and outside the classroom.

▼◄ ▲ ▼◄ ▲ ▼◄ ▲

This simpler solution, although not as dramatic as the rocket, enables the children to see things from a different perspective and to try to project what it would be like to be looking down from above. Polly's efforts to encourage the children to deepen and broaden their interests are successful.

A different perspective—the playground from up above.

Perspective-taking, which is the essence of this big idea, is an important part of what we want children to do when they encounter people who are different than they are in some regard. The extensions we can make in the arena of social studies are fairly easy ones. Posing questions to children about what it would be like to be seeing things from a different perspective can be done in the physical realm, as we saw with the study of the bird's-eye view, or from the social realm, as we see in conflict resolution. We can also try to put ourselves in the perspective of people whose everyday lives are different than our own, such as people who live in another country or culture.

One way you could do this is to introduce children to life in another country through a videotape. *Families of the World* (Master Communications, 1998–2002) is a series that profiles children from many different countries. These videos, made for children, walk you through the life of a young child in a particular country today.

Showing children one of these videotapes and then providing them with opportunities to explore more about that country and culture through books, music, materials, field trips, and visitors could stimulate the kind of perspective-taking that is necessary for intercultural awareness.

I'm not talking about the "tourist curriculum" that some criticize as an inappropriate approach to multicultural education. Too often that kind of approach fosters stereotypes and encourages children to see differences as "foreign" and as not really applying to them, which contributes to what Sonia Nieto (2003) called "exoticizing." Rather I am talking about introducing young children to the idea that their daily lives could be different than what they currently experience. We could also stimulate this perspective-taking by thinking about any children whose life experiences are different than our own, and there are often ways if you are teaching a diverse group of children to have a sharing of daily experiences be sufficient to make that point. However, sometimes it is helpful to make the differences clear enough and sharp enough so that children are not just personalizing what they see. This is the function that these videotapes could provide by encouraging the study of daily life in another country.

The second way you could extend perspective-taking to social studies is through conflict resolution. Through the everyday responses to conflicts between children, you can communicate a great deal about the importance of understanding that how you see the situation is not the way another sees it. Again, with young children it is sometimes difficult for them to see this in the heat of the moment. Young children will also find it difficult to detach their interests and needs from those of others in such a way that they can take the other's point of view. This social (and intellectual) egocentrism is natural for children, but there is much you can do to encourage the gradual construction of understanding of others' points of view. Making these conflicts explicit can be done through drama, role-playing, puppets, children's literature, and storytelling, and children can "hear" those lessons much better when they are not the players.

So, after a conflict has occurred that could be a learning opportunity for this purpose, you can search for resources and plan some activities that can depersonalize this conflict and help all the children look at it from another point of view.

Zooming is a big idea that can very effectively integrate so many curriculum domains—particularly because perspective-taking is such an important basis for scientific, mathematical, social, and cultural understandings. This is a big idea that has inherent appeal to children, so provoking interest and excitement in it is not difficult. It is also a big idea with particularly important social value. For all these reasons, the big idea of zooming is an appealing one to both teachers and children.

Resources

Teacher Resources

Arthus-Bertrand, Y. (2002). *Earth from Above*

Eames, C., & and Eames, R. (1977). Powers of 10. Available from www.loc.gov/exhibits/eames/science.html and www.powersof10.com/

Forman, G. E., & Hill, D. F. (1984). *Constructive Play: Applying Piaget to the Preschool*

Forman G. E., & Kuschner, D. S. (1983). *The Child's Construction of Knowledge: Piaget for Teaching Children*

Morrison, P., & Morrison, P. (1994). *Powers of Ten: A Book about the Relative Size of Things in the Universe and the Effect of Adding Another Zero*

Children's Literature

Zooming In and Out

Banyai, I. (1995). *Zoom* and *Re-Zoom*. Wordless picture books that consist of zooming pictures.

Brown, M. W. (1999). *The Train to Timbuctoo*. Illustrated by Art Seiden. This book has pictures zooming out on a bridge across a river and zooming into a piece of the bridge.

Keats, E. J. (2000). *Dreams*. Picture book showing the shadow of a mouse becoming bigger and bigger as the camera zooms in on it.

Shannon, D. (2000). *The Rain Came Down*. In this book there is a zooming in on the face of a policeman and a zooming out to the view from above the city block.

Wiesner, D. (1991b). *Tuesday*. This book includes several pictures that incorporate zooming in on a pond to see frogs, a turtle, and fish.

Zolotow, C. (1993). *The Moon Was the Best*. Photographs by Tana Hoban. For each photograph in this book, there is a small picture with a close view of a part of the larger photograph.

Perspective-Taking

These are good books for stimulating and exploring perspective-taking.

Browne, A. (2002). *Gorilla*. A view of a girl sitting in front of a television, from the perspective of the top of the opposite corner of the room.

Cronin, D. (2003). *Diary of a Worm*. A worm writes a diary about its life.

Joyce, W. (2000). *George Shrinks*. What happens when you are smaller?

Macaulay, D. (1982). *Castle*; (1981). *Cathedral: The Story of Its Construction*; (1982). *Pyramid*.

MacLachlan, P. (1980). *Through Grandpa's Eyes*. Illustrated by Deborah Kogan Ray. A grandson spends a day experiencing the world the way his blind grandfather does.

Mazer, A. (1991). *The Salamander Room*. Illustrated by Steve Johnson. A young boy gradually adapts his environment to reflect what the salamander is used to, transforming his room into the forest.

McCue, L. (1990). *Puppies Love*. This book includes the perspective of a dog looking at the feet of people.

Ryder, J, (1990). *Under Your Feet*. Illustrated by Dennis Nolan. This book offers the perspective from the ground, under children's feet.

Santore, C. (1997). *William the Curious: Knight of the Water Lilies*. This lovely book portrays life in a castle from the eyes of a frog, at boot-level.

Schuett, S. (1995). *Somewhere in the World Right Now*. This book illustrates perspective-taking by looking at what's going in different places in the world at the same time.

Sweeney, J. (1996). *Me on the Map*. This book walks the reader through a child's mapping of her world, starting with her room.

Van Allsburg, C. (1988). *Two Bad Ants*. In this book we see life as viewed by an ant exploring a kitchen.

Wood, J. N. (1990). *Survival: Could you be a mouse?* Illustrated by Derick Brown. This book asks you to take on the role of a mouse in going through your day, predicting what a mouse would do (or should do) in different situations.

Yolen, J. (1987). *Owl Moon*. Illustrated by John Schoenherr, This book shows scenes from the eyes of the owl up in a tree.

Young, E. (1989). *Lon Po Po*. This book shows the view from the tree top to the bottom, and from the bottom to the top.

100 Films and Videos

Families of the World (1998–2002)

The Films of Charles and Ray Eames, Volume I: *Powers of Ten* (1968)

Honey, I Shrunk the Kids (1989)

Men in Black (1997)

Osmosis Jones (2001)

To Make a Portrait of a Lion (Reggio Children USA, 1980)

Toy Story (1995)

Materials

digital cameras

magnifiers of all kinds, including jeweler's loupes

nesting toys

overhead projectors

CHAPTER 6

Playing with Sound

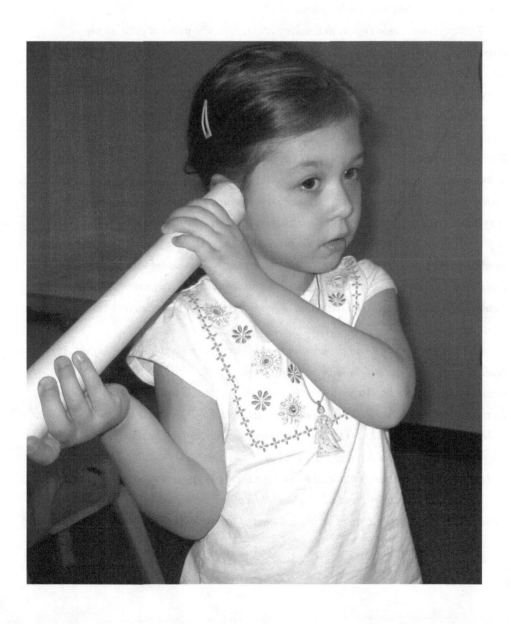

*T*he preschoolers in Devon's class had returned from a visit to a small local bakery. Sitting in a circle on a rug, they begin talking about the things they had seen and done. Devon asks them, "What were some of the things that you remember about our visit?" and after a number of the children put forth their ideas, Natalia says, "I really liked the way the door dinged." Surprised, Devon says she doesn't remember that. Cynthia says, "Yes, when you went through bells rang." The children begin talking about this, some of them remembering it. Another child says she remembers the bell that you had to hit to get someone to come to the counter.

The children decide, with Devon's encouragement, to try to make the door to the classroom ring a bell when it is opened.

This experience got Devon to thinking about how she was not even aware or thoughtful about the sounds that are a part of the learning experience, and how many of the children seemed to be more tuned into sound than she is. She decided to start exploring sounds with the children. Because the children had already noticed bell-like sounds at the bakery, she began to start with bells as an introduction to this exploration.

She began by seeing what was available already at the preschool that she could use and discovered a few toys, mostly musical instruments, that incorporated bells and other bell-like sound-making objects. She gathered them together. They included some musical instruments that have bells on them, such as tambourines, shaker sticks with several very small bells on them, and wrist ribbons covered with bells. She also found other objects that made bell-like noises—the pretend cash register, several timers that were used for games and for keeping track of turn-taking, and some wind chimes that were hung outside during good weather. She also noticed that there was a bell inside the bird case that the parakeet played with, and a gong that was used in the classroom to signify clean up time.

She shared what she had found with the children at circle time the next day. After some discussion about all the different ringing things, the children decided they wanted to make their own bells. An argument ensued over what you would need to make a bell. Dan said that you could make it out of paper and cardboard, and Leann said, no, it had to be out of something hard. The children examined the things Devon had shared, and they decided they would have to use metal or something hard like that. Devon asked the children to bring in empty cans and bottles for them to experiment with the next day.

The next day at the project table, the children tied string to the bottles and, with some adult help, fastened string to the bottoms of the cans. Devon had prepared a place *to hang the completed bells, and as each bell was completed it was hit with a drumstick to see what kind of noise it would make.*

Two of the children began trying to add a "ringer" to the inside of the can. Devon quickly sees how difficult this is, and provides metal spoons for them to use for this purpose, but they spend a great deal of time on the problem of how to get the ringer to hang inside the can so it can swing from side to side. As the children work, argue, and experiment, they keep looking at the bells Devon brought originally to the discussion, and they study them carefully.

Noticing that some of the children are frustrated by this problem, and others have given up and left the area, she decides they need to regroup. Coming back together, she suggests that they carefully study the bells that they have, as well as a book that has pictures of many different kinds of bells (Baker, 1998). Previously in this classroom, the children have been encouraged to sketch and draw real objects, and she suggests that they do some drawings of the bells they have been looking at.

▼◄ ▲▼◄ ▲▼◄ ▲▼◄ ▲▼◄ ▲▼◄ ▲▼◄ ▲

This is one example of how a group of children might embark on a study of some aspect of sound. Sound is a big idea that incorporates, in particular, much from the curriculum domains of science, mathematics, literature, poetry, and music. In considering sound as a big idea, we are able to go beyond each of these curriculum domains and consider the connections. In this chapter I will be describing some of the concepts underlying the big idea of sound, including sources and receptors; properties of sound; rhythm; and the reproduction of sound. By focusing on the concept of the source of the sound of bells, Devon's classroom engages in group problem solving that incorporates art and music, children's literature, and science. By seeing sound as a big idea rather than seeing "bells" as a project topic, Devon is able to generate many other curriculum extensions and capitalize on the children's interests and ideas in the process. Here is how Devon followed through on the bell-making experiences.

▼◄ ▲▼◄ ▲▼◄ ▲▼◄ ▲▼◄ ▲▼◄ ▲▼◄ ▲

Justin, one of the children in Devon's classroom, discusses his bell making with his family, showing them the booklet with his drawing of different bells. His mother notices that there is a performance coming to town of the show called *Stomp! Stomp!* is a show that features performances of percussion and other noisemaking using all kinds of objects and materials (see www.stomponline.com/show3.html for downloadable video and audio clips). She's seen excerpts of this show on television and thinks that Justin would enjoy seeing the show because of the work he's been doing making sound with cans. The family attends the show and purchases one of the videotapes of the performance. Justin excitedly brings the videotape to school and shares it with Devon and his classmates. The entire class watches the videotape together, and the children begin to try to reproduce some of the sound making that they see in the performance. They begin to generate so many sound-making objects and materials that they decide to convert the block-building area into a "stomp place." Over a long period of time, the children and the teacher develop this very popular area.

The "stomp place" includes:

a place to hang different objects

baskets of things with which to hit the objects

an assortment of percussion instruments—drums, maracas, bells, tambourines—from all over the world

a table on which children are constructing different versions of those instruments

an electronic synthesizer provided by a parent

compact disc and tape players with an assortment of music available for playing, some with headphones, some with speakers

a microphone and an amplifier

a basket full of things that make soft sounds, portable enough to be used throughout the classroom

recording devices

a video player with tapes of different musical performances

This area is constantly changing and expanding as children begin to inquire about different types of instruments. After about a month of experimenting with percussion, Devon notices some waning of interest and decides to introduce the children to other ways of making sound. One of the parents is a member of a fiddle band and comes in to play fiddle for the children, introducing them to the idea of stringed instruments. This leads to a new interest in sound making, and the "stomp place" is transformed, gradually, into a broader place for music making.

▼◄ ▲ ▼◄ ▲ ▼◄ ▲ ▼◄ ▲ ▼◄ ▲ ▼◄ ▲ ▼◄ ▲ ▼◄ ▲

While sound is itself a big idea, what are some of the concepts incorporated in experimenting with sound? Here are a few:

Sources and receptors—something that can make a sound and something that can hear the sound

Properties of sound—whether it is pleasant or unpleasant, melodic, discordant; emotions and reactions elicited by sound based on its properties

Rhythm—beats, regularity, predictability, timing

Reproduction—repetition, recording, variations

Sources and Receptors

When we consider what makes a sound and how it is received, we can see that each of these categories can be the subject of extensive experimentation, thinking of all the variables of making different sounds and then the variables of "taking in" the sound—hearing it, recording it, or registering it in some way through representation.

Sources   When we think about sources, we ask: Where does the sound come from? There are two different categories that can be considered.

Natural sounds: This category includes any sounds that are produced in nature, such as weather-related sounds (thunder, wind, rain); sounds produced by physical events (water flowing over rocks, branches falling off a tree); and animal sounds. Human sounds are, of course, a subset of animal sounds and include voice as well as other human-produced sounds (claps, burps).

Manufactured sounds: This category includes sounds created by machines and other sounds that do not occur in nature. This would include sounds created by musical instruments as well as engine-generated noises.

Receptors   The second question we ask is, How is it recorded? or How do we come to hear it? Is it represented, as with a recording device, or represented in another form, as in prose descriptions? Or is it directly experienced through our senses? If it is directly experienced, is it heard or felt, or both?

Let's look at one way you could explore the category of receptors.

Mary, who teaches in a first grade classroom, has been exploring sound with her children, and they've been focusing on producing sounds, using shakers

and musical instruments. She decides to focus the children on how they can change how they hear sound, rather than how they make it.

As the children sit around the rug in their morning meeting, Mary leads the class in humming a tune. Used to singing, humming is an interesting experience for this group, and they are enjoying it. She then asks for everyone to put their hands on their ears while they hum. The ensuing discussion focuses on how different the humming sound is when you put your hands over your ears. Then she pulls out a basket with some large seashells, cardboard tubes that are about four to five inches in diameter and of different lengths, a variety of noisemaker plastic cans with beans and other objects that the children had made in a previous activity, plastic cups, and funnels. She shows the children the items in the basket and says, "Here are some things you could use to explore how to hear noises differently. They'll be available over at the large project table for you to experiment with, to see how you can hear noises differently."

Chelsea, Frank, and Jessica all choose the project area as a place to work and begin by exploring all the objects, shaking the noisemakers, and putting the different objects to their ears—the shells, the funnels, the plastic cups, and the tubes. Chelsea hums while she puts each object up to her ear, and then Jessica starts shaking the noisemakers at her. "Wow, this sounds weird! Listen to this one!" Frank puts a tube up to each ear and then exclaims, "When you move around everything in the room sounds different." The girls all put cardboard tubes up to their ears and walk around the room.

Mary and the girls talk that afternoon at the group time about what they discovered, and they decide to create other shapes of "ear tubes" to try. Several of the children work to design ways to attach the ear tubes to their heads.

▲▼◄ ▲▼◄ ▲▼◄ ▲

▼◄ ▲▼◄ ▲▼◄ ▲▼

Everything sounds different with tubes on your ears.

Properties of Sound

What are the ways we can characterize what we hear and/or feel? How can we describe the sounds that we hear? We can think of this in terms of the different ways we experience the qualities of sound. Is it loud, soft, discordant, or harmonic? Is it pleasant, unpleasant, soothing, or upsetting? What are the emotions generated by listening to the sounds? Sounds can create moods and can serve as accompaniment to activities, such as dancing, marching, walking, even breathing.

Marianne decides to explore children's feelings about sounds by having a discussion with them after they've been exploring a variety of noisemakers. The preschoolers have been playing with a couple of large drums and a "thunder-making" object that is a can with a spring coming out of it. They discuss how the sound makes them feel. A couple of the children say that the sound makes them feel happy. Betsy says, "The squeaky sounds made me feel good," and Sonita says, "The sound was lovely and I liked it." Mike says, "The thunder thing makes me feel really scared, like there is thunder outside. I liked it."

Marianne then asks the children to draw how different sounds make them feel. After playing with maracas, Austin says, "It sounded like rain, so I painted it a soft color, because it reminds me of my kitty. When I'm cozy with my kitty there's soft colors. The music reminded me of that." Tyler says, "It makes me feel happy. I painted the hair of my person orange for happy."

Then the children play with metal sticks and a metal drum. Isaiah says, "It reminds me of really angry. I'm painting the fish angry." Tyler says, "The green is mad and the orange is mad." Dora says, "It reminds me of my Mom when she was a little kid and shocked herself. Her hair went kink." "It reminds me of a clock," Austin says. "It goes 'tick, tock, tick, tock.' The clock is orange, because it sounds like it's saying 'orange, orange, orange' over and over again."

Marianne is exploring the children's ideas as they express them both through their paintings and through their words and learns a great deal about their feelings about both sound and color, and the connections between them. The children start to spontaneously make these connections in the ensuing explorations of sound.

Rhythm

Not all sound follows patterns, but many sounds do and the characteristic of rhythm is an important part of thinking about sound as a big idea. Rhythm in sound captivates and engages; it is the structure of sound when structure exists. That structure embodies many essential mathematical concepts and can serve as the vehicle for categorization and conceptualization.

Providing children with instruments does not necessarily result in a focus on rhythm but providing children with instruments with background rhythms is likely to. Using a simple synthesizer keyboard can give children the option of trying different kinds of rhythms as background to their own productions or as background for movement or drawing. Start with a waltz rhythm, for example, and then switch to a reggae rhythm, and see how children's movements change. You can also show children videotapes of different kinds of musical performances that highlight rhythm, such as Taiko drumming, which involves very large drums, or the work of Blue Man Group, which uses unusual instruments. Explore the different kinds of drawing done to different rhythms as well as different rates of rhythm.

There are other sources of rhythmic sound as well. The ticking of a clock, a heartbeat captured by a stethoscope, rain falling, a metronome—all can be recorded, amplified, and listened to for their rhythm. A metronome can be the source of exploration by varying the timing.

Children with access to sound-making instruments, particularly percussion instruments, will often spontaneously begin to develop rhythms, and this can be facilitated by the teacher who can provide music as backdrop to their work. And a focus on rhythm can also be provoked purposefully. Here is an example of a teacher whose interest in different cultures and their music led to a focus on rhythm in her second grade classroom.

▼◂ ▲ ▼◂ ▲ ▼◂ ▲ ▼◂ ▲ ▼◂ ▲ ▼◂ ▲ ▼◂ ▲

Felicia, who loved to travel, made a habit of collecting samples of music from each country she visited. On her last trip to Japan, she purchased a compact disc of traditional Japanese music, and was struck by the lack of percussion in the music, which consisted of mainly stringed instruments without a clear rhythm to the music. She decides to share this music with the children and to provide the contrast of music with extensive percussion. She finds a compact disc with African music that has a vibrant percussion and begins by just having the music on at different times of the day. She is hopeful the children will notice the music and express some curiosity about it.

When some of the children ask about the "weird" music that is on when the Japanese music is playing, Felicia sees this as her opportunity to talk about different kinds of music with the children, both to increase their understanding of different cultures and to focus on rhythm. She plays excerpts to the children of the two forms of rhythmic and arrhythmic music—some from Japan and some from Africa—and asks them to imagine what kind of dancing you could do to each type of music. After a brief discussion, she asks for volunteers who would work to develop some kind of dance for each type of music, and two small groups are formed for this project. Each group is given the music and some time to work on this project, and they work over the next few days during their project time.

As they work, Felicia listens in on their conversations and makes some videotapes of their practices. They share their dances in their group meeting time, and the rest of the children respond by joining in after they are done.

The children get very excited by the percussion of the African music, and Felicia asks them if they would like to do some more projects on this type of music. She plays some other examples of percussion music from different countries and also discovers a videotape of African dance that is available at the library. Together they watch the African dance video, and the children try to reproduce the rhythms they hear with various instruments and noisemakers around the room. Felicia then suggests that they try to make the different rhythms only by clapping. All through this discussion, Felicia is tape recording their experimentation and listens closely to it later to see what she can learn.

Felicia also contacts a local music store that sells African drums and arranges for a field trip to the store. The owner also teaches African drumming and invites them to experience a minilesson in African drumming in the studio attached to the store. Felicia explains that she is particularly interested in focusing on different rhythms.

The field trip is a great success, and the children return from it with lots of questions and ideas for making different types of music. Felicia poses a question to them: How can they keep track of the different types of rhythms that they create? How can they represent them? One of the children remembers that the African drummer had some music that he was looking at, with X's on it to represent the beats. She suggests they try to figure out how to represent the different types of rhythms, to develop a language for it.

Some exploration follows with different children trying different types of representation. Many of the "codes" are very personal and idiosyncratic, and Felicia suggests that there be a test of the code to be sure it is something that anyone could read. She also acknowledges that sometimes a personal code is ok, if you are the one who needs to "read" it. The experimentation continues, with some children creating codes for others to read, and some writing their own personal codes.

Tim creates the following code:

X—a loud beat

O—no beat

Lowercase x—a softer beat

And represents one of the songs like this:

X O x X O x X O x X O

Felicia asks Joey to reproduce this rhythm, and Joey is able to do it successfully. Tim and Joey start writing codes for different rhythms together, and they present their new language to the class at the next group time.

In this way, Felicia is able to get the children to focus on rhythms more attentively since they are struggling to represent them in a way that they or someone else can play them again.

After some of this exploration of music with roots in another country, Felicia finds that the children are more interested in and less critical of the music they considered "weird" on first listening. She makes it a point to continue to bring music from many different countries and of different genre into the classroom. The awareness of cultural differences in taste and in ear for music is learned naturally rather than told to the children as a lesson.

▼◄ ▲▼◄ ▲▼◄ ▲▼◄ ▲▼◄ ▲▼◄ ▲▼◄ ▲

Reproduction

Much of what we do with sound involves reproduction of what we hear, imitation, or imitation with variation. In many ways, this element of sound as a big idea illustrates best how sound can be a vehicle for experimentation. In experimentation, we initiate something we predict and proceed to vary what we do more or less systematically. Think of repeating a rhythm, over and over, and, at some point, a mistake is made or a variation is interjected. This is incorporated into the rhythm, producing a new, more complex rhythm. Isn't this a microcosm of theory-building?

So take any of the previous rhythm-producing ideas and think about how children could reproduce and represent the different rhythms they hear. Explore the different timings of the metronome, for example, and see what children do to try to represent the range from fast to slow. Listen to heartbeats with a stethoscope at different points in time (for example, before and after running) and have children chart comparisons.

Here's an example of how preschoolers could explore the reproduction of sound.

Josh's group of three- and four-year-olds are interested in the construction going on next door, which for Josh, although interesting in terms of the building, has been a noisy intrusion into their classroom. Partly because it is so noticeable, Josh decides to explore the sounds of the construction. He starts by using a tape recorder to capture the sounds of the machinery that is crushing the concrete at the building site, and then finds that his recording includes many distinct loud noises. He plays the tape for the class at their group meeting, just to see what their interests and questions would be from listening to the tape. Some of them can readily identify a few of the sounds, and some of them express a curiosity about what is making a particular noise. Because of their attentiveness and interest, he suggests that they try to record, identify, and then reproduce some of the different sounds that they hear at the building site.

They begin by taking several tape recorders to the building site. Josh has selected several of the children to be "in charge" of each of the tape recorders, and the other children are assigned to help them by finding what to record. The children without tape recorders have clipboards with drawing paper and are to keep notes—consisting of drawings—of what is going on while the recordings are made so that they can remember. Josh also is taking digital pictures of the things that the children are sketching, so that they can match up the sounds to the pictures and drawings later.

When they return to the classroom, Josh encourages the children to work in their small groups to organize their tape recordings and pictures, and each group listens to the tape and shares their pictures. Meanwhile, Josh is printing out his digital pictures.

The next day Josh brings out an amplifier that they can use to play the tape recordings for all to hear, and over the next few days groups share their tape recordings and their pictures. Josh makes available copies of the digital pictures he took. While there is some overlap, some of the groups have recorded quieter machines or sounds that they encountered, including one group that recorded the workers having coffee and talking. Some of the children puzzle about how a particular machine is making a particular noise, and there is much discussion of the ways the machines work. These children ask to return to the construction site to look more closely at these machines, which Josh arranges. On the return visit, many of the children add to their sketches, and others just watch the machines more closely.

After working on connecting their representations with the tape recordings, children decide as a whole group to make a large scale display of the work, including tape recorders at each "station" of the display where the tape can be played for the accompanying picture. In preparation for this, some of the children take their sketches and, using the digital pictures, make a final drawing or painting of the sound maker that they focused on.

One of the parents in the preschool who helps out on occasion is skilled at technology, and Josh asks her for help in compiling the work into a form that can be saved. She scans the children's pictures and records the sound, creating a compact disc that can be looked at as a PowerPoint presentation. As each picture is viewed, the accompanying sound is played. She has several of the children help her do this during project time. The final result is presented at the end of the project, and with great fanfare and popcorn it is projected onto a screen. The children proudly present a copy of their movie to the workers at the construction site, who subsequently invite the children into the site as it is completed for a hard-hat tour of the construction.

Josh has been able to capitalize on the children's natural interest in the building site but directs it into a focus that they might not otherwise have chosen to explore. In the process they learn a great deal about representation, about the relationships between particular machines and the sounds they make, and, in particular, about using technology to represent what they are learning.

Children's Literature

There are so many good children's books that directly or indirectly raise issues of sound; the Resource section at the end of the chapter provides a sampling of the children's books that can be used as provocations and as resources for exploring sound. Look for both fiction and nonfiction books, as there are many in both genre that can be useful.

Children's literature that deals explicitly with sound or silence is a wonderful way to provoke children's interest in sound as a project, and each book can suggest different explorations to children. But be on the lookout, too, for books that have sounds incorporated into them less explicitly, either as accompanying "sound effects" to a story line about something else or where sound can be substituted for the words (one example is Barbara and Ed Emberley's *Drummer Hoff*, 1972).

Resource Books for Teachers

There are a number of good resource books for teachers about sound, many of them focused on music or on the scientific principles underlying sound. In the Resource section at the end of the chapter I've listed some that are particularly helpful. As with some of the other big ideas, resource books can strengthen your own understanding of the underlying scientific concepts, but be careful that these do not become the sole focus of the explorations, as in some cases they may be developmentally inappropriate and inaccessible to younger children. Children's natural interest in exploring sound should be your guide in the study of this big idea, with resource books serving as references for you.

Mathematics

Mathematics is clearly a curriculum domain that can be addressed by using sound as a big idea. The repetition and variations of patterns and seriation are the two predominant areas in which mathematics is explored by children through sound. Here is an example of four-year-olds exploring seriation.

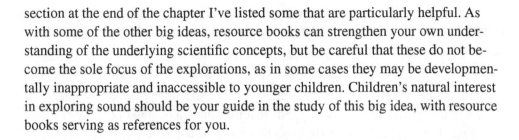

Elice's teacher, Ron, has acquired at a surplus store a set of metal pan lids without the knobs on top; they range in size from three inches to twenty-four inches. Ron has attached hangers to these metal lids with knotted rope and has suspended pieces of plastic pipe over the worktable from which he hangs the lids (see Figure 6.1). Elice and Mickey, who are four years old, have come to the work area to explore these materials. First, they hang as many of the lids as they can and begin banging away with the mallets provided on the table. Elice then says, "Shhh!" and proceeds to hit each lid, one at a time; Mickey follows after her, hitting each one again. Elice says, "I know, let's make a song!" They take all the lids off and then hang

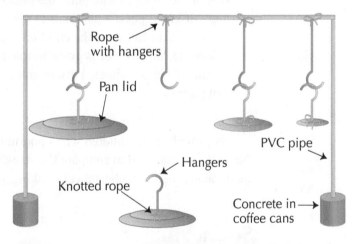

Figure 6.1 *Pan Lids Suspended in Order of Size*

one lid at a time, starting with the smallest one. When they have finished, they go down the row, hitting each one in turn. Then Mickey, laughing, starts hitting them randomly, and Elice joins in, laughing. "We're making a song, we're making a song!" they yell.

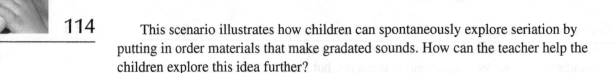

This scenario illustrates how children can spontaneously explore seriation by putting in order materials that make gradated sounds. How can the teacher help the children explore this idea further?

Ron notices what the children are doing, and when they appear to lose interest in the "performance," he suggests that they draw a picture of the series of pan lids they had constructed, "so that it can be constructed again." The children sketch the construction, and as they do, Mickey says, "Let's make this again tomorrow, ok?" They put their sketch up on the board by the work area and leave the activity.

Interested in this exploration, Ron puts pictures of other "seriated" instruments—marimbas, xylophones, and a wooden flute-like instrument in which seriated wood whistles are connected together with reeds. He also finds a large picture of the inside of a piano that shows the different lengths of the strings and a picture of a pipe organ's pipes. He puts these pictures on the worktable and on the wall by their sketch.

When the children return to the project area, a number of them look excitedly at the pictures, talking about their experiences with instruments. One of the children who plays the piano says, "My piano doesn't look like that!" Ron has put out materials to make different sized "drums" with paper stretched over cans, and the children begin to make and decorate drums. Dennis declares that he is going to make the loudest drum of all, and the children have an animated discussion about which can he should use for that purpose.

By providing the children with opportunities to vary the size of the materials that make sounds, and to compare the sounds produced by different sizes, Ron is encouraging logico-mathematical thinking, particularly regarding seriation.

Social Studies

How can the big idea of sound be used to explore developmentally appropriate social studies for young children? One way is inspired by some work done in Reggio Emilia. The documentation of the work is a compact disc recording of the sounds of the streets of the town of Reggio Emilia—a "sound tour" of the town. From the recording, it is apparent that the children were paying close attention to the different sounds in different parts of the town and decided to document it with this recording. Although we do not know what led up to this recording, we can imagine how teachers and children could be inspired by this idea to explore the different sounds heard in different parts of the children's world. A good approach to early childhood social studies is to begin with the child's immediate world and slowly branch outward into the environments of their experience. You could begin with the classroom, exploring different sounds of the classroom, in different areas, and at different times of the day. Then you could branch out to the school environment, different parts of school indoors and outdoors, the parking lot, the hallways, the offices, the bathrooms. The neighborhood surrounding the school could be the next circle of sound environments—streets, offices, stores, and parks.

A study mapping the sound environment could incorporate many different elements that integrate social studies with other curriculum domains. Mapping, in particular, could be a wonderful part of this exploration. As a way of doing that, children could read the book *Me on the Map* (Sweeney, 1996) about a child's mapping of her room and her neighborhood, and children could brainstorm how to map and document the sounds at different points of the map.

Let's look at how this might play out in a first grade classroom.

Sheryl's classroom is bustling with noise, on purpose. She and her students have been studying sounds for a month or more, and she and the students listened to the compact disc made by the children of Reggio Emilia. This provocation inspired the children to make their own audiotape of the sounds in their classroom. Dan and Brendan are the ringleaders of this project; they are in charge of keeping track of the tapes that have been made. To do this, they have designed a system of labeling and of describing each of the tapes. As the number of tapes increases, Dan and Brendan decide that they need a better way of keeping track. They pose the problem to the whole group, with Sheryl's urging. After looking at all the tapes that have accumulated, the children as a group brainstorm how they can keep track of where tapes had been made. Leslie suggests that they could use a map, and the whole group decides that they need a large wall map on which to keep track of where tapes had been made. The creation of this "sound map" of the classroom involves a small group of children for a week.

As they work on the sound map, the children extend the map outside the classroom, and begin to make a schoolwide sound map. As the map increases in scope, teams of children begin to make sound maps of other parts of the school. They carry their tape recorders around throughout the school and then carefully label each tape and mount it in an envelope on the sound map.

One of the children, Debra, goes for a visit over the holiday to see her aunt who lives across the country. While there, she and her father record the sounds in the airport and then the sounds in the neighborhood where her aunt lives. On her return, she and the children take out a map of the United States and put a mark on the map where Debra had been. This opens up a whole new chain of potential experiences for the children.

Another natural social studies exploration related to sound was described in the section on rhythm earlier in the chapter, where children listened to and studied music from different countries. Although the focus was rhythm, there are many ways the teacher could bring in differences in music across cultures, countries, and historical periods in ways that would enhance children's understandings of similarities and differences among people. To illustrate this, we return to the earlier example.

Felicia, the first grade teacher whose children studied rhythm from different parts of the world, decided to make this look at music and place more explicit as a way to extend the social studies learning. She puts a world map on the wall, and when music from another country is playing, she asks the children to find the place on the map where the music is from. There are reference books to help them, and she has several children work together to try to figure it out from the tape or compact disc that she is using. When they locate the area the music is from, they put a flag on the world map. Since they listen to a lot of music in her classroom, the children begin to anticipate this process and initiate it when Felicia has brought a new compact disc. She has also encouraged the children and their parents to share music they have at home, so sometimes the children will bring in a compact disc. The world map begins to fill with flags, and it becomes a game to figure out where the music is from. Sometimes Felicia or one of the children will play the music without showing the case it came in and will ask for predictions of what country or part of the world the music is from.

Some of the children start to notice that there are areas where there are no flags, and the class identifies some of those countries. They begin to search for music from countries that are not flagged on their map. They begin to see that there are many different types of African music by noticing the difference between a recording from Senegal and marimba music from Zimbabwe. They learn about regional differences by listening to zydeco music from New Orleans and comparing it to Hawaiian music. Felicia introduces the children to the legal ways of accessing music online and finds that there are some sites where music can be listened to without downloading it.

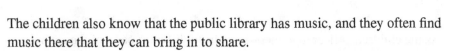

The children also know that the public library has music, and they often find music there that they can bring in to share.

▼◄ ▲ ▼◄ ▲ ▼◄ ▲ ▼◄ ▲ ▼◄ ▲ ▼◄ ▲ ▼◄ ▲

Felicia's focus on music from different countries is an intriguing entrée into the children's study of different countries. The differences and similarities in music spur their explorations of other areas, particularly as one or more children become intrigued with a particular country's music and rhythms.

Science

The connections with science predominate this big idea, as is true of many of the big ideas in this book. You've already seen a good example of science exploration in the bell-making experiences described at the beginning of this chapter. The key is to think about providing children with opportunities to experiment with materials that they can vary, so that they can (1) have good ideas, (2) try out their good ideas, and (3) see the results of their experiments. In the bell-making activity, the children were able to experiment with the sounds made by different materials used to make the bells (cardboard, metal) and different sizes of ringers hung inside the bells.

Here's another example of an activity that could provide children with the opportunity to experiment with the science of sound.

▼◄ ▲ ▼◄ ▲ ▼◄ ▲ ▼◄ ▲ ▼◄ ▲ ▼◄ ▲ ▼◄ ▲

Devon puts on the project table some plastic eggs and containers of a variety of materials such as rice, beans, marbles, small manipulative pieces, washers, and other things that can make noise when shaken. Chelsea, John, and Tim come to the table excitedly talking about creating shakers. John says, "My shaker will be louder than yours!" He puts the larges pieces of pasta into the shaker, closes up the egg, and shakes it. Chelsea puts rice in hers, closes it up, and shakes it. The two of them shake one after the other, and Chelsea declares, "Mine is louder!" Tim looks closely at the rice, putting some in his palm, then at the pasta, and then puts the washers in an egg, which makes an even louder sound. "These are heavier and harder, so they work even better!" he proclaims.

▼◄ ▲ ▼◄ ▲ ▼◄ ▲ ▼◄ ▲ ▼◄ ▲ ▼◄ ▲ ▼◄ ▲

Science inquiry can also emerge, with facilitation, from meaningful exploration in other curriculum domains. Here's how it could emerge in Sheryl's classroom when they were pursuing the social studies connection.

As the children collect tape recordings from different parts of the school, Sheryl asks them to find a short part of the recording that they would like to share with the rest of the class. Two of the children, Danielle and Justin, who are interested in computer technology, transfer the excerpt onto a computer so that the clip can be played over and over. Sometimes the excerpt is played for the group during their class meeting time, and questions or comments are generated by the whole group. Sometimes Sheryl will have the tape excerpts available at the computer area, and comments are written directly into the computer.

Over the first week of doing this, Sheryl notices that there are a number of questions raised about a few of the sounds and children are puzzling about what made the sounds. She decides to focus on these "unidentifiable" sounds and brings them to the whole group. She suggests that they embark on a project to reproduce these sounds in order to try to figure out what made them. The children respond enthusiastically and begin extended inquiry into the genesis of some of the sounds that they hear. Sheryl has the children document their inquiry in a logbook that is available for all children to look at, and they hold progress meetings to see which of the sounds the children have hypotheses about and which of them can be verified.

The resulting experimentation is rich and complex, and in addition to the experimentation, these first grade children are able to learn a great deal about scientific processes, terminology, and science experimentation (hypotheses, theory), and also learning the value of systematic variations, documentation of experimentation, and collaborative work. All of this process learning occurs spontaneously and naturally in the context of a highly motivating, meaningful experience that came out of the children's own questions.

It's important to think about how this entire scenario that we have seen in Sheryl's first grade classroom might play out differently for a group of younger children, who could very well engage in much of the same exploration. Here are some of the elements that might be different.

First, the idea of mapping may be too abstract for younger children or at least would have to be greatly simplified. Preschool children would probably focus more on the collection of the sounds, rather than the mapping of the sounds. This could lead to more focus on classification and comparison, rather than putting them into the more complex relationships that mapping incorporates.

Second, the experimentation to reproduce sounds would probably not be as systematic, largely because the focus on documentation would have to be minimized. Some simple techniques for playing back the sounds could be developed by the teacher, and there would most likely be less incorporation of technology into the exploration directed by the children.

So, with some different expectations and emphasis, you can consider developmental issues that can apply to just about any curriculum planning and the different capabilities and interests of children of different age groups.

Creative Arts

Musical creativity is an obvious way in which sound can be explored, and by providing children with opportunities to create sounds with many different types of objects, materials, and instruments we are facilitating this musical creativity. What may be less commonly considered is how some of the creative arts can overlap when we look at sound. Here is one fairly common example of how you could explore sound through movement and painting with preschool children.

Peter and Ashley stand in front of large sheets of butcher paper that have been tacked onto the wall. They turn on the tape recorder, onto which the teacher has recorded different excerpts of music, music that varies from fast and jazzy to smooth and dreamy. As the music plays, they draw on the butcher paper with markers of different colors. Their movements as they draw are choppy and jerky when the jazzy music plays and circular and larger when the dreamy music plays. As they draw to the changing music, Ashley says, "I think this is blue music, not red." Peter agrees, and they begin a discussion of the colors of the music and, when they are done, decide to label the drawings they have done to connect them with the music they were listening to. "Let's go make some orange music now!" Peter says to Ashley, and they run over to the area of the room that is filled with musical instruments for children to experiment with.

▼◄ ▲ ▼◄ ▲ ▼◄ ▲ ▼◄ ▲ ▼◄ ▲ ▼◄ ▲ ▼◄ ▲

Musical painting or drawing is just one example of how you can incorporate music and rhythm into activities. Sound and music can add a dimension to many activities that are not typically paired with it. As another example, think about older children writing poetry based on different sounds that are played, whether they be songs, rhythms, or sounds of nature.

Gradations of Sound

Another way of thinking about sound for children is to focus on gradation of sound, from none to lots. Silence is a very intriguing concept for children, and listening is a habit and a skill that can be played with. "Listen to the silence" was a game that my parents used to play with me and my three siblings; while it was clearly a tactic to give them some peace, I used to find it to be an exercise that was enjoyable, even delightful. What do young children think about silence? About quiet? What are some ways that children can explore silence?

Contrast is the key to exploring silence. Encourage noisemaking, then encourage silence. See how children respond to the silence and how the absence of sound generates interest and curiosity. Explore how sounds can grow from silence to noise and all the gradations in between. Forman and Kuschner (1983) encourage the development of children's understanding of continuity. While young children can easily talk about "noisy" and "quiet," it's harder for them to see the shades in between. "Down with dichotomies" is a slogan that Forman and Kuschner proclaim, representing the importance of helping children to see not only how something goes from point A to point B, but the points of transformation in between. The same slogan can be applied to sound.

How can sound be silenced? What are the ways of muffling sound or of reducing it? What can you do to a gong, for example, to make it sound quieter? This is an area where you could also explore deafness and what it might be like to be deaf, which could lead to looking at communication in deaf cultures—sign language, poetry, music—as another way of focusing on the absence of sound.

I'm concluding this chapter with an extended episode of how a kindergarten class explored sound.

The Sound of Water

After Alice's kindergarten class had been exploring sound for quite some time, they had the opportunity to go downtown to see a show for a field trip. Across the street from the theater was a large public fountain, and the class went to look at the fountain while they waited to go into the theater. Probably because of their explorations, the children started talking about how noisy the water was. "Water's always noisy," said Marisa. "No, it's not," said Jim. Jim goes on to say that sometimes water is real quiet, "like when you're in the bathtub and turn the water off." The children discussed this further, and Alice decided to revisit this question the next day. She sat down at their meeting time with a jar full of water and asked the children, "Does water make noise?"

The resulting discussion was a lively one, and the children who had participated in the fountain discussion made the connection, offering different perspectives on the question. After some discussion, the children decide that they want to try to have water make noise and launch into a series of different activities, mostly at the water table. Alice provides materials for them to use to experiment with, thinking about things that the water could fall on to make noise, as well as things the children could use to move the water or spray it.

Jim starts by pouring the water from a pitcher onto a metal cookie tray, and tries to put his ear down at the tray level while he pours. Marisa says, "I'll pour it while you listen," and Jim gives her the pitcher. As Marisa pours, she raises the pitcher up higher. "It's louder! Raise it higher!" Marisa takes a turn listening while Jim pours.

The next day at their class meeting, Marisa describes the comparison she and Jim made of the sounds made by water falling at different heights. Debbie says, "Just like the waterfall at the fountain!" Questions are raised about whether the water is noisier at the fountain when the water starts from higher up. "Let's go back there and see!" The children get excited. Alice acknowledges the good idea to test out their idea and tells the children that she doesn't think they can go on a field trip to the fountain. She asks if they have any other ideas about how they could find out the answer to their question without the whole class going to the fountain. "You could go and come back and tell us," suggests one of the children. Alice agrees to do this, but says she'll need help knowing what to do. She asks the children to help plan what exactly she will need to do and that they'll meet again to finalize it.

Some of the children decide to make a form for Alice to fill out and set out to work on that. Another group of children decide that she has to record the sound of the fountain, and they go to get the equipment ready for Alice to take. When they gather at the end of the afternoon before going home, they discuss what Alice needs to do and give her a clipboard with the form that they had made for her to fill out and the tape recorder with blank tapes. Anne says, "How about if we have Teacher Alice take some pictures too so we know which fountain goes with which tape?" She runs to get the digital camera.

Fortunately, it's a Friday afternoon, and Alice is able to go to the fountain over the weekend. She enlists the help of a couple of parents, whose

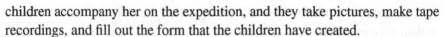

children accompany her on the expedition, and they take pictures, make tape
recordings, and fill out the form that the children have created.

On Monday, the children excitedly look at the pictures, the form, and
listen to the tapes. They carefully lay out the materials on a big table, match-
ing each picture with the tape that has been marked. There are three similar
fountains in the downtown park, each at a different height, so Alice has
focused on these three fountains for the comparison. The children lay the
materials on the table in order of height of the fountain, and after listening
to the tape, decide on a method for marking the degree of loudness—one
star for soft, with more stars for more loudness. Much discussion ensues
over the stars that are put on each fountain, with differing opinions on how
many stars each fountain should be given. Allison says, "Let's forget about
the stars." Sean says, "No, we need to know how loud each one is."

▼◄ ▲▼◄ ▲▼◄ ▲▼◄ ▲▼◄ ▲▼◄ ▲▼◄ ▲

The explorations of the kindergarten class continue. As you can see in this
episode, there are several different types of explorations going on that relate to different curriculum domains. First, the science domain is represented by experimentation that attempts to determine the relationship between the height of the fountain
and the sound that the water makes when falling from it. Second, mathematics is
represented by comparisons the children are making, by the seriation and variation
represented in the different heights of the fountains. Measurements have to be made
of the degree of loudness, and recording of differences has to be conducted. Third,
literacy is represented by the methods used for documenting the observation—the
form is made and tapes are labeled. Fourth, the children need to engage in complex
negotiations and collaborations to accomplish the tasks that they pose to themselves,
and to answer their own questions. In the process, they learn a great deal about each
other and gain skills in communicating their own ideas and listening to the ideas of
others. And fifth, they are able to bring to bear their creative ideas in determining
the different ways that the fountains and the sound can be represented, in this case
using digital photos and tape recordings.

As is evident from this chapter, the big idea of sound is manifested in so many
different ways and connects so many different curriculum domains that it is an ideal
concept for you to use to generate ideas. The critical issue, however, is that sound
is inherently fascinating and idea-provoking for young children, who will take your
ideas and travel in unexpected directions.

Teacher Resources

Baker, D. (1998). *Collectible Bells: Treasures of Sight and Sound*

Haslam, A., Parsons, A., & Barnes, J. (2000). *Make it Work! Sound*

Sabbeth, A. (1997). *Rubber-Band Banjos and a Java Jive Bass: Projects and Activities on the Science of Music and Sound*

Sayre, A. P. (2002). *Secrets of Sounds: Studying the Calls of Whales, Elephants, and Birds*

Children's Literature

Beeke, T. (2001). *Roar Like a Lion: A First Book About Sounds*

Berkes, M., & Noreika, R.I. (2003). *Marsh Music*

Boynton, S. (1982). *Moo Baa La La La*

Brown, M. W., & McCue, L. (2000). *Bunny's Noisy Book*

Carle, E. (1997). *The Very Quiet Cricket*

Carle, E. (2000). *Dream Snow*

Cazet, D. (1994). *Nothing at All*

Emberley, B., & Emberley, E. (1972). *Drummer Hoff*

Hearn, E., & Collins, H. I. (1983). *Woosh, I Hear a Sound*

Hutchins, P. (2000). *Ten Red Apples*

Martin, B., Jr., Archambault, J., & Endicott, J. (1988). *Listen to the Rain*

Mora, P., & Mora, F. X. (2001). *Listen to the Desert*

Munsch, R., & Martchenka, M. (1981). *Jonathan Cleaned Up Then He Heard a Sound*

Pearson, T. C. (2002). *Bob*

Pfeffer, W., & Keller, H. I. (1999). *Sounds All Around*

Seuss, Dr. (1996). *Mr. Brown Can Moo, Can You?*

Spier, P. (1979). *Crash Bang Boom*

Videos

Blue Man Group: The Complex Rock Tour Live (2003)

Other percussion groups, including Taiko drummers (large Japanese drums)

Website

Stomp. (1996). www.stomponline.com/show3.html

Materials

audio recorders

beans, pebbles, pasta, seeds, beads, pieces of metal (e.g., washers), etc., to put into noisemakers

bells of all kinds

cardboard tubes of various sizes to listen through

compact disc players

large seashells

loud ticking clocks

metronome

microphones with amplifiers, wireless microphones

musical instruments of all kinds and from different cultures, including
    percussion instruments, such as xylophones, marimbas, drums, maracas
    wind instruments, including flutes, recorders, whistles
    string instruments

objects that make noise when hit—pan lids, pieces of wood

plastic "eggs" and other sealable containers to make noisemakers

stethoscopes

synthesizer

timers

wind chimes

CHAPTER 7

Upside Down and Inside Out: Wacky Curriculum

T his big idea—upside down and inside out—is all about theory-building, about what you know—or think you know—about something and what you predict based on that knowledge. Anytime a theory is challenged, you are forced to reexamine the theory. Anytime you make a prediction based on what you know, you think again about what you know. In this way, this big idea is grounded in scientific inquiry, an intriguing way of thinking about scientific processes.

There are two ways that you can put this big idea into practice in the classroom. The first way is through "wackiness," the idea of turning what you know on its head. The second is through looking inside what you see or looking underneath the surface of things. Although the two go hand in hand, I will consider each in turn.

Wackiness or Upside Down

Wacky Wednesday (Lesieg & Booth, 1974) is a book that captures the essence of the big idea that is the focus of this chapter. In this book, everything is "off" enough to be silly. When something is off, such as shoes worn on ears instead of feet, it provokes the recognition of what is "normal" and usual. Wackiness intensifies your awareness of reality and of the taken-for-granted knowledge that has been constructed. The predictions that you make based on your previous experiences are not born out, and you are thrown back to relook at the assumptions you make. You must reflect on and reexamine your understandings.

Returning to the idea of theory-building can help us to understand this. We construct a theory through experimentation. Experimentation consists of acting in the world based on what we know and observing the impact of those interactions, processing them in ways that may either change or support what we already know. Theory-building is only possible where there is predictability—where we can anticipate what is going to happen because things occur the way we predict they will or the way they have happened, more or less, in the past. Once a theory is constructed, we apply it to the world in a taken-for-granted way. For example, when we build with unit blocks there are regular and predictable characteristics of the blocks that help us increasingly build with confidence without having to continue to go through trial and error.

Now imagine what would happen if, as a child is building a tower with blocks, they don't behave as he has learned that they behave. He finds that he is able to balance a block in a certain way when, under usual circumstances, it would fall off. Such unpredictability causes him to puzzle: Why is this happening? This puzzlement brings into his awareness what he is used to taking for granted. This puzzlement makes his theory about how blocks balance visible to him in a way that it is not when it goes unchallenged.

Weighted blocks challenge children's theories of building.

Returning to the book *Wacky Wednesday*, it's important to see that one of the main sources of humor is this violation of predictability, through the introduction of the unexpected or unpredicted. This element of silliness can, if thought about this way, lead to reflection. In fact, when children are building with blocks that have weights in them so that they do not act like normal blocks, they often laugh while they are building. The laughter heralds an understanding of the disconnection between their predictions and the actions of the objects.

Here's an example of how the book *Wacky Wednesday* could be used as a provocation.

▼◄ ▲ ▼◄ ▲ ▼◄ ▲ ▼◄ ▲ ▼◄ ▲ ▼◄ ▲ ▼◄ ▲

Ellie reads the book *Wacky Wednesday* to her kindergarten students. The children laughingly point out all the discrepancies that the book illustrates, and, throughout the day, refer back to the book as they play.

For example, five-year-old Kim is playing in the sandbox, and she scoops up sand in a cup and pours it into a bucket. Then she scoops up sand and jerks the cup so that the sand flies upward out of the cup. She says, laughing, "Look, the sand is pouring up!" After seeing several other instances of this kind of play, Ellie decides to introduce some new elements to the classroom the next day.

When the children come into the classroom, there are some new activities that Ellie introduces to them at group time. The unit blocks have been replaced by cardboard boxes with weights in them. In a large plastic bin are bowls of cornstarch and water to pour into it. Next to the block area is a large board suspended from the ceiling onto which are duct-taped giant LEGOs, where the children can "build down."

Mark goes to where the LEGOs are suspended and begins to build. He starts by taking one block at a time, connecting with the suspended LEGO. After he connects two, they fall. He tries again, one at a time. Then he tries two at a time, but they fall too. He looks at it, thinking, and begins to build a long chain of LEGOs on the ground. Standing it up on end and lining it up with the suspended LEGO, he realizes that the chain is upside down, with the "teeth" of the LEGOs pointing up so that they can't connect. He turns the chain over, with some difficulty. In the process, the chain breaks, and he patiently rebuilds it. He finally gets it lined up, but it is not long enough, so he lays it back down and adds one more block. Standing it up on end, once again it is upside down, so he turns it over again and connects it from top to bottom. Triumphant, he stands back and applauds himself.

▼◄ ▲▼◄ ▲▼◄ ▲▼◄ ▲▼◄ ▲▼◄ ▲▼◄ ▲

Building Down

What's going on here is that Mark is applying his theories of how to build from the bottom up. However, they don't completely work, and he has to modify his theories to accommodate the force of gravity. Building one at a time is a strategy that works when building from the bottom up. Gradually, through applying his theories and modifying them, he is able to expand his theories and accommodate the differences in this context.

The importance of challenging theories is that Mark is made more cognizant of what is working in one situation, in this case building from the ground up. This is knowledge that he may not have been consciously aware of. This reflection on what is taken for granted is important for solidifying those theories as well as helping to expand them to incorporate the disparate experiences of having to build from the

top down. One of your roles as a teacher is to encourage this kind of reflection on the taken-for-granted knowledge, and one way of doing this is by providing discordant experiences, such as this one, which may not be common in our everyday lives.

Any connecting building toys can be used for "building down," as illustrated in the photo.

▼ ▲▼ ▲▼ ▲▼

A challenge to children's thinking— building down.

Crazy Blocks

Blocks that are weighted in different ways act differently than "normal" unit blocks. Ellie has taken cardboard boxes and wrapped them carefully with newspaper and tape. Some of the boxes are empty; some of them have weights inside them (e.g., sacks of beans taped inside, sometimes in the middle and sometimes on one side of the box); and some of them have moving weights in them (e.g., a can that rolls from one end of the box to the other or a loose sack of beans that shifts around inside the box). When children build with these crazy blocks, they balance differently, and constructions can be made that appear to defy gravity or at least stretch the common ideas of balance. Commercial crazy blocks are also available, as shown in the chapter opening photograph.

Oobleck

A substance you are probably familiar with, oobleck is a mixture of cornstarch and water. It does not respond like a liquid, nor does it respond like a solid, but it responds like each in different ways. In other words, it tends to challenge the experience children are accustomed to when playing with a liquid, such as water, or a solid, such as sand, in the sensory table. The act of pouring oobleck causes one to wonder about its properties and in the process to think about the processes of pouring water or sand and how they are similar or different.

Building down, crazy blocks, and oobleck are just three examples. Once you have the idea of challenging theories by turning an activity or an experience upside down, it is an interesting process to generate other examples. At the end of this chapter, I've provided lists of some of the common activities and materials used in early childhood classrooms and some ideas of how you could modify them to challenge children's thinking in the same way that Ellie did with her children.

Explorations of Wackiness

Let's see how a first grade teacher could explore the idea of upside down or wackiness using one of the books about the Stupid family written by Harry Allard and illustrated by James Marshall, *The Stupids Step Out* (1974). Some of you might object to the emphasis on "stupid," not wanting to support children's labeling of what is different in such a manner. My experience with these books is that children (and teachers) find them delightful, not offensive; however, there are alternative books that you could use.

Yumiko reads the story, *The Stupids Step Out*, to her first grade children. They giggle and laugh, and thoroughly enjoy the story. As they discuss what's different and "off" in the Stupids' house, Yumiko has them make a chart: on one side of the chart it says "Normal" and on the other side "Stupid." As they go through the differences, the children write on each side of the chart. So, a "normal" picture on the wall in the living room would be of a person; the "Stupid" picture is of a tree named *flower* or a flower named *tree*. Yumiko asks them to imagine what it would be like if the Stupids came to their classroom—what would be different? She tells them that they are going to create a classroom in which the Stupids go to school, and she asks for each table group to take a different area of the room to redesign. They are to write out a plan for this using a chart similar to what they used in describing the Stupids' house. They have the following groups: the block area; the literacy corner, with books and writing; the project area (where there are resources for creating things); the game and manipulatives area; and living things, which are scattered throughout the classroom (birds, hermit crabs, plants, and a turtle).

The children are excited and enthusiastically go to work in their groups, which they are accustomed to working in. As they fill in their charts, they have arguments and discussions about what should go in the "normal" column, and what should go in the "Stupid" column. Yumiko goes from group to group, helping them clarify the task, but they do not need much direction. When one group is done, they go around and look at what other groups are doing, and the classroom is soon full of activity, with children discussing each other's charts.

The class gathers for a class meeting, and each group presents their charts and ideas. Here is one example of a chart for the literacy corner.

Normal	Stupid
Books	Blank books (or some other object)
Pencils, pens	Feathers, sticks
Computer	Computer writes in another language
Paper	Tin foil
Word lists on wall	Number lists
Dictionaries	Maps and atlases

Yumiko poses the challenge—which of their ideas could they try out and which could they not? What would it be like to be in a classroom like this? They have a lively discussion about how much they want to change and decide as a group to try just a couple of changes to see what happens. They exchange the lists with each group and decide which of the things they want to try out to see what will happen. For example, they decide to change the paper in the literacy center to see what happens when they only have tin foil or paper towels to write on instead of regular paper. Another group decides that they will swap the block area to have only Styrofoam blocks instead of wooden blocks. And another group decides that they will swap the signs for the animals, so that the sign that says the bird's name and some information about their bird is hanging by the hermit crab. This group rejects the idea of moving the hermit crab to the birdcage!

▼ ◄ ▲ ▼ ◄ ▲ ▼ ◄ ▲ ▼ ◄ ▲ ▼ ◄ ▲ ▼ ◄ ▲ ▼ ◄ ▲

Now let's look at how a preschool class could explore wackiness by playing with various substances, including oobleck, and experimenting with the idea of liquids and solids.

▲ ▼ ◄ ▲ ▼ ◄ ▲ ▼ ◄ ▲

Karen, the teacher of four-year-olds, has given the children lots of opportunities to play with different substances in the sensory table. They have played with water, of course, but also with flour, rice, beans of different sorts, and snow during the winter. The children never seem to grow tired of playing in this area. She decides to challenge their theories about different substances by introducing them to a couple of different ones—oobleck and "gak." She hopes to learn more about their ideas about liquids and solids and to force them to think about different qualities of the substances they play with.

▼ ◄ ▲ ▼ ◄ ▲ ▼ ◄ ▲ ▼

Oobleck—cornstarch and water—acts like a liquid and a solid.

In one of the sensory tables, she puts cornstarch in bowls and water in pitchers. In the other sensory table, she puts a large quantity of flubber, which she has made the night before. Later she'll involve the children in making flubber, but for now she wants them to experience its qualities without thinking about how it is made. Flubber (also called gak) is the same substance as Silly Putty, but Karen makes it a little runnier, so that it will flow, very slowly, through the large funnel that is suspended over the table. She places a large amount of the gak in the table and fills the funnel with it too.

During the class group meeting, Karen introduces the two substances, and asks the children not to mix the two for now, which is a constraint she normally wouldn't put on the children because she likes to encourage reciprocity across different parts of the room. The children express some interest in the materials, but no more than usual—until they start playing with the two substances!

Much excitement starts to generate in the sensory area when they begin playing. Fiona starts to exclaim, "Weird! It's like a powder sometime!" about the oobleck, and calls her friend Tara over to see. "But it can pour, too!" The two girls play with the oobleck, feeling it and trying to make it flow sometimes, then break off into powder the next minute.

At the gak table, the children are trying to pour it into different patterns, watching as it slowly, slowly drips from the faucet into a puddle underneath. Mia discovers that you can roll it into a ball and put it on your hand and it will slowly ooze around your hand out of the ball shape.

Play with these substances continues over several days, and Karen replenishes the supplies each day as needed. After a period of a week, she asks them at group time to talk about what is going on with the two different substances. "What are they, anyway?" Mia asks, and different children have different ideas. Karen poses the question, "Is each substance more like water or more like clay?" As the children debate this, they start to list the reasons they've chosen water or clay, and soon they have a list of properties of water and a list of the properties of clay. The result is a Venn diagram that shows the places of overlap, showing the children that in some ways each substance is like a liquid and in other ways like a solid.

In the following period, Karen shows the children how to make flubber, but she doesn't give them the exact recipe. Instead, she says that she misplaced the recipe and needs their help in figuring out how to make it. The children spend quite a bit of time trying different combinations of the ingredients, and making comparisons of the resulting substance. With Karen's help, they keep track of each attempt and have a display of the different types of flubber created. After a number of different experiments, the children vote on their favorite, and this recipe is sent home with the children in their monthly newsletter.

▼◄ ▲ ▼◄ ▲ ▼◄ ▲ ▼◄ ▲ ▼◄ ▲ ▼◄ ▲ ▼◄ ▲

While Karen's purpose in introducing these substances isn't to "teach" them what a solid and a liquid is, it is an experience that provokes children's thinking about what is different about each substance and why each of them doesn't act quite the way you would think it would based on certain properties.

Another way of introducing the idea of "wackiness" to the curriculum is to think about the premises on which we operate and to tweak them in some important way that makes everything different. This changing premise is what occurs when you build from the top down, as Mark did earlier in this chapter. It can be used to generate a lot of different ways of implementing this big idea. Anything that can be framed as a "what if" question is included here, such as "What if insects were bigger than people?" "What if we had Styrofoam blocks instead of wooden ones?" or "What if I was the teacher and you were the student?" Such a change in premise requires the kind of radical reexamination of why we do what we do or why things are the way they are—or at least what our theories are about these things. So, if I (the child) become the teacher then I have to think about what I believe a teacher does and how a teacher acts in certain situations, and I also have to think about what I believe I do as a student. Role-playing and switching roles requires an active understanding of your own role as well as the one you are switching to. Role-playing is therefore a good gauge of children's understandings and theories about whatever it is that is being flipped around. Let's look at the idea of building down in more detail as an example of changing the premise on which we act.

▼◄ ▲ ▼◄ ▲ ▼◄ ▲ ▼◄ ▲ ▼◄ ▲ ▼◄ ▲ ▼◄ ▲

In a second grade classroom, Claire has decided to try to challenge her children's ideas by doing more with building down, similar to what we saw earlier in this chapter with Mark and the large LEGOs. In Claire's classroom they have been studying structures, focusing largely on stability of structures. They have constructed different types of small-scale buildings and have subjected them to an "earthquake" by putting each structure on a board with springs underneath it. But Claire feels that the children are losing interest and that they are just copying what they see that works without much enthusiasm.

She poses the following question: What if everything that we built had to be suspended from above instead of built from the ground up? What would happen? How would things be different? Now this, the children think, sounds fun! They excitedly begin to talk about what would happen, and Claire has set up some opportunities for them to experiment with this. She has suspended from the ceiling a large pegboard, onto which different things can be attached to build from. She also suggests that the large tables be used so that they can build from underneath the tabletop. For this purpose, she has attached Styrofoam to the underside of each large table.

For the next several weeks, a number of different projects unfold. Some of the children try to simply reproduce what they have done with structures. They soon find that the things that kept their structures up are different, and they're forced to reconsider how to build the structures. Other children try to build "swinging structures" that capitalize on the property of hanging things. And still others spend some time trying to figure out how people would live in these structures. With Claire's encouragement, a number of the children begin writing stories about the people who live in these hanging villages.

Following up on this aspect of the project, Claire finds some pictures of unusual dwellings, such as cave dwellings, where accommodations have to be made to the space available, similar to the hanging villages the children have created. The blown-up pictures of these cave dwellings are consulted now and then by the children doing the construction. She also finds a picture of climbers who suspend their sleeping bags on cliffs.

▼◄ ▲▼◄ ▲▼◄ ▲▼◄ ▲▼◄ ▲▼◄ ▲▼◄ ▲

Claire feels that this extension of the architecture study enhances children's understanding because it forced them to reexamine some of the assumptions under which they were working with "normal" buildings. And sometimes the introduction of a premise—the premise that everything has to be hung instead of built from the ground—that is imaginative and, yes, wacky, can generate interest and spark the enthusiasm that may have been waning.

Inside Out

The second category of this big idea has to do with what's inside, or underneath the surface—the unknown. Inquiry into what lies underneath is often provoked by trying to figure out why something is acting the way it's acting—particularly when it is unpredictable.

Let's imagine the children playing with crazy blocks—boxes covered with newspaper that are weighted in different ways. Some of them have weights taped inside in different parts of the box; some have a sack of beans or a can that rolls inside so the weight moves around. Some are heavy all over, and some are very light. These different characteristics are not linked to any shape or size of box. So a small box might be very heavy and a large box very light. Playing with crazy blocks of this kind would be a great example of providing children with the kind of wacky experiences that we talked about in the previous section of this chapter. But let's see how this could extend children's inquiry into being interested in what's inside.

▼◄ ▲▼◄ ▲▼◄ ▲▼◄ ▲▼◄ ▲▼◄ ▲▼◄ ▲

Ron and Doug are building with crazy blocks and have created a tower that looks like it would fall over because of how the weighted blocks are able to support what's on them in interesting ways. Ron starts holding one block at a time and notices that the newspaper covering of one of the blocks is a little torn. He starts to peel the newspaper off and opens up the block. "Look, there's a sack of beans in here!" He shakes the box from side to side, noticing how the sack of beans moves from one side of the box to the other. "This is how it works!" Carol, the teacher of this preschool classroom, sees what's happening and goes over to where Ron and Doug are playing. "How interesting!" she says. Ron says, "I'll bet you made these, so you know what's in them, right?" Carol says, "Actually, no, Reiko's mother made them, so I have some ideas but don't know for sure. Do you want to guess?" Carol has decided, in this very moment, that this inquiry is important enough to sacrifice a few of these well-used crazy blocks to the children's experimentation.

The children pick out several of the blocks, and they hold them and shake them back and forth and up and down to see whether there is something stable inside or whether there is something fixed. Then they listen as they shake them to try to see if they can hear what's inside. Carol gets a piece of chart paper and says, "Let's make some predictions." The children tell her what to write on the chart, and she has them draw on the chart the type of block, and then she writes their prediction next to the picture.

As they do this, other children start to notice what is going on and want to make predictions too. Carol calls all the children together for a spontaneous group meeting, and the class makes predictions. Where there are different ideas, she lists the different possibilities and the children vote on what they think by putting dots under the prediction.

Then, with great fanfare, children unwrap one box at a time, and then the children circle which of the predictions was correct. The entire process is full of shouting and laughter.

When they are all done, she asks the children if they have ideas of other things that could be in crazy blocks. She asks them to think about it and to come to school the next day with ideas. With two of the children, she writes a letter on the computer to the parents asking them to help with this "assignment" and to send to school things that could be put into the crazy blocks. She also asks for parents to send boxes of different shapes and sizes. The children excitedly take home the newsletter to their parents, and the next day boxes and sacks of things to put into the boxes start coming into the classroom.

One of the parents has offered to help make the new crazy blocks, and Carol tells the children that even she won't know what the new crazy blocks contain. She has the parent design a secret code so that she can keep track of what's in each block and actually has her take a digital picture of the contents of each block so that in the future they don't have to unwrap and rewrap each block. In this way they have a library of the crazy blocks.

Once the crazy blocks are all made and ready to go, the children are excited to play with them. Carol and the children decide that they will play with the blocks for a week or two before trying to guess what's in them. But just in case they have ideas before that time, she puts another chart on the wall next to the crazy blocks where children can write or dictate their ideas about what's in the blocks.

As the children play, Carol notices a lot of informal predictions, and some of the children are very systematic in their explorations of each block. One of the children knows that their parents sent in some feathers, and she tries to figure out which of the blocks would contain the feathers. Her prediction is that it will be "light as air," just like feathers.

After awhile, the children's interest in the crazy blocks begins to wane, and Carol decides it's time to wrap up this inquiry. She announces that this is the last day to "place your predictions," and that they will have a ceremony that afternoon to unveil the contents of the new blocks. Before the unveiling, the children have a discussion about the predictions, with Carol encouraging them to explain the reasons for their predictions.

▼◄ ▲ ▼◄ ▲ ▼◄ ▲ ▼◄ ▲ ▼◄ ▲ ▼◄ ▲ ▼◄ ▲

This classroom exploration of crazy blocks is a good example of how important theories, hypotheses, and predictions are in the investigation of the unknown, particularly the unknown that violates expectations in some ways. Carol is pleased that through this kind of exploration she's able to make meaningful and explicit the articulation of predictions for children this young. She's also pleased at the natural and meaningful use of literacy in this project and the many opportunities it offers to connect print with meaning. And communicating with parents about the crazy blocks was another important application of the children's literacy abilities as well as an opportunity to use technology (word processing).

Some Underlying Concepts of Upside Down and Inside Out as a Big Idea

While the discordance and the motivation to make predictions is an important part of this big idea, there is another reason why it is so significant for children's cognitive development. Theories are evidence of prior knowledge and making predictions is only possible when children have ideas. Piaget, in his work on genetic epistemology (the study of how knowledge develops), talks about the development of "the necessary and the possible." What this means is that there are certain constraints in a given situation in which one makes a prediction, and those constraints relate to what is possible and what is necessary. Think about a box, for example, with a pyramid coming out of the top of it (see Figure 7.1).

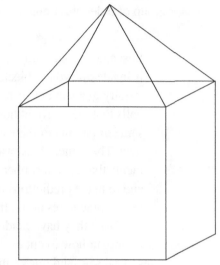

Figure 7.1 *Box with Pyramid Coming Out*

There are predictions one can make about what is inside the box, and these predictions are based on two things. First, what's necessary is that what is inside the box cannot be larger than the box. What's possible is anything that fits inside the box. But when you ask children what they think is inside the box with the pyramid sticking up, they will often reply "a pyramid," as shown in Figure 7.2. This is possible but not necessary. Predictions can thus be a clue to how children are thinking about what they see and a look at their thinking about what is necessary and possible. In other words, you get insights into children's thinking that you wouldn't get otherwise.

By making some of this thinking explicit, you are also in a position to encourage children to think broadly and creatively about possibilities. Through reflection on what is possible and necessary in a given situation you can challenge the limitations of your thinking.

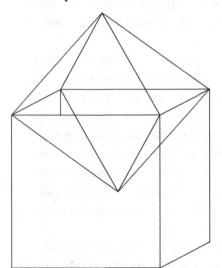

Figure 7.2 *Box with Pyramid Inside*

Aside from the inherently intriguing aspects of this big idea, this is one of the underlying reasons why it is an important one. This is also an important way to emphasize the processes of scientific inquiry in developmentally appropriate ways, processes that many schools and districts focus on in curriculum guidelines.

Now let's see what an exploration of the idea of inside would look like for a group of older children.

▼ ◄ ▲ ▼ ◄ ▲ ▼ ◄ ▲ ▼ ◄ ▲ ▼ ◄ ▲ ▼ ◄ ▲ ▼ ◄ ▲

Susan, a second grade teacher, is interested in exploring the idea of what is inside everyday objects, primarily as a way to meet some of the science inquiry goals in her district. She begins by asking children to bring in any balls that they have at home that they don't mind giving up and also asks the same of parents in their weekly newsletter. She also brings in a few of her own. These include a baseball, a tennis ball, a Ping-Pong ball, a golf ball, a racquetball, and a rubber ball. She asks the children to think about the balls and to make predictions about what is in them. She asks for each child to make some notes about their predictions, including reasons for each one.

Once they have made their predictions, Susan and the children try to figure out how to cut each ball in half. In some cases they need to use a special saw, and one of the parents offers to cut the balls in half at home and bring them in. In other cases they are able to do it in the classroom, with the small saw that they have available.

The children write about how each of their predictions fare given the results, and they discuss the properties of the different insides of the balls. They also talk about how the insides of the ball are hard to discern from the outside.

Susan asks the class if they have questions about the insides of other things that are around the house, and several of the children respond with ideas, including small electrical appliances, cameras, and clocks. Together they decide to have a place where discarded appliances and other similar objects can be safely taken apart, a project table that has tools, goggles, and equipment for dismantling the appliances. Susan checks on each one to make sure there are no toxic parts that the children will be exposed to. Again, the children are encouraged to write their predictions, and a pad of paper for each appliance or object is posted on a clipboard next to the project table.

Then Shawnese brings an orange in to group one day, and she asks everyone to predict what the inside of this orange looks like. Of course, they all laugh like she's tricking them and say "like an orange." "Ha!" Shawnese says, and she opens up the orange, which has been cut in half, and it is bright red, a blood orange her mother brought home from the store. This leads to a discussion of other fruits and vegetables and whether we always know what the insides look like from the outside. The children decide to bring in different kinds of fruits and vegetables to try to trick each other, and Susan joins in.

▼◄ ▲ ▼◄ ◄ ▲ ▼◄ ◄ ▲ ▼◄ ◄ ▲ ▼◄ ◄ ▲ ▼◄ ◄ ▲ ▼◄ ◄ ▲

This extension of the examination of what is inside things and how predictions are based on our experiences with similar objects occurs because the children are tuned into this big idea and start to make their own extensions as they encounter new things. Without the focus in class on this big idea, they might not have paid attention to the discordance between a blood orange and a regular orange and they might have found it only mildly interesting. And Susan is pleased because such spontaneous extensions demonstrate that the children are really thinking about a big idea if it transcends the particular types of objects they were originally focusing on. Such generalization is a sure sign that the children have really understood the underlying concept.

Extensions in Social Studies

Thinking about the application of this big idea in the arena of social studies is an interesting exercise. Probably the most appropriate way to connect this is through the inside out idea. Studying the way people look and what this tells you about how they are thinking and feeling is an important aspect of children's developing social competence. One way of doing this is through the study of faces, particularly facial expressions of emotions and communication through expressions. Even very young children can engage in meaningful study of faces and emotional expression, using a variety of media and strategies. There has been a good deal of influence in this area from Reggio Emilia, whose work documenting children's studies of faces has been disseminated throughout our early childhood community. This has inspired others to attempt the study of faces in a variety of different ways.

▼◄ ▲ ▼◄ ◄ ▲ ▼◄ ◄ ▲ ▼◄ ◄ ▲ ▼◄ ◄ ▲ ▼◄ ◄ ▲ ▼◄ ◄ ▲

Susan's second grade class, described earlier, had been studying what the insides of everyday objects look like, with the focus on hypotheses and pre-dictions. Susan is interested in extending this study to the social realm, and she decides to provoke the children's interest in studying the expression of emotions. She begins by collecting a set of photographs taken of the chil-dren's faces and attempting to capture as many different emotional states as she can. She catches Celia in a yawn, Darrell in a laugh, Rose looking puzzled, and Peggy looking upset. She makes these pictures into transparencies and projects them onto the wall without comment.

The children start talking about the pictures and right away pick up on the different facial expressions. The children whose pictures were taken talk about what they were doing at the time and how they were feeling. Susan pays close attention to these conversations, recording them when she can to capture the children's initial ideas and comments about the pictures.

She then asks them if they are interested in studying how we express our emotions through our faces, and the children are enthusiastic about the idea. Together they generate a number of ways they could do this, many of them related to different ways of representing their own or others' faces. Susan also suggests other media, such as verbal descriptions. They decide to begin by drawing their own faces, so mirrors are provided to the children for this purpose. Some of the children prefer working in clay, and since the class has the resources and background for this Susan provides this opportunity as well. Another group of children decides to look in magazines for pictures of other people expressing emotions and puts together a large collage that many children add to as the project unfolds. And yet another small group of children who like using the digital camera decide to collect more photographs of each other making different facial expressions. The children start to become self-conscious about facial expressions and often exaggerate them when they are aware that the picture-takers are around.

After many different representations of facial expressions are displayed around the room, some of the children begin writing stories and poems to go with the pictures. Susan has encouraged this by bringing in poetry books and picture books (some for younger children) that talk about different emotional states. Because they have already studied a couple of different forms of poetry, she encourages them to try using these forms with this focus—the expression of emotions. Haiku, in particular, is a form of poetry that the children really enjoyed studying, and many haikus are produced to accompany pictures and sculptures of faces.

▼◄ ▲ ▼◄ ▲ ▼◄ ▲ ▼◄ ▲ ▼◄ ▲ ▼◄ ▲ ▼◄ ▲

You can see in this classroom that it is hard to separate the different curriculum domains. Children's work on faces integrates social studies, creative arts, literacy, and technology in many different forms. Yet Susan is able to make sure that a number of different required skills and content areas are covered in the process. In fact, she has so much documentation that her challenge is to be selective in what she uses for assessment purposes, a problem that she prefers to have.

The books mentioned earlier, the Stupids series and *Wacky Wednesday*, are just two of the books that exemplify this big idea. The Amelia Bedelia series by Peggy Parish includes excellent "wacky" stories. There are other books listed at the end of this chapter whose premise is that things are not what we expect. Another way of thinking of this category of children's books is to reconceptualize fantasy. Using the numerous variations of fairy tales, such as *The True Story of the 3 Little Pigs!* by Jon Scieszka and Lane Smith (1999), is one way to do this. More examples are given in the resource list at the end of the chapter. Any book in which animals talk or inanimate objects are alive can be the provocation for a wacky investigation. Take any book that children already know in which the animals talk—*Charlotte's Web* (White, 1974) or the George and Martha series (Marshall, 1974–1991)—and after reading one of these books as a group pose the "what if" question to the children. What if animals could talk? Or take a book like *Diary of a Worm* (Cronin, 2003) and pose the question, What if animals could write? Or take a version of the *Peter Pan* story (Barrie, 2003, originally published in 1903) and pose the most-favorite question of children: What if people could fly? Each of these questions should generate a lot of ideas that could be child-initiated springboards to explorations with wackiness as a premise. Here is what this could look like in a preschool classroom.

▼◄ ▲ ▼◄ ▲ ▼◄ ▲ ▼◄ ▲ ▼◄ ▲ ▼◄ ▲ ▼◄ ▲

Louise reads the book *Flat Stanley* (Brown, 2003) to her class of four-year-olds, and when she is done, she poses the question, "What if we were *all* flat like Stanley?" This leads to a lively discussion about how things wouldn't work the way they do. Crystal says, "we couldn't sit in our chairs anymore," and some of the children start talking about what kind of chair they would have to have in the classroom if they were all flat. Then Louise holds up a rubber ball and asks the question, "What if we were *all* round like a ball?" After much laughter, the children start talking about the chair they would need to sit in if they were shaped like a ball. Louise suggests that they might want to try to design chairs in the project area for this "new world" in which the people are shaped like balls.

In the project area, Louise has provided tape, newspaper, wire, and pipe cleaners for the children to use, although they know they can have access to other materials if need be. The children create lots of different types of containers to hold the balls, and as they do so they begin to have the balls "talk" to each other and create families with balls of different sizes. After some chairs are made for the ball family, the play moves over to the block area, where a few of the children begin to create a house for the ball family. "We have to have a way for them to get downstairs because they can't walk!" The children use blocks and a flat board to create an incline the "ball people" can go down.

During their group meeting the following morning, Louise asks the children to share what they were doing in the block area. As they do, other children pose questions: How can the ball people go *up* the incline? Some of the children work to solve this problem during project time later.

▼ ◂ ▲ ▼ ◂ ▲ ▼ ◂ ▲ ▼ ◂ ▲ ▼ ◂ ▲ ▼ ◂ ▲ ▼ ◂ ▲

This use of children's literature to serve the purpose of provoking interest in a big idea is an example of how you need to be intentional in your provocations and find creative ways that will intrigue children and result in the kind of further inquiry and problem-posing that we see occurring in Louise's classroom.

You can see that this big idea really focuses on inquiry skills—on generating curiosity in how something works and why, on making predictions based on previous experiences, on making comparisons between what we know and what we don't know. In many ways, this big idea is the core of all theory-building, despite the apparent silliness of some of the activities and ideas described. It's important to recognize the underlying seriousness of children's interest in this big idea and to pay attention and really listen to what it is that the silliness is representing to children—the deviation from their prior knowledge and experience. Such deviation is an indication that the prior knowledge and experience exists, because without it there would be no discordance.

Being able to articulate the value of this big idea is a challenge, but thinking about it this way can help impress upon parents, administrators, and peers why engaging in this focus on wackiness can in fact be some of the most serious work children can do.

As you can see, the big idea of upside down and inside out, or wackiness, can easily be extended and applied in many different curriculum areas, including language and literacy, science, mathematics, creative arts, and social studies.

Resources

Children's Literature

Barrie, J. M. (2003, originally published 1903). *Peter Pan*
Brown, J. (2003). *Flat Stanley*
Bunting, E. (1999). *Night of the Gargoyles*
Cronin, D. (2003). *Diary of a Worm*

Goffin, J. (1991). *OH!*

Lesieg, T., & Booth, G. (1974). *Wacky Wednesday*

Marshall, J. (1974–1991). *George and Martha* (series)

Allard, H. (1974). Illustrated by J. Marshall. *The Stupids Step Out*

Allard, H. (1981). Illustrated by J. Marshall. *The Stupids Die*

Meddaugh, S. (1997). *Cinderella's Rat*

Parish, P. (1963–1995). *Amelia Bedelia* (series)

Perry, S. (1995). *If . . .*

Scieszka, J., & Johnson, S. (1991). *The Frog Prince Continued*

Scieszka, J., & Smith, L. (1992). *The Stinky Cheese Man and Other Fairly Stupid Tales*

Scieszka, J., & Smith, L. (1999). Illustrated by L. Smith. *The True Story of the 3 Little Pigs!*

Slepian, J., Seidler, A., & Freem, E. (1990, 1992). *The Hungry Thing* (series)

Trivizas, E. (1997). Illustrated by H. I. Oxenbury. *The Three Little Wolves and the Big Bad Pig*

White, E. B. (1974). *Charlotte's Web*

Wiesner, D. (1991a). *Free Fall*

Wiesner, D. (1991b). *Tuesday*

Wiesner, D. (1992). *June 29, 1999*

Wiesner, D. (1999). *Sector 7*

Wiesner, D. (2001). *The Three Pigs*

Materials and Other Ideas

Blocks

blocks that change shapes (e.g., beanbag blocks)

building down with all kinds of materials

> suspend a sheet of Styrofoam, use toothpicks and pieces of Styrofoam to build down

> suspend a metal cookie sheet and attach magnets onto it or hang magnets and build down from them

styrofoam blocks

weighted blocks

Creative Arts

invisible ink

mirror painting

painting on a dry surface with water

painting on a Plexiglas easel, then turning it around

painting underneath a sheet of Plexiglas

white on black painting

Games

Play a game in which the rules are reversed— e.g., the fewest points win instead of the most

Play a game in which you play for your partner and your partner plays for you

Combinations

oobleck (be sure to add just a small amount of water to the cornstarch)

flubber, gak, or Silly Putty—children can make it and then play with it to explore how it is different than other substances

any other substance that children can make and play with—different kinds of playdough or other modeling mixes

Role-playing

Reverse the "normal" roles—children pretend to be the teacher, older children pretend to be younger children, boys pretend to be girls

Reading and Storytelling

Start with the end of a story and tell it backward

Read a book backward

"Fractured" fairy tales—variations on the same fairy tale

Numbers

Change the numbers—have a 1 be a 9, for example

Create other kinds of "codes" using letters instead of numbers or numbers instead of letters

The Natural World

Create alternatives and explore what would happen—e.g., where insects are bigger than people or where dogs and cats can talk

CHAPTER 8

Chain Reactions: One Thing Leads to Another

I started thinking intensively about chain reactions—or cause and effect—as a big idea that could be used with children after seeing an art exhibit featuring a video created by Peter Fischli and David Weiss, *The Way Things Go* (1987). In this work of performance art, they create a complex series of constructions. The film opens with a suspended trash bag unwinding, and, as it unwinds, it lowers until it hits a tire, which then rolls. Incorporating everyday objects, chemical reactions, fire, water, and different forms of movement, the entire film is one huge chain reaction. Because of the chemical reactions, explosions, and fire, it may not be appropriate for young children, but for adults it is breathtaking and amazing. It also introduced so many different takes on how things move that I couldn't help but generate lists of different things children could do to try to move objects.

It also reminded me of my childhood fascination with Rube Goldberg, whose cartoons in the *New Yorker* magazine were the source of intrigue and ideas. Rube Goldberg would create "machines" where one object's movement kicked off a chain reaction (see Wolfe, 2000). The popular children's game, Mousetrap (Milton Bradley), is based on this same Rube Goldberg–like idea, as is the practice of setting up dominoes and knocking them over.

Once you start thinking of chain reactions, you begin to see them in many places and you start seeing how the beginning action may be unrelated to the end product. This relationship—between one action and another action unrelated to the first—is the basis of much mystery. How can one thing that I do have such an unforeseen outcome? What are the complex sequences of events that can be traced, one after another? The connections between and among seemingly unrelated actions and reactions also underlie the ideas of complex systems, in which one thing is affected by another. Think of ecosystems, in which the disappearance (or introduction) of one species of plant or animal can have devastating effects on the entire system, even destroying it. This is the "butterfly" effect, which has been described in nonfiction and in fictionalized

▼◄ ▲▼ ◄ ▲▼ ◄ ▲▼

Playing with the Mousetrap game.

accounts of the far-reaching impact single events can have. Isn't this the basis for legislation designed to protect animals at risk of extinction—recognizing the importance of seemingly "insignificant species" and the need to preserve them to maintain the complex relationships among plants, animals, and the inorganic world?

Given all of this, let's begin to think about what we can do with children to explore and experiment with cause and effect.

First, cause and effect can be a simple relationship—one thing leads to another. When I do this, this other thing happens. When I throw a ball at a target, it is knocked over. This focus on simple cause and effect is a traditional curricular focus in much early childhood science education.

A chain reaction, on the other hand, goes beyond simple cause and effect, and implies that the effect is also a cause. It looks like this:

Initiating event ➜ effect/cause ➜ effect/cause ➜ effect/cause ➜ ultimate outcome

So, when I throw a ball at a block that has a bucket of water sitting on it, the block is knocked over *and* the water is spilled. The spilled water can move a toy boat that is sitting on the dry ground.

These are fascinating events for young children when they occur accidentally. The intent of this chapter is to explore how chain reactions can be set up so that they occur purposefully and so that children think about the ultimate outcome rather than just the immediate outcome. What can we do to facilitate a focus on the intermediary steps—the process of change—as well as the outcomes? I will be exploring two major categories of cause and effect—chain reactions and gears.

Chain Reactions

I'll begin with the idea of chain reactions by looking at it and exploring it in the physical world, through the domain of science. But the idea of chain reactions has many other extensions, and I will be going beyond science to think about how children can explore chain reactions in the domains of social studies, language arts, and mathematics as well.

I'll begin by looking at a classroom of three- to five-year-old children whose teacher, Marjory, decided to explore the idea of chain reactions. Previously, the children had been doing extensive exploration of balls and ramps.

Scott and Jeff take several of the large-sized dominoes and run over to where they had constructed a ramp out of plastic tracks and blocks. They

place the dominoes on their ends, one after another, at the bottom of the ramp, four in a row. Scott rolls a car down the ramp, and when it hits the first domino, it falls over; but the second domino is placed too far away from the first one to fall over. Jeff, watching at the bottom of the ramp, laughs excitedly, and adjusts the placement of the first domino so that it will hit the second one. Scott retrieves the car, then says "Watch out," letting the car go down the ramp again. It hits the domino, and they fall over in a row.

Antonia, who is building a tower with small blocks next to the ramp, watches Scott and Jeff for a short while, then, without talking to them, brings two small blocks and places them at the end of the row of dominoes, which Jeff has set up a third time. Scott excitedly releases the car again, and as the last domino falls it hits the blocks, knocking them over. The three of them jump up and down, and the play continues for some time as they set different toys on top of the block construction.

▼ ◄ ▲ ▼ ◄ ▲ ▼ ◄ ▲ ▼ ◄ ▲ ▼ ◄ ▲ ▼ ◄ ▲ ▼ ◄ ▲

Now let's look at what happens when Ned, a second grade teacher, decides to explore the idea of chain reactions.

▼ ◄ ▲ ▼ ◄ ▲ ▼ ◄ ▲ ▼ ◄ ▲ ▼ ◄ ▲ ▼ ◄ ▲ ▼ ◄ ▲

Ned introduces the children to the idea of chain reactions showing a videotape clip, the beginning of *Pee-wee's Big Adventure* (Warner Bros., 1985). This sequence shows Pee-wee's alarm going off, which sets off a sequence of events that cooks his breakfast. After watching it once, with much laughter, he asks them to watch it again, and to pay attention to the sequence of events. They talk about the sequence and attempt to outline it on the board.

He then asks the children to design and build a chain reaction that would pop a balloon. The children are to work in groups of four or five, as they are used to doing for many purposes. The materials that are provided include a variety of craft materials, including cardboard and craft sticks, as well as some sets of building materials such as Tinkertoys. They are not yet given the needles necessary to pop the balloon, which Ned tells them he will help each group with when they are ready. Ned also posts the assignment on the overhead, specifying that the machine they design must have at least three different elements to it; they had already defined an "element" as one sequence of cause and effect.

The children are impatient during Ned's instructions, excited to get on with the project. They work for the half hour that they have during their designated "science time," and at the end of the half hour are not quite done. The constructions are left untouched on the floor where they are being worked on while the children go out to lunch. After lunch, the class is scheduled to have a reading/language arts time. Ned, seeing the children's excitement about the uncompleted projects, decides to have them spend the time documenting where they are in the process. As they individually write and draw their chain reaction projects, Ned visits each project and takes digital pictures of the works in progress.

They continue on with the rest of the scheduled day, including a school-wide assembly. The next day, Ned adjusts the schedule so that they can complete their projects first thing, which takes another thirty minutes. At the end of the project work, the children have reading and journal time, during which Ned meets in turn with each group, helping them to attach the pin for popping the balloon to the appropriate part of the machine.

After recess, the class has a sharing fair during which each group presents their machine to the rest of the class. Two of the groups have succeeded in making the machines pop the balloon; the rest have some kind of design flaw that wasn't apparent until the pin was attached. The class decides to take some additional time to correct the flaws, and twenty minutes later they resume the fair. Later that day, Ned takes digital pictures of the completed projects, and each group writes up their project on the computer. He asks each group to describe one or two problems they had to solve while they constructed their chain reactions. The finished documentation will be displayed outside the classroom and will be sent home as a class newsletter. In that newsletter, Ned will add footnotes to explain how each element of the project work fits the needed curriculum work in reading/language arts, in science, and in math.

▼◄ ▲▼◄ ▲▼◄ ▲▼◄ ▲▼◄ ▲▼◄ ▲▼◄ ▲

Notice how Ned has modified his schedule, in fairly minor ways, to accommodate the project work but has also planned that the work will bridge a number of scheduled activities. Note also how Ned has incorporated documentation and assessment into the project itself, so that the children are busy writing and drawing the projects and analyzing them as they go. This documentation is useful both for communicating with parents what they are doing and why and for keeping track of how each child is doing.

Let's return to the preschool classroom where Scott, Antonia, and Jeff are working on the domino constructions and see how the teacher, Marjory, extends their work with chain reactions.

One of the children in the class notices that there is a picture of just such a chain reaction with dominoes in the book *I Spy School Days* (Marzollo & Wick, 1995, p. 16) that she had been looking at. She brings it to her teacher to look at, who places it next to the area where the children are constructing.

Scott and Antonia see the picture, and begin to trace the pathway of the ball through the picture with their fingers, talking excitedly. They decide to make a bell-ringing part of the ramp construction, and, taking an arch-shaped block, they tape a bell to the inside of the arch so that the ball, as it goes through the arch, will ring the bell.

This leads to lots of discussion about other ways to incorporate bells into the domino construction, and they begin to construct a series of modular archways out of Tinkertoys that can be moved around. In the process, they have to solve numerous problems, such as how to attach a bell to the archway so that it will still make noise.

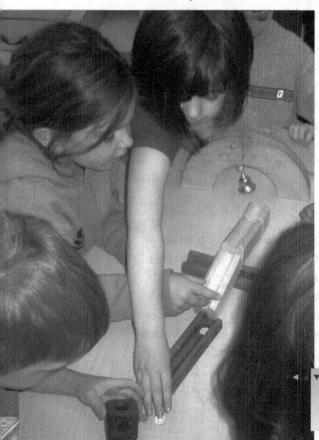

Making the bell ring with a block construction.

Jeff, working on another project, comes back over and begins to look at the *I Spy* book. He notices the balloon-popping segment, and suggests that they try to figure out how to incorporate that into their constructions.

Later, as the children sit in the circle at group time, Marjory asks Scott, Antonia, and Jeff to talk about their work, and the whole class looks at the *I Spy School Days* picture. Marjory has made copies of the picture for the children to look at more closely. Jeff shares his idea about making a balloon popper. Marjory asks for other ideas about things that could be built, and the children raise their hands to share their ideas. To each idea, Marjory says, "That's a great idea, tell me more," encouraging them to think more carefully about how they might do it. The group generates a list of materials they might need to create some of their ideas. At the end of the group time, she reminds the children that they could try out some of their ideas during tomorrow's activity time. Then, when the children's parents come to pick them up, she asks some of the parents to bring specific materials that the children have brainstormed.

▼◄ ▲▼◄ ▲▼◄ ▲▼◄ ▲▼◄ ▲▼◄ ▲▼◄ ▲

As you can see, Marjory plays a critical role in extending the children's activities and helping them to generate more ideas. She also plays the role of encouraging the sharing of ideas with each other and, in so doing, generating more interest across the group of children.

Also notice the similarities and differences between Marjory's preschool classroom and Ned's second grade classroom. While both are addressing the same big idea—chain reactions using dominoes—Ned's format is more complex and more structured, which is appropriate given the constraints on the older grades that are common in our schools today. It is also more developmentally appropriate in many ways, since second grade children are capable of the kind of structured group work that Ned has facilitated. In Ned's school, expectations are clear about how much and what children are to learn in the different curriculum domains, and through this kind of appropriate structure Ned is able to ensure that he documents what and how children are learning in each domain.

Resources for Exploring Chain Reactions

Precipitating Videotapes

In addition to the video clip mentioned earlier from *Pee-wee's Big Adventure* (1985), there are other clips that show cause and effect. One such clip can be found in the movie *Home Alone* (Twentieth Century Fox, 1990) in which the child left home alone has set up an elaborate system for foiling the men breaking into the house. There are also episodes in *Wallace & Gromit in Three Amazing Adventures* (1996), and in the movie *The Goonies* (Donner, 1985) that could serve this purpose.

The picture mentioned earlier in this chapter from *I Spy School Days* illustrates an elaborate cause and effect construction that stimulated children to construct replicas. The photographer, Walter Wick, had to actually construct the mousetrap-like scene in a way that worked, and his website shows the trial-and-error work that went into the construction of the scene that was photographed for the book (www.walterwick.com, go to "features"). This would be interesting either as a precipitating event, after looking at the picture in the book, or after the children had engaged in their own constructions and experimentation.

Children's Literature

One type of children's literature that illustrates the idea of chain reactions is represented by books such as *This is the House That Jack Built* (Taback, 2002) and *There Was an Old Lady Who Swallowed a Fly* (Taback, 1997). These books involve one small thing leading to another thing, eventually resulting in a larger consequence. One way of incorporating such literature would be to introduce one of these books to the children (of any age) and then to write a story about a chain reaction the children have designed and/or constructed using the patterns of the book. Additional books with this theme are *Snail Started It* (Reider & Von Roehl, 1999); *The Napping House* (Wood & Wood, 2000); *Why Mosquitoes Buzz in People's Ears* (Aardema, 1975); and *When the Wind Stops* (Zolotow, 1995).

Games

Aside from Mousetrap, there are many domino sets available that can be used for domino constructions as opposed to playing the domino game. There are even domino sets that are made solely to construct with, and some of these include accessories such as flipping windmills and bells. There are also large-sized dominoes that lend themselves more easily for use by young children, but that also can be incorporated into larger constructions by older children. Unit blocks or boxes can also be used as dominoes in much the same way as larger-scale dominoes. Noncommercial games that involve chain reactions include "telephone," in which children whisper a message from one to another and see how it changes after passing through many ears.

Language Arts

You can also plan a number of activities that involve "growing" stories or poems, where one child writes the beginning, the next child writes the next piece building on the first, and so forth. This is an excellent and nonthreatening way for children who have difficulty with larger-scale stories to participate in creating something. Younger children can engage in this orally; older children can do it in writing.

Creative Arts

In a similar fashion to the story chains described above, children can make picture chains. A picture is passed from child to child, and each one adds to it. This can be structured in a number of ways; one way that I have seen it done is to have children in table groups of five or six and give each child a different color of pastel chalk or marker pen. Then children are told they will be given a limited amount of time after which they must pass on the drawing to the next child. Every child begins with a blank piece of paper and passes it to the right when the timer goes off. The results are fascinating, and children can discuss the changes in each picture that occurred as they went around the table.

Murals also can lend themselves to chain reaction projects if they are seen as representing sequences of events rather than just large-scale pictures. Murals can be many sizes and can be created by large or small groups of children. One way of creating a chain-reaction mural is to propose to the children that they document a construction in segments and then display the segments sequentially across the wall. Children could delegate parts of the construction to draw and then put the mural together as a group. The result would portray the entire construction in sequence.

These visual representations consist of another form of reflection, since the process of reproducing the constructions visually requires children to think through what each element is, as well as how the elements of the chain go together—in what sequence, and with what consequences. A book could also be made that consists of each segment as one page in the book, with or without narration describing the action.

Gears

Gears, which in themselves are fascinating objects, make up the second category of the big idea of cause and effect. Basically, a gear is defined as an object that, when turned, turns something else, either by being connected with teeth or by the use of bands.

A good place to start to get inspiration for this idea is by exploring a commercial set of gears. Gears, Gears, Gears! Gizmos, Gears, Gears, Gears! Super Set, or Gears, Gears, Gears! Dizzy Fun Land (all by Learning Resources) and Georello Kaleidogears (Quercetti Toys) are all good choices. When you begin exploring these materials, you can see that there are lots of different ways of putting the gears together, making them a good constructivist set of materials to have available in your classroom. The reason for this is that children can take on different challenges, simple or complex. The more complex sets of gear toys have incorporated gear elements that do something else besides turn around. For example, one gear element, as it turns, might cause a bell to ring; another one might make a clicker go off.

Once you've explored a commercial set, you can start to think about ways to construct your own different types of gear sets. Many gear elements can be purchased at surplus stores or hobby shops. Then, you can either create a pegboard mounting structure for placing the gears or you can set up a system for older children where they can stick pins into the gears to hold them onto a Styrofoam base and figure out the placements themselves. Gears can be made out of any material—clay that hardens, or even slices of potatoes or apples, as you can see in the photograph. Let's look at a class of five-year-olds playing with a commercial gear set.

▼◄ ▲▼◄ ▲▼◄ ▲▼◄ ▲▼◄ ▲▼◄ ▲▼◄ ▲

When the class visited a fire station and looked closely at the fire truck, some of the children noticed that there were large gear mechanisms that were used to roll up the hoses. They asked the firefighters about them, and one of the firefighters demonstrated how by turning the crank, one gear linked to another one to roll the hoses onto the truck. This event stood out as the most important of the field trip for a number of the children, so when they returned to the classroom, they decided to try to make a similar hose-rolling machine.

Elaine began by saying that they needed to get some large gears first. "You know, those things with the wedges in them that hook onto the other gear." Hillary, the teacher, suggests that Elaine draw a picture of what she means, so she draws a sketch of what she means with her help.

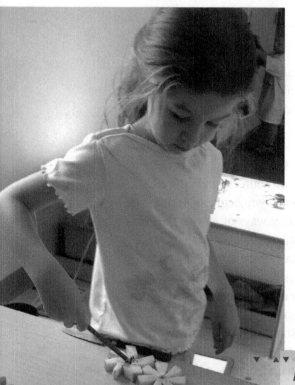

The children decide to make a set of gears out of cardboard and enlist the help of a parent who is working in the classroom. They find some thick cardboard and draw the gear onto the cardboard. The parent cuts it out and then is asked to cut out a second one.

When Emily and Megan try to make the two gears work together, they discover that they are too thin to work. They decide they need to use something thicker and, after some heated discussion, finally decide to glue the cardboard pieces together to make it thicker.

Meanwhile, Sam and Becky are working to make gears out of Play-Doh, only to discover that the gears need to be less pliable. They ask Hillary if there is anything they can use that would be hard, and she gets out some clay that

▼◄ ▲▼◄ ▲▼◄ ▲▼

Making gears out of apple slices.

can be baked, which she has in the storage room. They roll out the clay and begin to cut forms with jagged edges on them, using the commercial gears in the classroom as a model. When they are done, Hillary says she'll bake the clay overnight and they can try it out in the morning. They continue working on their plan for the hoses and the cardboard fire truck that is taking shape in the dramatic play area.

▼◄ ▲▼◄ ▲▼◄ ▲▼◄ ▲▼◄ ▲▼◄ ▲▼◄ ▲

As is evident in this example, much of the work of the children involves problem solving and trial and error—trying out different materials, some that work and some that do not. The high motivation of the children to complete the project carries them through the difficulties they encounter. If the children had not been as creative and motivated as they were, Hillary could have helped facilitate their problem solving in a more active way. As it was, she did not need to, and the children came up with two very different ways of making gears.

This is a great example of how a focus on something like gears can be stimulated quite inadvertently, and how important it is to be able to be flexible enough with your curriculum plans to accommodate the children's newfound interest and high motivation. In primary classrooms, it may be difficult to be so flexible, given the demands placed on you to more systematically cover material mandated by the state or the school district. In the more constrained primary classroom, you would have to be more purposeful in stimulating the children's interests to fit the timing of your curriculum plans. Here is an example of how you might do that.

▼◄ ▲▼◄ ▲▼◄ ▲▼◄ ▲▼◄ ▲▼◄ ▲▼◄ ▲

In planning her curriculum Casey had decided to focus on gears and pulleys in her second grade classroom, in part to meet the science standards of her district and in part because she felt it would be a good overarching focus to connect a number of different curriculum domains. Plus, she had noticed that there was a large-scale building project going on one block away from the school, and the equipment at the site included very large cranes and pulleys that were used to lower pipes and construction materials into the hole that had been dug.

She began by taking some pictures of the pulleys and the large equipment that included a number of gears. She enlarged the pictures and posted them up on the wall in her classroom before she began to talk to the children about her plans.

The pictures immediately elicited talk and interest among the children, many who walked by the construction site every day. They began discussing the construction at their class meeting time, and Casey posed some questions to them as they talked, trying to focus them on the gears themselves. She asked, "How do you think those gears work?" and "Why are they shaped the way they are?" Most important, she did not answer the questions she asked but let the children put forth different ideas, which she recorded on a chart. The children also added questions of their own: "Why does the gear need to be so big?" and "Who makes the gear?"

"How do you think we could find the answers to our questions?" Casey asks. One of the children, Eric, says that his neighbor works at the construction site and suggests that maybe he could ask him. "That's a great idea!" After school, Casey calls Eric's mother and explains the children's interest in the construction site. A visit to the construction site is arranged, and Eric's neighbor agrees to talk to the children when they visit. He tours them around parts of the site, and, as Casey has specifically asked, directs their attention to the various machines that have gears and pulleys. The children draw sketches, ask questions, and take pictures with the classroom's digital cameras.

Casey has brought to class a number of gears and pulleys for the children to examine, and they spend part of their language arts time describing and drawing the materials that are spread out in the classroom. They then look as a whole group at two books that she has brought in, David Glover's *Pulleys and Gears* (2002) and Angela Royston's *Pulleys and Gears* (2001). As she reads the books to them and they look at the pictures, more questions come up. Casey has prepared some overheads of some of the illustrations that she projects onto the wall so the children can examine them closely in a larger scale while she reads. She poses the question to the group when they've finished the story: "Now that we've looked at gears and pulleys, how will we go about making a display that will show everyone how they work?" She asks them to all think about that, and the next day they'll form project groups to work on this.

The next day, each small group decides how they want to do the assigned project. One group decides to make a tabletop model. Another group decides to make a poster; yet another decides to write a book, using pictures the children have taken and drawn. For the next week, the children work in their project groups every day for about thirty minutes, and the resulting work is ready to be displayed for the parents at the Open House. They invite the construction workers to the Open House, and Eric's neighbor comes with a couple of his coworkers, where they are the honored guests.

Casey has been able to meet a number of the prescribed goals for her second grade classroom, including science benchmarks and language and literacy activities, and she has integrated creative arts and mathematics in some of the small-group work. She also feels the children have experienced a rewarding culminating experience that connected them to the larger community of parents and neighbors, which is a one of the primary initiatives her principal has spearheaded among staff at the school.

Casey's job in facilitating such projects is not an easy one. She must monitor the work that each small group is conducting, helping them move along as needed. However, Casey has set up her classroom in such a way that her children are experienced and well versed in how to manage projects such as the gear/pulley projects. They have had to learn specific skills that enable them to do cooperative group work, so that Casey's facilitation job is taken on by different members of the group. For example, one of the group members is the documenter, who summarizes the group's progress each day and reports to Casey and the rest of the class on how they are doing. Casey has found that behavior problems in work like this are few, because the children enjoy what they are doing and many of the children who can be distracting to the whole group when they all try to work together are actually the most involved.

The biggest problem Casey experiences is a common one to project work, and that is that some groups complete their work more quickly than others. It is up to Casey to make sure that the children have other options for activities when they are done with their projects. She has found that groups that finish earlier can be helpful in planning the culminating activity. The book-making group finished first in this case, and Casey put them to work planning for the Open House celebration. They used their book to make labels for the different parts of the projects and designed the invitations they sent home to parents.

▼◄ ▲ ▼◄ ▲ ▼◄ ▲ ▼◄ ▲ ▼◄ ▲ ▼◄ ▲ ▼◄ ▲

As you can see, the study of gears, as with many studies focusing on big ideas, can take many different directions. The direction you may take will depend upon a number of things, including your need to cover different aspects of the curriculum or your ability to respond to the children's initiating interests; the continuing interest and motivation of the children; the ages and capabilities of the children; and the availability and access to interesting resources and motivators, such as the construction site that Casey's classroom visited.

Making the Big Idea Even Bigger

I have described how resources from many curriculum areas—language and literacy and creative arts, for example—can be drawn on when examining cause and effect in the scientific and mathematical realm. But there are larger issues and implications when considering causal relationships that have to do with the sociocultural realm. The importance of understanding the far-reaching impact our behaviors can sometimes have is aptly illustrated by the ecosystem example given at the beginning of the chapter. Here are some ways of looking at cause and effect relationships in the sociocultural realm.

Cause and effect—A leads to B. A simple example of this is when I give you something I am playing with and you feel happy or when I knock over your block construction and you get upset.

Chain reaction—A leads to B leads to C. I give you something I am playing with, so you feel happy, so you share with another child, or I take something you're playing with, so you get angry and knock over someone else's block construction.

Mutuality–A influences B, which influences A. I treat you kindly and you, in turn, treat me kindly. I share my toys with you, and you share toys with me.

Causal relationship with mutuality—A leads to B, which leads to C and A. I give you something I am playing with, you reciprocate by sharing with me, and then we both feel happy and share with others.

Some of the ideas of causality in the social and emotional realm are highly abstract, but there are ways children can be introduced to them that are quite appropriate. As is often the case, children's literature can be a good provocation for such an exploration.

Jannelle notices that the children in her kindergarten class have been reading the book *This Is the House That Jack Built* (Taback, 2002) over and over. She has been wondering how much they could grasp about the concepts of interdependence and decides to embark on a series of explorations relating to interdependence using the book as the starting point. She decides to start without focusing on the social realm and then to move to it.

She lays it out directly to the children. "I'm interested in seeing if we can create our own story like this based on what we do every day. This way we could tell people who don't know the story of our classroom, just like this book tells the story of Jack and his house. What do you think?" Before beginning, she has thought about the difficulty children of this age might have in coming up with a starting point, so she suggests one to them. She begins with the mural on the wall that documents the work they did studying the marshy woods outside their classroom. She suggests that they start with the statement. "This is the mural that the class made." She gives one example. "This is the tree that is drawn on the mural that the class made," and asks for other examples. They excitedly generate lots of other examples, mostly based on those aspects of the mural that they worked on personally.

In order to help them visualize the chains of relationships they are creating, Jannelle puts the elements of the story onto pieces of paper and lays them out on the blackboard with magnets so they can move them around. The story elements are:

Mural that the class made ➜

Tree in the mural that the class made ➜

Jon, who made the tree in the mural that the class made ➜

The desk that Jon worked at when he made the tree in the mural that the class made ➜

The colored pencils from the desk that Jon worked at when he made the tree in the mural that the class made

Jannelle predicts that some of the children may not be able to make these connections beyond one causal link, and she wonders if this is too complex for this group of children. She decides to use this as an opportunity to explore what they do understand about cause and effect. Children are given the opportunity to work on this project during a period of about one hour of work time they have in the morning, and about six children choose this project to work on together.

The children focus on creating each page in the book, and as they do there is lots of discussion about which page will go first and which will go second. As they work, they go back to the blackboard, checking the order of the pages with the list on the board. When each page is finished, they mount the pictures onto the board with magnets, and, each time, the child who puts the page up tells the story.

Over the weekend, the pages on the board are accidentally taken off by the janitor, and on Monday morning the children are upset that their story is ruined. Jannelle decides this is a great opportunity to challenge their understanding of the relationship between the story elements, and she begins putting the story up in the wrong order. After much uproar and laughter, the children correct her, but not before she's had an opportunity to pursue their ideas about why it wouldn't work that way. As they work to put the story back up on the board, Jannelle takes notes for herself about what the children said. One of her notes is about Jackie, who says, "It has to go this way, because it's like one thing is inside the next thing." Later that day, when the occasion arises, Jannelle asks Jackie to explain what she meant by one thing being "inside the next thing." Jackie says, "Well, it's like this [she points to the crayons] is inside this [she points to the picture of Jon drawing with the crayon] and this one [the same picture] is inside this one [the tree on the mural]. It's like each one is a part of each one. Like one thing happens, then the next, and so on."

Jannelle contemplates how to move this focus into the socio-emotional realm and decides to stay with the genre of a story building that is parallel to the mural story. She tells the children she wants them to help her make a new story, one that is about children's feelings. Recently they have been talking about how words can effect how you feel, both good and bad, and so they begin by discussing this again. In another part of the room, the children have put pictures they've taken of each other showing different emotions. Jannelle asks them to pick which of the pictures they want to write a story about, and the children pick a picture of three children laughing while they are building in the construction area. Together they generate different "captions" for the picture. "The children are laughing and happy." "They are having fun." "They like building the building."

They begin with one of the captions and Jannelle tells them that this is just an example and that they can make their own stories and do it differently. They choose "The children are laughing and happy." Jannelle reads the first statement of the *This Is the House That Jack Built* again to remind them, and together they figure out that the caption should read, "These are the children that are laughing and happy." Jannelle asks them to predict the things that could lead to one of the children feeling happy and laughing, and Jennifer says, "Maybe Bobby is happy because he's having fun."

Jannelle realizes that somehow she has to interject the idea of time, so that they can better sequence the story line, and so she says, "That's a good idea, let's put this up on the board and try to put things in order the way we did with the mural story." When they do that, Dori says, "Oh, but what made him happy was that he got to play with the blocks." So they put the next element of the story, "This is the boy who chose to play with the blocks, that made him laughing and happy." Although this is complex for the children, they begin to see the different ways they can write the story, and Jannelle patiently encourages them to write the things that came before each element of the story.

▼ ◀ ▲ ▼ ◀ ▲ ▼ ◀ ▲ ▼ ◀ ▲ ▼ ◀ ▲ ▼ ◀ ▲ ▼ ◀ ▲

Here's an example of how a teacher of younger children was able to expand the idea of cause and effect to the communication (and literacy) realm for her preschool children.

▼◄ ▲ ▼◄ ▲ ▼◄ ▲ ▼◄ ▲ ▼◄ ▲ ▼◄ ▲ ▼◄ ▲

Dana's four-year-old children have been exploring cause and effect with domino-type constructions, mostly using blocks and ramps. She would like to extend this big idea and decides to try to introduce the idea of communication. During group time, she asks the children if they have ever played the game "telephone." None of the children have heard of this game, and so she tells them the rules: One person is chosen to decide on a word and this person whispers the word, very quietly, to the next person. Each person whispers it around the circle, until the last person is able to call out the word.

"Easy game!" Tony says, and they begin. Dana puts some music on so that the room has some distracting noise in it, and she starts with the first word, "banana," and whispers it. As the word goes around the circle, the children get antsy, but when the last child calls out "Potato!" Dana says, "No, it's banana." The children are puzzled, and Dana decides to try again. So Tony chooses the word and starts the telephone game. When his word, "purple," becomes "paper" some of the children are intrigued, and Dana decides they need to explore the path of the word. So she asks each child to think and to remember what they said the word was. As they call out the word, the group is able to trace how it changed from the original word into the final word.

Dana decides not to make the connections explicit at this point, since the children are so young. She is hopeful that later, after they've explored more about cause and effect, she can return to the telephone game to show the relationship between different ways of looking at cause and effect.

The children like this game, and Dana notices that some of them play it spontaneously. However, when only a few children play the game, it is not as interesting, since there are fewer opportunities for the word to transform into a new word. So she decides she needs to instigate the game more often, and she also decides to make it more of a literacy experience for them.

The next time they play the game, when it is over, Dana asks for help from the group. She says she wants to trace how the word changed. She writes in large letters the beginning word and then the ending word. Then, as they go around the room, she writes the words in between. As she does it, some of the children notice the point at which the word looks (as well as sounds) different and say so. Dana suggests that they make a mark by the words that are different from the previous words in the list (see p. 162).

Teacher's chair
    Teacher's chair
  X Teacher's hair
    Teacher's hair
    Teacher's hair
  X Peter's hair
    Peter's hair

In this way, Dana is able to draw the children's attention to the relationship between the sounds of words and the print that represents the words, so that even if some of the children don't understand this relationship they are seeing it in action. Some of the children already have that knowledge and are able to model the awareness they have about the print/sound relationship. Dana takes note of which children seem to grasp this and finds that this simple game is a great tool for seeing which of her preschool children are emerging readers.

Dana decides that the key to making the connections across the different curriculum domains lies in the public documentation that she is using to display the different types of relationships that are transforming. So, the "word trail" that she makes in the telephone game becomes her model for the representation of transformation that occurs in other domains.

▼◄ ▲▼◄ ▲▼◄ ▲▼◄ ▲▼◄ ▲▼◄ ▲▼◄ ▲

You can see how the lines between chain reactions or cause and effect in different domains can blur, which is something you want to happen. Documentation is one thing that helps to blur the lines, since it incorporates language arts as well as creative arts in the process of representing what is happening. You can also see that cause and effect can be seen in so many aspects of what we do that it is easy to generate these and many more ways to explore it. Children's understandings of the complexity of relationships in all domains provides an important foundation for the understanding of interconnections that is so critical for much learning in the future.

Resources

Teacher Resources

Glover, D. (2002). *Pulleys and Gears*
Royston, A. (2001). *Pulleys and Gears*
Wolfe, M. F. (2000). *Rube Goldberg: Inventions!*

Children's Literature

Aardema, V. (1975). *Why Mosquitoes Buzz in People's Ears: A West African Tale*

Marzollo, J. (1998). Illustrated by Walter Wick. *I Spy Gold Challenger! A Book of Picture Riddles*

Marzollo, J. (1995). Illustrated by Walter Wick. *I Spy School Days: A Book of Picture Riddles*

Reider, K., & Von Roehl, A. (1999). *Snail Started It*

Taback, S. (2002). *This Is the House That Jack Built*

Taback, S. (1997). *There Was an Old Lady Who Swallowed a Fly*

Wood, A., & Wood, D. (2000). *The Napping House*

Zolotow, C. (1995). *When the Wind Stops*

Videos

The Goonies (1985)

Home Alone (1990)

Pee-wee's Big Adventure (1985)

The Way Things Go (1987)

Websites

Walter Wick, balloon-popper: http://walterwick.com (go to "features" for the clip "making a balloon popper")

www.enchantedlearning.com/graphicorganizers/causeandeffect/

Toys and Games

Gears! Gears! Gears! Dizzy Fun Land (Learning Resources)

Gears! Gears! Gears! Gizmos (Learning Resources)

Gears! Gears! Gears! Super Set (Learning Resources)

Georello Kaleidogears (Quercetti Toys)

Mouse Trap (Milton Bradley)

Dominoes

Materials

balls and ramps

blocks

CHAPTER 9

Transformation

C hildren are fascinated with transformation. You can see this in their play, in which they are transforming the world physically as well as symbolically. We construct an understanding of things by changing them and, when possible, changing them back. There are many ways of thinking about transformation. In this chapter, I will consider transformation as a big idea, as an umbrella that subsumes all the kinds of transformation that make up the physical and social world that children must understand and construct.

In order to look carefully at this big idea, I am first going to describe the different kinds of transformation. Once we have considered the different types of transformation, you will be able to look at what you can do to help children make connections and to see the relationships among all kinds of transformation.

Movement of Objects

The first kind of transformation we will look at has to do with the movement of objects. The position of objects and materials can be changed by moving them. Balls can be rolled, pendulums can be swung, water can flow, and air can blow. Children construct a great deal of physical knowledge by moving objects. The construction of this physical knowledge is best described by Constance Kamii and Rheta DeVries in their classic book *Physical Knowledge in Preschool Education* (1978). In this book, they describe numerous ways that you can encourage the construction of physical knowledge by providing children with activities and experiences that allow them to experiment with the physical world. This means that the children have opportunities to act on objects and materials, to vary their actions, and to see the results of their actions. In *The Young Child as Scientist* (Chaillé & Britain, 2003) we build on the work of Kamii and DeVries by describing a curriculum model for early childhood science education based on children's questions, and the question appropriate for this type of transformation is "How can I (we) make it move?" While this is a great science-oriented question, the way to think of this as a big idea is to think of the movement of objects as just one component of transformation.

For the purposes of delineating a big idea, I find that one of the key differences between the different kinds of movement as well as the different kinds of transformation is whether or not they are reversible or irreversible.

Reversible Movement

I'll start with a focused and specific idea to make reversible movement clear. Reversible movement—or "back and forth"—can be illustrated by pendulums.

Children's experimentation with pendulums is rich with possibility because of all of the variables that children can control—the weight of the bob, the length of the string, the strength of the swing, and the size and weight of the target hit by the bob. And things that swing are common in the child's world, on the playground and in the environment. Back and forth also implies a much bigger notion, that of reversibility —what goes in one direction comes back in the opposite direction; what goes up comes down; that which is changed can be returned to its former state. So while I am going to begin with the idea of pendulums, keep in mind that this is just the start. We will be extending this to be a bigger concept—that of reversible transformation.

▼◄ ▲ ▼◄ ▲ ▼◄ ▲ ▼◄ ▲ ▼◄ ▲ ▼◄ ▲ ▼◄ ▲

Micki and Vangie have set up a tower made out of cardboard blocks to serve as a target for their pendulum game. Micki is standing with the pendulum bob in her hand—a bob made out of a plastic bottle—and is calling out instructions to Vangie. "Put one more block on top!" Vangie adds another block, and then Micki walks the pendulum with the bob over to the construction and tests out the swing to see if it will hit the target. Returning to her original place, she lets the bob go, and it swings toward the target, missing it by only a couple of inches. The girls laugh, and then Micki catches it when it swings back and quickly releases it again, changing her aim slightly. When it hits the target, it bounces off the cardboard blocks. Vangie says, "Let's use this one," and gets another plastic bottle that is filled with sand, "It's heavier." They fasten the new, heavier bottle onto the rope and try again. The block structure collapses.

▼◄ ▲ ▼◄ ▲ ▼◄ ▲ ▼◄ ▲ ▼◄ ▲ ▼◄ ▲ ▼◄ ▲

In order for Micki and Vangie to experiment as they have and succeed in their self-appointed task, they need to pay attention to several things. First, they need to think about the weight of the pendulum bob, a variable made possible by the provision, by the teacher, of the differently weighted plastic bottles that are easily attached to the pendulum rope. Second, they need to think about the angle of their swing, as we see when Micki modifies her aim to hit the target. Third, they need to think about the pathway of the pendulum bob—the trajectory—in order to anticipate whether or not it will hit the target. Fourth, they need to think about the target—how high is it, how wide is it, how heavy is it, and what will knock it down. The many possibilities for varying actions and seeing what happens makes this a good activity for promoting experimentation and problem solving. In Kamii and DeVries (1978) and in my previous book (Chaillé & Britain, 2003) we articulate the criteria for "good" physical knowledge activities, and this activity meets those criteria—the variables are under the child's control, the results of the children's actions are visible to them and are immediate—and thus they have the possibility of constructing an understanding of pendulums.

You could extend the activity that Micki and Vangie are engaged in by the introduction of some children's literature that highlights the act of swinging. Here are a few examples of books that incorporate the act of swinging in some of the illustrations:

Johnston, T. (2002). *Yonder*. Illustrated by Lloyd Bloom. In one picture in this book, a young girl is swinging with her bare legs and feet high up in the sky; her head is down but her face is up to keep her balance.

Gershwin, G. (1999). *Summertime*. Illustrated by Mike Wimmer. In this book, a girl swings as she sits on the knotted end of a rope that is hanging from a tree.

Zolotow, C. (2000). *My Friend John*. Illustrated by Amanda Harvey. In this book, one picture shows that the two friends are pulling a rope through a wheel with a suspended chair at the other end of the rope holding a dog and some other things.

After reading one of these books to the children, Micki and Vangie's teacher could see if any of the children comment on the swinging—if not, she could ask the question directly. "Look at how she is swinging back and forth on this rope—isn't this a lot like something some of you have been experimenting with?" The discussion that follows would be a rich source of information for the teacher about whether or not the children are able to see the relationship. It's probable that they will, and the resulting questions from the children will also guide the teacher in seeing what kinds of things they might be interested in doing next.

Changing the scale of the initial pendulum activity and using their own bodies as a "bob" would be an extension sure to capture their interest and might even come out of their discussion. It is possible to safely construct a child-sized pendulum using a rope from a tree, ropes in a gymnasium, or a rope you have attached to play equipment on a playground. Then, with proper supervision, begin some experimentation with swinging.

Reversible Transformation: Combining Materials and Structures

To extend the idea of reversible transformation, let's now look at the parallel form of transformation that can be constructed when objects and materials are combined in different ways. Let's think about what happens when children build with blocks.

168

They are putting one block on top of another block, and once the structure is built, it can be unbuilt. Building up and taking apart—we see this kind of play occurring for its own sake, over and over. Children do not play with blocks to create a permanent structure; it is the process that is the focus, the process that enables children to do what they want and then undo it if they want. Here's what this kind of transformation looks like.

▼◄▲▼◄▲▼◄▲▼◄▲▼◄▲▼◄▲▼◄▲

Katrina, a kindergartner, is building with LEGOs, and she carefully, and over a fifteen-minute period, creates a structure with four walls, which she calls her "house." She places a toy cow in the middle of the structure, and then decides to try to build the roof of the house. She begins to try to bridge the blocks from one side to the other and soon finds that the LEGOs don't connect in such a way that she can cover the top. After the first attempt falls into the structure, she begins creating spaces within the larger structure, and declares that it is a barn for all the farm animals.

Katrina's construction is planful, but she adapts her plan based on her capabilities to make the materials work, to do what she plans on doing. The play is fluid despite the plan.

▼◄▲▼◄▲▼◄▲▼◄▲▼◄▲▼◄▲▼◄▲

Now think about a different material, such as clay. As children play with clay, they create one thing, and then as they work with the material it becomes another. Here is an example of how fluid the transformation is when children play with clay.

▼◄▲▼◄▲▼◄▲▼◄▲▼◄▲▼◄▲▼◄▲

Four-year-old Jason is rolling a ball of clay into a log-like shape, and as he does so he is saying "I'm baking a cake!" As he continues to roll it, it becomes skinnier and longer, and he starts chanting, "Snakey, snakey." He picks up scissors and starts cutting it into pieces, saying, "Babies, I'm making babies!"

▼◄▲▼◄

Clay continuously transforming.

Different materials contribute different possibilities for children's play. This is important to think about when you want the focus to be on transformation. Children will bring to their play opportunities lots of ideas and experiences, but the nature of the materials and toys that they interact with will also shape their play. So the type of transformation that is "afforded" by the materials is critical.

Construction with blocks and other construction materials and working with materials such as clay are traditional activities almost unquestioned as valuable in preschool and many kindergarten classrooms. In some kindergarten classrooms and certainly in the primary grades, such exploration of transformational materials is rare, or, if there are opportunities for construction, they are task-oriented or goal-directed. For example, children in a second grade class may have as an option for a "book talk" to create a diorama or a display representing the story they have read. The focus here is on the product and on the representation, not on the act of construction or on transformation itself.

Why is this? Why do we not give primary grade children the same opportunities to experiment, problem solve, and theory-build that we assume younger children need? Part of the answer to this question lies in the structures of time and space in which education occurs for the primary-age child; and part of the answer lies in the different professional education that many of our teachers have access to. Whatever the reason, it is important to think about how and why we should give all young children opportunities to engage in experiences focused on transformation. And there are ways to do this even if you are constrained in what you teach and how you teach it.

So let's imagine a second grade classroom in which the teacher begins to incorporate a focus on the big idea of transformation.

▼◄ ▲▼◄ ▲▼◄ ▲▼◄ ▲▼◄ ▲▼◄ ▲▼◄ ▲

Suzanne has a discussion with her class about recycling, based on a newspaper article that one of the children brought in to share. The discussion focused on paper recycling, and although the class had a recycling bin for papers it was not being used as much as it could be. As a group, they decided to study recycling.

Suzanne planned several things to stimulate their study. She asked the community recycling coordinator for resources, which included some curriculum ideas and materials. As the children went through the materials, Suzanne noticed that a lot of interest focused on how paper was recycled. Based on this, she decided that papermaking would be a good way to make the process concrete.

Suzanne begins the project posing questions to the children: How do you think we could recycle our own paper? How do you think paper gets recycled? She asks the children for their ideas. Some of the children say they already know—that you need to cut the paper up and put it in water. Others say that first you need to shred the paper. She suggests they all do some research on the question. Some of the children volunteer to go on the Internet in the computer lab to look up the process, and a couple of children volunteer to go to the library after school to see if there are any books on the topic. Susan has already collected some resources of her own, but she wants the children to participate in the process.

The children find a wealth of information, both in the library and on the Internet (such as Grummer, 1992; Levine, 1993). The children decide to begin with a few pieces of paper in order to see if the process works before they go "large scale" with their experiments. They find a few different techniques in the books and decide to try a couple of those described.

In the first, the paper is soaked, then mashed up by hand into a pulp, and then laid out on a screen. In the second, the paper is soaked and then put into a blender. They decide to try both techniques. Sarina has gone to an art media store with her mother and has brought in some beautiful art paper that has flowers in it, and she suggests that they try putting things in some of the experimental paper batches. They try different things—glitter, flowers, pieces of colored tissue paper, and confetti.

Some of the early experiments do not result in paper that is very useful. It is either too thick, or it falls apart, and the children try adding things to the paper mush to help it bind together.

In the end, the children find a number of different ways to make the paper, and although the process is a tedious and long one, they decide to carry it on over time, because they are so excited about trying to add different things to the paper to create different effects. They use the resulting "art" paper for many things, including note cards that they use to write messages to each other.

One of the after effects of this project is that Suzanne finds that the children are much more diligent about recycling, because they have discovered how complex the process of papermaking is. She overhears them catching each other when they waste paper or when one of the children accidentally throws into the wastebasket a piece of paper that should go into the recycling bin.

Suzanne asks them how they want to communicate all that they've learned about paper recycling and papermaking. The children decide that they need to make a poster to put in the school hallway that explains why it is important to recycle. They also create a booklet for the other classes using the word processor that describes how to make new paper with their recycled paper. The cover of each pamphlet incorporates a piece of the recycled paper that they made in class.

As this project wraps up, some of the children start to ask about other things that are recycled, including plastic. They wonder how that process occurs. And so the inquiry continues, extending into other directions as the year progresses.

▼◄ ▲▼◄ ▲▼◄ ▲▼◄ ▲▼◄ ▲▼◄ ▲▼◄ ▲

Here the children in a second grade classroom are given opportunities to experiment with transformation in the context of study appropriate for their grade level, and they can learn a good deal of content in a meaningful context. And although it could be argued that papermaking is not an example of truly reversible transformation, paper *can* be made back into paper.

Now that we've seen how older children might engage in exploration of (semi-) reversible transformation, let's see how it might look different with a group of younger children.

▼◄ ▲▼◄ ▲▼◄ ▲▼◄ ▲▼◄ ▲▼◄ ▲▼◄ ▲

Andy, the teacher of three-year-old children, is, like Suzanne, interested in reversible transformation. After an ice storm, some of the children start asking where all the ice is going to go. Andy decides instead to focus on the transformation of water to ice and ice to water.

Anthony and Katie, both three-year-olds, are at the water table where Andy has placed a large block of ice. They are pouring water over the ice and chipping it with tools. Andy brings over a cup of salt with spoons and sets it on the ledge of the water table. "Why don't you see what this does?" he asks. Anthony and Katie begin sprinkling the salt on the ice, exclaiming as it melts where the salt hits it. "We're making it all go away!" they exclaim. They work with the salt, using basters and droppers, until the ice is largely melted.

Later in the day, at story time, Andy shares the picture book *The Snowman* (Briggs, 1978). The children see the connection between what they're doing with ice and the snow in the story. Anthony and Katie get very excited, "We made the ice go away, just like in the book!" Andy asks if anyone has an idea of how to get more ice, and Steven says, "At the grocery store," and Lynn says, "My refrigerator makes it." They take the water from the melted ice and put it into plastic buckets and put the buckets into the large freezer in the kitchen of the school. Every couple of hours some of the children check on it and report back to the class on how the water is doing.

The process takes quite a while, because the buckets are large. When they are finally fully frozen, the buckets are returned to the water table, and the process begins all over again.

Andy suggests that they try different sizes of containers to see if the process could be hastened, and the children experiment with smaller plastic containers, concluding that they can do it faster that way.

▼◄ ▲▼◄ ▲▼◄ ▲▼◄ ▲▼◄ ▲▼◄ ▲▼◄ ▲

Children's Literature Relating to Reversible Transformation

Here are a few examples of books that could support the study of reversible transformation.

Jonas, A. (1983). *Round Trip*. This book can be read cover to cover and then turned upside down and read again. The illustrations are flipped over and fit the new text in their upside down state.

Macaulay, D. (1980). *Unbuilding*. This is another good book related to reversible transformation. It shows the process of building and dismantling the Empire State Building.

Hutchins, P. (1987). *Changes, Changes*. A classic wordless picture book that takes the reader through blocks being constructed and reconstructed to make different scenes.

Nonreversible Transformation

When something changes, and it cannot be changed back to its original state, we call this nonreversible transformation, and it is another fascinating idea for young children to explore. This category of transformation can be further divided into change that occurs because of something we do and change that occurs over time.

Nonreversible Change That We Create

In this category we find all of the transformation that can't be undone. When children build with scraps of wood by nailing them or gluing them together, the resulting construction is not readily undone and is intended to be nonreversible. When children mix glue with water and paper and let it dry, you are not able to change it back to what it was before.

Cooking is on many occasions a good example of nonreversible transformation. By combining ingredients and applying heat, we create something different from the process that cannot be reversed. Bread making with children provides a good way for experimentation with different amounts of the ingredients, and, although the processes of change are not visible, the beginning and end points can be compared. Popcorn popping, butter churning, ice cream making, and drying fruits are other popular transformation activities. And what happens to the food we eat? The book *What Happens to a Hamburger?* (1985) by Paul Showers and illustrated by Anne Rockwell describes the process of digestion and the transformation of food in the body.

One of the difficulties with nonreversible change is creating conditions under which the transformation is clear and visible to children, since the beginning state is replaced by the ending state. There are ways that you can try to make the transformation more evident and visible. One way is by making sure that there is some sample of the beginning state available when the ending state occurs so that comparisons can be made. All too often we make it into a sort of magic trick. Here is the popcorn unpopped, and now it is popped. Children rarely are given the chance to directly compare the unpopped and the popped corn. Without such a comparison, the transformation is easily missed, particularly by younger children. Another way to make the transformation more evident is through technology—for example, taking pictures before and after—and making comparisons of the representations of the change.

Even better is when the change can be captured as it occurs. Some things lend themselves to this and some do not. We'll see some examples of how to capture transformation as it occurs when we look at change over time. When children are directly mixing glue with paper and water they can feel and see the changes as they occur, as they can with many mixture activities. But providing the opportunity to capture the transformation at different points can prove difficult. In the case of a wood scrap sculpture, for example, you could take pictures of the sculpture at different points in its creation, and have a sequenced description of the transformation in this way.

Using popcorn as an example, you could have fresh corn—on the cob—available for the children to see and taste. You could also have dried popcorn on a cob for the children to look at and compare to the fresh corn. You could then set up a hot-air popcorn popper on a sheet, have the children help put the kernels in the popper, and sit in a circle at the edges of the sheet to watch the kernels pop out onto the sheet. In this way you are helping to make visible the transformation as it occurs, as well as helping children make direct comparisons between the transforming material at different points in its transformation.

Change That Occurs over Time

This category is one that is commonly addressed in early childhood curriculum by focusing on growth, particularly in the natural sciences. Seeds turn into plants, caterpillars turn into butterflies, tadpoles turn into frogs, and the transformations involve dramatic changes. As Kamii and DeVries (1978) and I (Chaillé & Britain, 2003) have described, when children are exploring the physical world, it is easier for them to construct understanding when the transformations are (1) due to variables that they control, (2) observable, and (3) immediate. The difficulty with studying growth in the natural world is that many of the variables that result in the transformation don't easily meet these criteria. First, the variables that affect the growth of a plant or the development of a frog generally involve steps to allow the change to take place or the growth to occur. Most importantly, it is inappropriate to experiment with nature by altering these steps. For example, you could stop feeding the tadpole, and the result is that it most likely would die. You could stop watering the plant, and it would wither and die. Second, the change that occurs is not directly observable. The change from point A (the seed) to point B (the plant) is impossible to see as it is occurring, although representations of the growth are possible (e.g., graphs or photographs). And third, the change is not immediate but occurs over time. Teachers generally choose plants and animals that are fast growing and visibly changing to maximize the change that can be observed.

In addition, the variables that govern these kinds of transformation are not ones that you necessarily want children to learn to experiment with, as is evident from the tadpole example. Putting the tadpole in different environments or treating it in ways that might lead to its death is not experimentation that is to be encouraged! While natural experiments that lead to an animal's death can precipitate learning, this is one of the areas where experimentation is to be discouraged and is an issue that I discuss in *The Young Child as Scientist* (Chaillé & Britain, 2003). One of the major goals in studying the natural world is to develop a deep respect and appreciation for nature that leads to a focus on more passive observation rather than active experimentation.

There are ways of studying change over time that do not involve experimentation on the natural world. For example, there are many inanimate "growing" materials that can be experimented with, such as natural sponge materials or the material (a superabsorbent polymer) from which a number of popular toys are made that expands a great deal when put in water.

As opposed to growth, a less common focus of the study of change over time is loss. Yet, the study of decay, decomposition, or disintegration can be as valuable as the study of growth. And, although generally speaking decomposition and decay are very gradual processes, it is possible to create opportunities to explore decay, to represent the process, and even to accelerate the process. Here is an example of preschool-age children exploring disintegration.

The pumpkins from their field trip to the pumpkin patch are in the window, and Anne, the teacher of this group of four-year-old children, decides to leave them there to focus on disintegration, something that occasionally happens spontaneously. She tells the children that they are going to watch carefully to see what will happen to the pumpkins over time, and that they are going to keep track of the changes that occur. She asks them how they could do that, and they suggest taking pictures and drawing pictures. So some of the children draw pictures of the pumpkins, and others help Anne take digital photographs of them, which they put up on the window by each pumpkin.

Each day the children run to the window to check on the pumpkins, and compare the pictures with the pumpkin. At their group time, Anne and the children discuss what is happening with the pumpkins. She puts out things they can use to look closely at the pumpkins, including a projecting microscope. Periodically, she and the children take samples from inside the pumpkin, and look at the results under the microscope. Fairly quickly mold and soft spots start to appear, and the children carefully document the different things they see in the pumpkins, putting the pictures onto the growing wall display of changes in the pumpkins. Anne has set up the wall with headings, Day 1, Day 2, and so on, so that the changes over time are clearly visible.

After still more time, the pumpkins fall in on themselves, and become very soft. And after still more time the pumpkins turn more mushy and begin to smell. Anne and the class decide to move the experiment outside, and set up a small area where they can continue to watch the pumpkins. Pictures and samples continue to be taken until the pumpkins are no longer visible in the dirt.

The children call their display "The Death of Our Pumpkins" and culminate the project by taking samples of the pictures and making it into a class book.

Now let's look at how a first grade teacher explores decomposition with her class.

▼ ◄ ▲ ▼ ◄ ▲ ▼ ◄ ▲ ▼ ◄ ▲ ▼ ◄ ▲ ▼ ◄ ▲ ▼ ◄ ▲

In the late fall, Shoshana takes her class for a walk to collect leaves as a way of beginning to look at change over time. When they return to the classroom, they spread out the leaves on a large white paper, and Shoshana asks if anyone notices anything about them. Tristan says, "Look, some of them are full of holes!" And Kiernan says, "But not all of them . . . some of them are thick and some are thin." At afternoon recess, some of the children find a pile of leaves next to a tree, and begin digging in it. "Teacher, look, the leaves under the pile are like the ones with holes!" Shoshana gets a shoe box and puts some of the leaves into it to bring into the classroom, where the children get out jeweler's loupes (see Ruef, 1998) and examine them, comparing the ones that were buried and the ones they found on their walk.

After a good deal of discussion and reading of resource books, the children decide to see what will decompose if buried in dirt, so, after the children have made written predictions about what will happen, Shoshana sets up a box with dirt in the corner of the classroom where a number of different items are buried. They choose to bury things made out of different materials—paper, metal, plastic, cloth—and label each buried object. Every few days the children carefully dig into the dirt to see what is happening, and are surprised at how quickly the paper disintegrates compared to the other materials. The children compare their predictions with the actual findings and after three weeks decide to continue the experiment until the metal and plastic are gone. This experiment goes on for a very long time, and the children finally conclude that the metal and the plastic will *not* disintegrate, leading to a discussion and an extended project on recycling and waste.

▼◄ ▲▼◄ ▲▼◄ ▲▼◄ ▲▼◄ ▲▼◄ ▲▼◄ ▲

There are many resources available to examine things closely and having these on hand will be helpful. Jeweler's loupes are very easy for children to use, much easier than hand-held magnifying glasses, and relatively inexpensive. But bug-viewers and water magnifiers, in which you put material into a magnifying container, are also good tools for any activity that involves observation and close study.

▼◄ ▲▼◄ ▲▼◄ ▲▼

Looking closely with a jeweler's loupe.

There are many good sources for reading about change over time.

> Taback, S. (1999). *Joseph Had a Little Overcoat*. A good example of a children's book that raises the issue of something changing over time, becoming one thing after another. In this book, a piece of cloth is used over and over, becoming a part of different things.

> Johnston, T. (2002). *Yonder*. This book shows, as seasons change, children growing up, marrying, babies being born, and parents getting old and dying.

> Munsch, R. N. (2001). *Love You Forever*. A similar story to *Yonder* in which the same song is sung by a mother to her baby, and then to her progressively older boy until he sings the song to his own baby.

> Leopold, N. C. (1999). *Once I Was . . .* Another book that illustrates growing and changing as things come together—a trickle becomes a lake, a baby becomes a grown-up, the alphabet becomes books.

> Zolotow, C. (1992). *This Quiet Lady*. This book traces a child from being born to becoming a mother herself.

These are just a few examples of the kinds of books that you could incorporate into the study of the big idea of transformation and change over time.

Looking at History as Change over Time

Expanding the idea of change into the arena of social studies, we can view the study of history as an example of change over time. The study of history is often presented as too abstract for young children and outside the realm of what it is possible for them to understand. But I would contend that, on the contrary, children can comprehend and will be fascinated with history to which they perceive a connection when you have cultivated and excited their interest. For younger children the connection will need to be concrete and clear, visible and of importance to their lives.

But if you think about it, much of the most important literature that resonates with children is telling stories that are outside their lived experiences. Books and other media become the connection with children's lives. Similarly, we can document events and experiences in children's lives in ways that become historical accounts, and through documentation we can facilitate this interest in what has happened before the present.

Thus, one of the keys to making history meaningful and interesting to young children is documentation. Documentation is a form of reflection on the present, and becomes a portrayal of the history of the experiences in the classroom. Presented in a sequential way, or organized by themes or topics, documentation can be the source for considering history.

Here is a way that children can study transformation that is occurring in their environment and then extend this to study historical transformation.

Next door to the school where Stephanie teaches her preschool children, an apartment building is being built. Of course the children are fascinated by it and talk about it on a daily basis. Stephanie decides to use this as an opportunity to study transformation since the children are already very involved in watching the building process. She encourages the children to write and draw in their journals what they are seeing each day, and the class begins to document each day's changes as they occur. This includes the children's dictated descriptions of what is going on, their drawings (often copied out of their journals), their paintings, and the class-taken digital pictures. All of these go on the wall, starting on one side of the room and progressively moving across the wall space. When they run out of space for all the documentation, they number the documents and store them in a book.

Two of the children, Ramon and Miranda, create an elaborate reproduction of the foundation of the apartment building, using a box for the basement and elevator shafts, and begin to build with cardboard what they see each day. As they do this, Stephanie takes more pictures to put on the wall, capturing the in-process construction.

Now and then the children will walk over to the building site and watch from the sidewalk. The workers notice the children, and the foreman comes and talks with them. The children decide to invite him into the classroom to see what they have done. He comes for a visit, and they ask him lots of questions about what the workers are doing and what will come next. Impressed by their interest, the foreman suggests that they talk with the architect, who is happy to visit the preschool and share with the children the architectural drawings of the apartment building and even brings the model that he has constructed out of balsa wood. The children have so many questions about how she did her work that the architect comes back for a second visit after the work is underway. This time she brings her laptop computer and shows them the graphics program that she used for the initial designing of a building, a three-dimensional design program. Although the program itself is too complex for preschool children to use, they are fascinated by it and she prints off some of the images that the group helps her to make.

These images and copies of the architectural plans also go onto the table where the children have accumulated all the documentation about the apartment building, and children spend a good deal of time studying the different materials that they have, going back and forth between their artistic representations of buildings—both cardboard constructions and paintings—and the actual architectural renderings and computer-generated images.

This project in itself is a rich and wonderful study of something relevant to the children in their immediate environment, and Stephanie capitalizes on this by facilitating more intensive study and documentation of what the children are seeing. She is interested in using this interest as a way of provoking the children's understanding of and interest in history. She decides to do a parallel study of historical buildings that extends off of the study of the apartment building. Stephanie has herself been intrigued by historical architecture and in her travels has taken pictures of many important buildings. She has a personal hobby of reading about the time periods of the buildings she has been particularly drawn to. Based on this, she decides to choose something for which she already has some resources. Since the children seem to be intrigued by the way the apartment is getting taller and taller, she decides to focus on skyscrapers to feed their interest. She begins her efforts to expand their interest in the height of the buildings by showing them some of her pictures of skyscrapers she has visited throughout the world. She also finds a large number of children's nonfiction books that tell the story of different tall buildings. And, since these are children who had some knowledge of the World Trade Center bombings, she knows there are issues that may come up relating to how structures stay up and what can make them fall down. Instead of shying away from this and from the possible social and emotional issues that could be uncovered, she decides this is a meaningful way to explore the children's understanding and feelings about an important event in their recent histories.

But to start, she shows them books such as *Skyscraper* (2004) by Susan Goodman and Michael Doolittle, and *Up Goes the Skyscraper!* (1990) by Gail Gibbons to provide stories and descriptions of the construction of several different skyscrapers. She tells them that she would like to study one of them in more detail just as they are studying the apartment building in some detail. The children decide that they particularly like the Empire State Building, mostly because one of the children excitedly shares a book about King Kong with pictures of the giant ape hanging onto the building. This intrigues them, and so they begin to explore the Empire State Building.

Stephanie has done some homework, and has identified a number of resources for the children to use in this exploration, including one book specifically about the history of the Empire State Building (*Empire State Building: A Wonders of the World Book,* by Elizabeth Mann and Alan Witschonke, 2003). She brings the book in, and makes some enlarged copies of some of the pictures in the book. These pictures include New York at the time the building was being constructed, and her hope is that the old cars and dress of people in the picture will provoke the children's interest in the historical aspect of the project. She thinks that by enlarging the pictures that show the cars and the people they will be highlighted and more noticeable to the children, and it turns out that she's right. The children ask a lot of questions about why people are dressed funny and why the cars are different. Jon says that they're only like that in New York, but Sammy says that he's seen pictures of his grandparents in Nebraska that look like that. Stephanie lets the children raise questions about it and keeps notes on the things the children talk about and the questions they have. She suggests to the class that maybe they could do some work together to find out what they can about that time in history in both New York City and in their own town of Portland, Oregon.

In this way Stephanie has stimulated the children's interest in history and how their own town has changed over time, an interest that is dynamic and is fed by a visit to the historical society's educational resource center in downtown Portland.

▼◄ ▲ ▼◄ ▲ ▼◄ ▲ ▼◄ ▲ ▼◄ ▲ ▼◄ ▲ ▼◄ ▲

From this example, you can see how a focus on transformation of a building can be extended, quiet naturally, into transformation over time and a study of historical change as well.

Creative Arts

Transformation captures the essence of much of the work children do in the creative arts. Taking materials, whether they be paints, clay, or paper, and creating something out of them—whether two- or three-dimensional—is a form of transformation. One of the interesting things that we can do as teachers is to facilitate children's awareness and acknowledgment of the processes of transformation. As with other big ideas, a key element in doing this is representation and documentation. Finding ways of recording and displaying what is going on can help draw attention to the transformation, both while it is occurring and in reflecting back on what has been done. When representation, documentation, and reflection become a part of the classroom culture, it is natural for children to think about processes.

▼ ▲ ▼ ◄ ▲ ▼
Creating a flower on the grass.

How can you capture process through documentation? Lucy, the teacher of preschool-age children, documented Charlotte's creation of a flower by sketching and taking notes while Charlotte created this flower on the grass.

When Charlotte finished, Lucy went over her sketch with her and asked her some questions about what she was doing as she created the representation.

Lucy's final sketch and notes looked like Figure 9.1.

Let's see how a class that is accustomed to focusing on processes engages in a creative activity and how the teacher documents the process.

▼ ◄ ▲ ▼ ◄ ▲ ▼ ◄

Jenna, a six-year-old, has decided to join the group at the project table that is creating horse sculptures out of clay. Her first grade class has been studying horses, an interest that came out of a visit to a nearby ranch where they saw many horses, some very young. While at the ranch, the children sketched the horses, took digital pictures, and their teacher, Traci, made videotapes of the horses walking, trotting, and running. In the subsequent discussions, the children talked a lot about how differently the horses moved depending on their speed. Several of the children began to try to reproduce the horses in different poses out of clay. This group of children had a fair amount of experience working with clay and the required tools, and so it was a natural thing for them to do. They worked at the project table on which large copies of the digital pictures had been placed. Next to the table

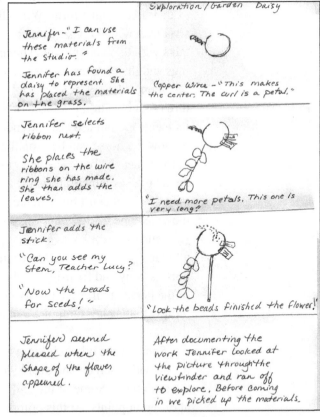

Figure 9.1 *The sketch and notes taken by the teacher of the flower creation.*

▼◄ ▲▼ ◄ ▲▼ ◄ ▲▼

Teacher reviewing her sketch and notes with the child.

was the television on which the video was playing, and now and then the children would replay the video or pause it at certain points to look at the horses in a particular position.

Traci is documenting what the children are doing as they create their horse sculptures. She is recording their conversations with a tape recorder, taking pictures of their work, and sketching the progression as their horses take form. When the children come back after lunch, Traci sits down with the group that has been working on the horse sculptures and talks with them about what she has been seeing. She shows them her drawings and the pictures and asks them what they are thinking as they work.

Jenna's horse sculpture began with her studying very carefully one picture of a horse in the middle of a gallop. The horse's legs are extended and its mane and tail are also extended. As she begins to work, she is puzzled by how the horse can be propelled into the air in this way and can't figure out whether the back legs are pushing the horse or if the front legs are "reaching" as they go forward. Jenna tries to reproduce the gallop with her own body but can't quite make a similar action. Traci suggests they look at the videotape in slow motion, and they stop the action as it goes.

Jenna stops the video at one point and, through Traci's suggestion, actually tapes a piece of paper over the video screen, tracing the shape of the horse's body and focusing on the legs. She makes three different pictures of the horse at different points in time and then says, "I've got it now!" She returns to the clay sculpture and refers to her sketch while she works with the clay.

Some of the other children become interested in how Jenna is tracing off the video screen and decide to focus on tracing and drawing rather than the sculptures. Some of the children draw a series of pictures of the horse at different points. At this point Traci finds a flip book—the kind where you flip the pages to see something move—and places it nearby, thinking that it might suggest a new extension to the children. However, the children don't make the connection, and Traci decides that it would probably take too many duplicate pictures to make an effective flipbook. She decides to think about this for later project work, however, perhaps with some other medium that doesn't require such careful work to make each picture, like a series of digital pictures of the same thing over time.

The children continually revisit the videotapes of the horses that they saw at the ranch, and one of the children brings in a videotape of the movie *Seabiscuit* (Ross, 2003) so that they can watch the race scene in the movie to see how horses move when they go as fast as they do in a race. Traci finds some excerpts to show the children, and again they watch these excerpts over and over and discuss why the movement is different when the horses are going at different speeds.

One of the children wonders whether the same thing is true for people as for horses. They decide to go outside and do a comparison of the different ways they move when they walk, jog, and run, and the children reproduce some of the horse study using videotapes and images of their own movements. Just as with the horse study, the children (and Traci) find other videotapes of people running (the movie *Prefontaine* [James, 1997], has some good race sequences in it, and there are many others). This extension to human movement is done with Traci's active encouragement. She is very pleased because she is expected to cover some aspects of the study of the human body in first grade in her district, and this is the perfect introduction to the study they will embark on as a class.

▼◄ ▲ ▼◄ ▲ ▼◄ ▲ ▼◄ ▲ ▼◄ ▲ ▼◄ ▲ ▼◄ ▲

This episode from Traci's first grade classroom illustrates how their work in creative arts is indissociably integrated with their work in science. They also have many opportunities to bring in children's literature, and mathematics plays a role in their discussions of comparisons and measurements. And clearly the use of technology plays an integral role in their study.

Transformation, probably more than any of the other big ideas described in this book, captures the essence of what children do and are interested in. It is hard to do it justice, and I know that you will be inspired to think of many ways you could capitalize on this interest and facilitate the making of connections across curriculum domains that are so natural to do with transformation.

Teacher Resources

Grummer, A. (1992). *Tin Can Papermaking: Recycle for Earth and Art*
Levine, S. (1993). *The Paper Book and Paper Maker*
Ruef, K. (1998). *The Private Eye*

Children's Literature

Briggs, R. (1978). *The Snowman*
de Paola, T. (1978). *The Popcorn Book*
Gershwin, G. (1999). *Summertime.* Illustrated by Mike Wimmer
Gibbons, G. (1990). *Up Goes the Skyscraper!*
Goodman, S. E., & Doolittle, M. (2004). *Skyscraper*
Hutchins, P. (1987). *Changes, Changes*
Johnston, T. (2002). *Yonder*
Jonas, A. (1983). *Round Trip*
Joyce, W. (2000). *George Shrinks*
Leopold, N. C. (1999). *Once I Was . . .*
Macaulay, D. (1976). *Underground*
Macaulay, D. (1980). *Unbuilding*
Macaulay, D. (1982a). *Cathedral: The Story of Its Construction*
Macaulay, D. (1981). *Castle*
Macaulay, D. (1982b). *Pyramid*
Mann, E., & Witschonke, A. (2003). *Empire State Building: A Wonders of the World Book*
Munsch, R. N. (2001). *Love You Forever*
Showers, P. (1985). *What Happens to a Hamburger?*
Taback, S. (1999). *Joseph Had a Little Overcoat*
Zolotow, C. (1992). *This Quiet Lady*
Zolotow, C. (2000). *My Friend John*

Ideas from Different Curriculum Domains

Science

Reversible (or semireversible) transformation:
> block building, Play-Doh
> pendulums, swinging
> recycling, papermaking
> some architecture, building construction

Nonreversible transformations:
>   some kinds of construction (gluing wood)
>   some kinds of combinations (cooking)
>   decomposition, loss, disintegration (melting ice)
>   growth (plants, insects)

Social Studies
>   history as change over time

Creative Arts
>   representation of change over time (through documentation)
>   representation of movement (through drawing, sculpture)

Mathematics
>   measurement

Technology
>   digital photographs
>   videotapes

Materials
>   materials for construction play (in addition to unit blocks)
>   modeling materials (Play-Doh, clay, other types of dough)

Epilogue

We've journeyed through seven big ideas in this book: light, balance, zooming in and out, sound, upside down and inside out, chain reactions, and transformation. For each big idea, I've tried to paint a picture of how you as a teacher could develop curricula grounded in it and how you could explore some of the facets of each big idea that might inspire curricula for your classroom. In so doing, I've also shared with you some of the resources that I have found for each big idea in the form of materials, books, websites, videos, and toys.

It is my hope that in the process of exploring these seven big ideas you have gained some knowledge of what makes a big idea, of how one would go about planning and implementing curriculum based on a big idea, and of how each big idea has its own unique emphases and directions. I also want to repeat that the ideas presented for each big idea represent only *my* thoughts and ideas on how you might proceed to work with these particular big ideas. There are many other directions one could go in with each of the big ideas, and I have only sampled some of the possibilities. The possibilities are truly endless, and part of the joy of working with big ideas is the opportunity to play around with all the possible directions. In exploring each big idea, I used a variety of strategies to do so, and in this chapter I will share some of the strategies that I used to find and screen resources. What I would like you to take from this book is the understanding that this process of developing curriculum and ideas is one that stimulates your own interest and one that is quite exciting. Perhaps you'll try out one or two of the ideas in this book and see where they go. Perhaps you'll try to develop a focus on one of the big ideas and explore it with your children in many different ways. Perhaps you'll embrace the idea of big ideas and develop some of your own. Whatever you do, what I'd like to do in this final chapter is to discuss some of the issues and strategies that you might encounter in putting these ideas into practice. I'll start with discussing the planning process, including strategies for pulling together resources.

Identifying a Big Idea

The key to identifying a big idea is to think of it as a topic that subsumes many different types of projects and activities. One way to identify a big idea is to take something that has emerged as a possible project for the class and map it out. Ask the following questions: What are the underlying ideas for this project? What are the concepts that children will be exploring when they pursue this project?

187

For example, let's say that your community has experienced heavy rainfall leading to flooding in some areas. Some of the children in your preschool class have been talking about the flooding, and you see them in the construction area creating rivers and dams and talking about how the water is rising. A project on rain and flooding could emerge from this initial interest. Stepping back from that, think about what the children would be exploring and experimenting with in the course of doing this project. One underlying concept is the idea of contraction and growth, which might be what you see the children "playing around" with. What you as a teacher can do is play around yourself with the idea of growth as a big idea. Another underlying concept has to do with movement, which children could be exploring through the movement of the water—through the streets, through the river. Movement or growth as big ideas could come out of the initial project work that is focusing on the flooding. Either one would be rich with possibility.

As another example, let's say that you have just visited some caves with your family while on vacation and become fascinated with caves yourself. You start reading about caves and want to share your excitement with the children in your second grade classroom. One of the things that children often become excited about when they explore the idea of caves is the darkness of the caves—and light as a big idea could result. But another aspect of caves is the idea of enclosures, which is something children are also interested in. This could lead to a big idea of enclosure and spaces, which could subsume work on habitat. The study of caves, then, would become a provocation for work on the bigger idea of spaces and enclosures.

Searching for Resources: Strategies and Considerations

So once you have identified a potential new big idea, how do you proceed? I found myself, at different points in researching the big ideas described in this book, totally obsessed with each of them. When I was studying light, I would see reflections everywhere I looked. I would notice how much music and poetry makes allusions to light, and I would notice how many toys and play materials allow for experimentation with light. I also discovered how many other teachers have played around with light in a similar way and have shared their experiences in books and teacher resources. Similarly, when studying balance, I discovered quite a selection of toys that involve playing with balance, as well as some naturally occurring interests of children that lend themselves to the exploration of the ideas of balance. When traveling in Korea and Japan during the period I was writing this chapter, I found numerous games from both countries that involve balance, and I'm not certain I would have paid as much attention to them as I did had I not been thinking about balance during that time.

So it is helpful to give yourself time to do this kind of thinking and obsessing. Once you have decided to pursue a particular big idea, let it become your focus for some time. This will give it time to percolate and will allow this kind of serendipitous discovery to happen.

Begin by looking at what has been done by other teachers. Do a literature review to see what has been written in the education arena on curriculum relating to the idea. Read those that sound interesting. Talk to other teachers to see what they have done. Post a question on a teacher Listserv to see what comes up. Do an Internet search including the word *curriculum*; Google became my best friend during this process. This kind of search will most likely yield too much information, and much of it will be uninteresting or not applicable. So be selective in what you read and look at. This is a process that should be inspiring and fun, not dreary.

As you do this, also broaden your search to include any literature or material related to the topic. I found myself doing very unusual Google searches on broad topics, such as "mirrors," when I was exploring light. This led me to books on the history of mirrors and other nonfiction, poetry, and much fiction that was largely metaphorically related and therefore of limited use. I also found a large number of art books that included work on capturing light in paintings and other artwork, which I found very inspiring.

But you also have to think creatively, beyond what comes up as a directly connected search word. For example, looking through some of my favorite children's books, I would find illustrations that included shadows, sunlight, reflections, and light through water. I began exploring glass and glassblowing, which is how I came across the video of Dale Chihuly's work described in Chapter 2.

At some point fairly early in my explorations, I would try to write out the characteristics of the big idea that might lend itself to categories of activities and materials. For the big idea of zooming, for example, there seemed to be two main categories—one around changing size (micro and macro) and the other around perspective-taking. Perspective-taking as an umbrella covers both physical and social perspectives, and each of those categories could be expanded into numerous curriculum domains and ideas. For the big idea of sound, I categorized the concepts underlying sound into sources/receptors, properties of sound, rhythm, and reproduction of sound. Once I had some categories, I could go into more depth in each one.

There is, however, a big difference between writing this book and deciding to explore a big idea with children. You may say to yourself, "Oh come on, I don't have time to do this kind of research." You don't have to. You can decide on one thing to try out, and then research further as children's interests and explorations unfold. However, it is a good idea to do some of the research on an ongoing basis to feed your knowledge base and to stimulate new directions that you might provoke through the provision of materials or an experience. I had no idea how interesting it would be to think about some of the big ideas. For example, I anticipated sound would be fairly straightforward to explore. Wrong! It was quite complex, and there was much I didn't know or understand about the concepts that I began to explore. Keeping files or crates with ideas and materials related to a big idea that interests you is a good way to let the ideas percolate and grow.

I also think that teachers of young children often get into ruts when it comes to their professional reading and often focus on curriculum ideas rather than the broader (and more interesting) literature that can stimulate their own intellectual growth as well as help them to feel children's growth and understanding. In one of the seminars in Reggio Emilia, Sergio Spaggiari, speaking to the Reggio Study Tour in 2004, suggested that a teacher should read something outside the field of education every day. We have to nurture our own intellectual development. And spending a half hour looking through a book of art prints that illustrate all the ways that painters have represented light in paintings is incredibly inspiring and can yield lots of ideas for provoking children's interests in representation and in activities related to light.

I also found that I had to stretch myself to think of connections in some of the curriculum domains for some of the big ideas. As an early childhood educator who's focused on science education, working in the curriculum domains of literacy and social studies was sometimes challenging. There were times when I think I might have gone too far in making connections with the big ideas! And while I've witnessed the use of all of the activities and approaches that are described in this book, the ultimate test of whether these connections are the result of too much of a stretch depends on what happens with your children in your own classroom setting and in the context of thinking about the big idea over a period of time with children. Implementing a curriculum grounded in a big idea is a process, and it is a process that requires you as a teacher to be constantly listening in the broadest sense of the word and responding to what you see and hear, asking questions, and paying attention to what you learn from children. At times it may involve you provoking children to make connections without manufacturing the relationships that children might construct among ideas.

In this sense, the process of attempting to implement a curriculum grounded in big ideas can be characterized as representing the teacher as theory-builder at its finest. Experimenting with curriculum, looking for connections, provoking relationships, even stretching the concept (too far at times!) embodies the principles of experimentation and requires you to be a reflective practitioner in the best sense of the word. The theory-building teacher is one who is willing to take risks and has fun in the process—playing around with ideas, activities, and materials as much as the children are, sometimes succeeding, and sometimes failing—but always learning.

Some Considerations in the Choice and Use of Resources

There should be no constraints in the brainstorming and self-education process that I've described above. You should feel free to look at things that may not be appropriate for children. However, once you've garnered your own thoughts about the big idea and some directions in which you could go, you do need to take into account several issues relating to the particular group of children with whom you work. Three types of issues are paramount—developmental considerations, cultural considerations, and community considerations.

Developmental Considerations

As I am focusing on early childhood—defined as preschool through the primary grades—I primarily distinguish between what I call "younger" children —preschool age—and "older" children—kindergarten through second grade. This dichotomy works for some broad differences. But a better way to think of development is in terms of developmental sequences, since there are obvious differences between working with three-year-olds and working with five-year-olds.

1. *Physical activity.* All young children need to engage in physical activity, but younger children need even more physically active engagement, and our schools and schedules usually provide for this.

2. *Capability for abstraction.* As children get older they become increasingly able to think abstractly, to make mental predictions, and to represent their thinking.

3. *Representational capabilities.* While the work in Reggio Emilia has demonstrated even very young children's competence at representing their thinking in many different "languages," the complexity of those representations does change with age as well as experience. This is particularly true in the area of verbalization. Older children are better able—and more disposed—to express verbally what they are doing and thinking without it interfering in their actions.

4. *Complexity of social interaction.* Again, all children are social beings, and need opportunities for social interaction. But younger children's social interactions are less complex in some ways than those of older children. We see more elaborated social scripts, for example, in the pretend play of older children than in the pretend play of younger children.

These developmental considerations shouldn't be too constraining, however. It is always important to assume competency of young children and try things that we may think they are not capable of. We are very often surprised at what young children can do and are much more likely to water down what we share with them. It's good to get into the habit of anticipating the most and the best from children.

Cultural Considerations

Promoting an interest and awareness in diversity is a strong value in the field of early childhood education. The study of big ideas is an ideal arena in which to explore diversity, and it is one that we must make a conscious effort to address. Every classroom most likely includes diverse cultures of some kind or another, and whether or not that diversity is evident, we value children seeing themselves as part of a global community. So considering culture consists of two commitments—consideration of the culture of your own classroom and community and consideration of the child as part of the world with all its diversity.

One of the ways that we can show this consideration is in the selection and use of materials and resources. In images and references always make a conscious effort to include authors, painters, and actors from different cultures and countries. This should particularly—but not solely—target those cultures represented by the children in your classroom and school. If you have refugees from Somalia, for example, you would want to make sure to include in your exploration of the big idea of sound music and instruments from Somalia in particular and Africa in general.

Community Considerations

As you have seen, exploring big ideas involves capitalizing on the resources of the community in which you teach and learn. It is essential to build awareness of the local community and establish relationships within the community in order to do so. In Reggio Emilia the teachers brought the classroom to the community by physically setting up spaces in the town where children would work and share their work with people in the town of Reggio Emilia. This was a purposeful effort to build connections and collaborations, and over time those relationships become very important to the working of the school. Such community collaborations can happen anywhere and require cultivation on the part of the teacher. Parents can be an important part of this process, since they are themselves a part of the community and play different roles that can enhance community connections.

This kind of connection can be spectacular—as in the children of the Diana School making the theater curtain for the Municipal Theatre of Reggio Emilia (Vecchi, 2002)—or more mundane—as in children walking to the bakery near the school. Either way, community connections need to be intentional and frequent. Depending on the project work that children are engaged in, communication with community resources can become an important part of the project. Children studying bells can write a note to the local music store to see if they can come for a visit to see the different percussion instruments. A classroom engaged in studying perspective-taking as part of a focus on zooming in and out can contact the owner of the tallest building in the neighborhood to see if they can look out the window onto their school and playground from the top story of the building.

Considering the community, however, means also being sensitive to the issues and values of that community. If your school is in a part of town dominated by a particular ethnic or religious group and you as the teacher are not familiar with the values of that group, you must become more knowledgeable in order that communication with the local community is respectful and compatible with the community's values.

Beyond Resources and Ideas

There are a number of elements of the curriculum that you can and should anticipate and prepare for, remembering always the principle of intentional planning combined with flexible and responsive implementation. There are several categories in which you can make some plans: provocations; planned exploration of materials; collections of children's literature and other resource materials; community resources for field trips, visitors, and materials; and culminating activities or projects.

Provocations

A provocation is an event or activity designed to capture children's interest in a big idea and to generate excitement and thinking. There are times when provocations are suggested by things that are already occurring—as when a big storm hits town or a circus is coming to a site near the school. Other times, you as the teacher can provide the provocation to generate interest. A provocation could be as simple as reading a book or story to the children, as we saw in Chapter 7 when the teacher read *Wacky Wednesday* (Lesieg & Booth, 1974) to children to generate interest in the wacky big idea. A provocation could involve showing the children a video, such as the Dale Chihuly video about glass, *River of Glass*. A provocation could involve a visit from a family member who is a percussionist, stimulating the children's interest in rhythm and sound, or a shell collector, stimulating interest and attention to symmetry in nature. A provocation could also involve the exploration of materi-

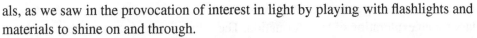

als, as we saw in the provocation of interest in light by playing with flashlights and materials to shine on and through.

Every big idea that does not arise spontaneously from children involves provocation as an initiator of the big idea. But provocations can be used throughout exploration of a big idea, as ways of suggesting directions or paths or of supporting the directions children are taking in their work around a big idea. Waning interest in a big idea can be restimulated through intriguing provocation. In this way, the teacher is supporting, facilitating, and feeding the children's interests and ideas through ongoing provocations.

Providing Materials for Exploration

Planning for big ideas also involves provision of materials that allow for children to explore and experiment, raise questions, and generate interest. Materials are themselves a form of provocation. During the exploration of light, the teacher could set up large mirrors at different angles in the construction area and provide children with numerous small mirrors to work with as a way of directing interest toward reflection and symmetry. Similarly, while studying perspective-taking, the teacher could provide numerous different magnifying devices for children to use in many areas of the room. Parents can be of help gathering together materials appropriate for the big idea you're exploring. A note to parents giving the overall focus of work on a big idea might bring in materials that you never thought of.

Children's Literature and Resource Books

In planning for a big idea, you'll want to gather together all the children's books and adult books, as well as videos and visual displays, that could be used as reference material. Many libraries have book sets that can be checked out on different topics, and these may be appropriate for the big idea you are taking on. This is also a good area for you to keep accumulating ideas, because, as I said earlier, once you explore a big idea you'll continue to see it everywhere you look. As stated earlier, it helps to have a set of crates for the big ideas you've developing where you can put materials and resources as you come across them.

Community Resources

Think creatively about what's available to you in terms of the neighborhood of your school, parents and family members of the children in your classroom, and more distant resources that might be available over the Internet. Getting to know your students' families, their occupations, and their hobbies can help you greatly when you're brainstorming resources. A parent who is a chef in a restaurant can host the class for an exploration of transformation. The same is true of the neighborhood of the school and accessible parts of the city in which you teach. A visit to the art museum could be focused on how artists depict light in their paintings, for example. Parents and the community are important sources for materials as well.

Culminating Activities

It's neither necessary nor even a good idea to plan culminating activities in advance, because you do not know what directions children may go in with the big idea that you're exploring. It is important to be alert and open to the possibilities as the work unfolds. If children exploring balance become interested in mobiles, you might have an opportunity to construct a large mobile for a particular place in the school or classroom. Introducing that as a possibility to discuss with the children could be itself a provocation for collaborative work that would lead naturally to the culminating act of presenting the mobile to the parents and other children in the school. A culmination of the work is an important part of the process of reflection and documentation because it allows children, teachers, and parents to look at the connections across all the projects and activities that occurred.

Final Thoughts

To end this book, let's return to the beginning. What can we do to make teaching and learning full of joy? We can provide opportunities for children to explore ideas that are rich and valuable, ideas that cut across curriculum domains, and ideas that allow for children to make connections in ways that make sense to them. We can be intentional in our planning, providing an array of provocations, materials, and experiences, and also be responsive to the wonderful ideas children come up with and the directions that they decide to go in. We can decide as collaborators in the curriculum process to get excited about learning with and from children. We can dedicate ourselves fully to the value that there should be "Nothing Without Joy" for ourselves and for the children we teach.

References

Aardema, V. (1975). *Why mosquitoes buzz in people's ears: A West African tale*. Pictures by L. Dillon & D. Dillon. New York: Dial Press.

Abbott, L., & Nutbrown, C. E. (2001). *Experiencing Reggio Emilia: Implications for preschool provision*. Philadelphia: Open University Press.

Adkins, J. (1980). *Moving heavy things*. Boston: Houghton Mifflin.

Adoff, A., & Steptoe, J. (1982). *All the colors of the race: Poem*. New York: HarperCollins.

Allard, H., & Marshall, J. P. (1974). *The Stupids step out*. Boston: Houghton Mifflin.

Allard, H., & Marshall, J. P. (1981). *The Stupids die*. Boston: Houghton Mifflin.

Allsburg, C. V. (1984). *The mysteries of Harris Burdick*. Boston: Houghton Mifflin.

Anno, M. (1988a). *In shadowland*. New York: Orchard Books.

Anno, M. (1988b). *Upside-downers: Pictures to stretch the imagination*. New York: Philomel Books.

Arthus-Bertrand, Y. (2002). *Earth from above*. New York: Harry N. Abrams.

Asch, F. (1999). *Moonbear's shadow* (Rev. ed.). New York: Aladdin.

Bailey, V. (1990). *Shadow theater (Rainy days)*. New York: Franklin Watts.

Baker, D. (1998). *Collectible bells: Treasures of sight and sound*. Atglen, PA: Schiffer.

Banyai, I. (1995a). *Zoom*. New York: Viking Penguin USA.

Banyai, I. (1995b). *Re-Zoom*. New York: Viking Penguin USA.

Barrie, J. M. (2003). *Peter Pan*. New York: Henry Holt.

Beeke, T. (2001). *Roar like a lion: A first book about sounds*. London: Quilane Children's Books.

Bentley, W. A. (2000a). *Snowflakes in photographs*. New York: Dover Publications.

Bentley, W. A. (2000b). *The snowflake man*. Jericho Historical Society. Retrieved from http://snowflakebentley.com

Berk, L. E., & Winsler, A. (1995). *Scaffolding children's learning: Vygotsky and early childhood education* (Vol. 7). Washington, DC: National Association for the Education of Young Children.

Berkes, M., & Noreika, R. I. (2003). *Marsh music*. Brookfield, CT: Millbrook Press.

Bodrova, E., & Leong, D. J. (1996). *Tools of the mind: The Vygotskian approach to early childhood education*. Englewood Cliffs, NJ: Merrill.

Bova, B. (2001). *The story of light*. Naperville, IL: Sourcebooks.

Boynton, S. (1982). *Moo baa la la la*. New York: Little Simon.

Brallier, J. (2000). *No sweat projects: Shadowy science*. Illustrated by B. Staake. New York: Planet Dexter, Penguin Putnam Books.

Briggs, R. (1978). *The snowman*. New York: Random House Books.

Brooks, J. G., & Brooks, M. G. (2000). *In search of understanding: The case for constructivist classrooms*. Washington, DC: Association for Supervision and Curriculum Development.

Brown, J. (2003). *Flat Stanley* (40th anniversary ed.). Illustrated by S. Nash. New York: HarperTrophy.

Brown, M. W. (1991). *Goodnight moon*. Illustrated by C. Hurd. Brdbk Rei ed. New York: HarperFestival.

Brown, M. W. (1999). *The train to Timbuctoo*. Illustrated by A. Seiden. New York: Golden Books.

Brown, M. W., & McCue, L. (2000). *Bunny's noisy book*. New York: Hyperion Books.

Browne, A. (2002). *Gorilla*. Cambridge, MA: Candlewick Press.

Bruchac, J., & London, J. (1992). *Thirteen moons on turtle's back: A native American year of moons*. Illustrated by T. Locker. New York: Philomel Books.

Bulla, C. R. (1994). *What makes a shadow?* (Rev. ed.). Illustrated by June Otani. New York: HarperCollins.

Bunting, E. (1999). *Night of the gargoyles*. Illustrated by D. Wiesner. New York: Clarion Books.

Cadwell, L. B. (1997). *Bringing Reggio Emilia Home: An innovative approach to early childhood education*. New York: Teacher College Press.

Cadwell, L. B. (2003). *Bringing learning to life: A Reggio approach to early childhood education*. New York: Teachers College Press.

Carle, E. (1997). *The very quiet cricket*. New York: Grosset & Dunlap.

Carle, E. (2000). *Dream snow*. New York: Philomel Books.

Castle, K. (2004). The meaning of autonomy in early childhood teacher education. *Journal of Early Childhood Teacher Education, 25*(1), 3–10.

Cazet, D. (1994). *Nothing at all*. New York: Orchard Books.

Chaillé, C., & Britain, L. (1990). The "permissive" early childhood environment and knowledge construction. Paper presented at the American Educational Research Association, Boston.

Chaillé, C., & Britain, L. (2003). *The young child as scientist: A constructivist approach to early childhood science education* (3rd ed.). San Francisco: Allyn and Bacon.

Chaillé, C., & Young, P. (1982). Some issues linking research on children's play and education: Are they "only playing"? *International Journal of Early Childhood, 14*(2), 52–66.

Cherry, L. (1990). *The great kapok tree: A tale of the amazon rain forest*. New York: Voyager Books.

Cherry, L. (1992). *A river ran wild: An environmental history*. New York: A Gulliver Green Book.

Chihuly, D. (1999). *River of glass* [Video].

Cronin, D. (2003). *Diary of a worm*. Illustrated by H. Bliss. New York: Joanna Cotler Books.

Curtis, D., & Carter, M. (2000). *The art of awareness: How observation can transform your teaching*. St. Paul, MN: Redleaf Press.

Demi. (1987). *Opposites: An animal game book*. New York: Gosset & Dunlap.

de Paola, T. (1978). *The popcorn book*. New York: Scholastic.

DeVries, R., & Zan, B. (1994). *Moral classrooms, moral children: Creating a constructivist atmosphere in early childhood*. New York: Teacher College Press.

Dibble, C. H., & Lee, K. H. (2000). *101 Easy wacky crazy activities for young children*. Beltsville, MD: Gryphon House.

Donner, R. (Director). (1985) *The Goonies*. [Motion picture].

Doris, E. (1991). *Doing what scientists do: Children learn to investigate their work*. Portsmouth, NH: Heinemann.

Eames, C., & Eames, R. (1968). *Powers of 10*. Available from http://www.powersof10.com and http://www.loc.gov/exhibits/eames/science.html

Edwards, C., Gandini, L., & Forman, G. (Eds.). (1993). *The hundred languages of children: The Reggio Emilia approach to early childhood education*. Norwood, NJ: Ablex Publishing.

Edwards, C., Gandini, L., & Forman, G. (Eds.). (1998). *The hundred languages of children: The Reggio Emilia approach to early childhood education* (2nd ed.). Norwood, NJ: Ablex Publishing.

Emberley, B. (1972). *Drummer Hoff*. Illustrated by E. Emberley. New York: Aladdin.

Farber, N. (1992). *Return of the shadows*. Illustrated by A. Baruffi. New York: HarperCollins.

Farrelly, B., & Farrelly, P. (Directors). *Osmosis Jones*. [Motion picture].

Fischli, P., & Weiss, D. (1987). *The Way Things Go*. [Video].

Forman, G. E. (2001). Ordinary moments. Paper presented at the National Association for the Education of Young Children, Anaheim, CA.

Forman, G. E., & Hill, D. F. (1984). *Constructive play: Applying Piaget to the preschool*. Reading, MA: Addison-Wesley.

Forman, G. E., & Kuschner, D. S. (1983). *The child's construction of knowledge: Piaget for teaching children*. Washington, DC: National Association for the Education of Young Children.

Gandini, L. (1993). *Fundamentals of the Reggio Emilia approach to early childhood education* (Vol. 49). New York: Teachers College Press.

Gedin, M. (1998). *About listening: Discovering the inquisitive child*. Stockholm, Sweden: Reggio Emilia Institute.

Gershwin, G., & Wimmer, M. I. (1999). *Summertime*. New York: Simon & Schuster Books.

Gerstein, M. (2003). *The man who walked between the towers*. Brookfield, CT: Roaring Brook Press.

Gibbons, G. (1990). *Up goes the skyscraper!* New York: Aladdin Books.

Glanz, J., & Lipton, E. (2003). *City in the sky: The rise and fall of the World Trade Center*. New York: Times Books, Henry Holt and Company.

Glover, D. (2002). *Pulleys and gears (simple machines)*. Portsmouth, NH: Heinemann.

Goffin, J. (1991). *OH!* New York: Harry N. Abrams.

Gold-Dworkin, H., & Ullman, R. K. (1999). *Exploring light and color*. New York: McGraw-Hill.

Goldsworthy, A. (2000). *Time*. New York: Harry N. Abrams.

Goldsworthy, A. (1990). *Andy Goldsworthy: A Collaboration with nature*. New York: Harry N. Abrams.

Goodman, S. E., & Doolittle, M. (2004). *Skyscraper*. New York: Knopf Books.

Gordon, S., & Wyman, J. (1967). *Primer of perception: Handbook for artists & teachers*. New York: Reinhold Books.

Grummer, A. (1992). *Tin can papermaking: Recycle for earth and art*. Appleton, WI: Greg Markim.

Guidici, C., Rinaldi, C., & Krechevsky, M. (Eds.). (2001). *Making learning visible: Children as individual and group learners*. Reggio Emilia, Italy: Reggio Children.

Harter, P. (1994). *Shadow play, night haiku*. Illustrated by J. Greene. New York: Simon & Schuster.

Haslam, A., Parsons, A., & Barnes, J. (2000). *Make it work! Sound*. Princeton, NJ: Two-Can Publishing.

Hearn, E., & Collins, H. I. (1983). *Woosh, I hear a sound*. Toronto, Canada: Annick Press.

Helm, J. H. (2001). *Young investigators: The project approach in the early years*. New York: Teachers College Press.

Hendricks, J. E. (1997). *First steps toward teaching the Reggio way*. Upper Saddle River, NJ.: Prentice-Hall.

Hoban, T. (1973). *Over, under and through*. New York: Aladdin Books.

Hoban, T. (1990). *Shadows and reflections*. New York: Greenwillow.

Hoban, T. (1993a). *Black on white*. New York: Greenwillow.

Hoban, T. (1993b). *White on black*. New York: Greenwillow.

Hoban, T. (1995). *Colors everywhere*. New York: Greenwillow.

Hoban, T. (1997). *Exactly the opposite* (Reprint ed.). New York: HarperTrophy.

Hoban, T. P. (1992). *Look up, look down*. New York: Greenwillow.

Hogrogian, N. (1971). *One fine day*. New York: Trumpet Club.

Hutchins, P. (1987). *Changes, changes*. New York: Aladdin.

Hutchins, P. (2000). *Ten red apples*. New York: Greenwillow.

James, S. (Director). (1997). *Prefontaine*. [Motion picture].

Jipson, J., & Johnson, R. T. (Eds.). (2001). *Resistance and representation: Rethinking childhood education*. New York: Peter Lang Pub.

Johnston, J. (Director). (1989). *Honey, I Shrunk the Kids*. [Motion picture].

Johnston, T. (2002). *Yonder*. (Reprint ed.) Illustrated by L. Bloom. Layton, UT.: Gibbs Smith Publishers.

Jonas, A. (1983). *Round trip*. Hong Kong: Greenwillow Books.

Jonas, A. (1987). *Reflections*. New York: Greenwillow.

Joyce, W. (2000). *George shrinks*. New York: Laura Geringer Books.

Kamii, C. (1985). *Young children reinvent arithmetic: Implications of Piaget's theory*. New York: Teachers College Press.

Kamii, C., & DeVries, R. (1978). *Physical knowledge in preschool education*. Englewood Cliffs, NJ: Prentice-Hall.

Katz, L., & Chard, S. (2000). *Engaging children's minds: The project approach*. New York: Ablex.

Keats, E. J. (2000). *Dreams*. New York: Puffin.

Lasseter, J. (Director). (1995). *Toy Story*. [Motion picture].

Leopold, N. C. (1999). *Once I was . . .* Illustrated by W. Hubbard. New York: Putnam Publishing Group.

Lesieg, T., & Booth, G. (1974). *Wacky Wednesday*. New York: Random House.

Levine, S. (1993). *The paper book and paper maker*. Illustrated by J. Weissmann. New York: Hyperion Books.

Libbrecht, K. G. (1999). Snow crystals. Retrieved April 30, 2005, from http://www.its.caltech.edu/~atomic/snowcrystals

Line symmetry (2005). Retrieved from http://www.adrianbruce.com/Symmetry

Lynch, D. K., & Livingston, W. (2001). *Color and light in nature*. New York: Cambridge University Press.

Macaulay, D. (1976). *Underground*. Boston: Houghton Mifflin.

Macaulay, D. (1980). *Unbuilding*. Boston: Houghton Mifflin.

Macaulay, D. (1981). *Cathedral: The story of its construction* (Sandpiper). Boston: Houghton Mifflin Books.

Macaulay, D. (1982a). *Castle*. Boston: Houghton Mifflin Books.

Macaulay, D. (1982b). *Pyramid*. Boston: Houghton Mifflin Books.

MacLachlan, P. (1980). *Through grandpa's eyes*. Pictures by D. K. Ray. New York: Harper & Row.

Mann, E., & Witschonke, A. (2003). *Empire State Building: A wonders of the world book*. New York: Mikaya Press.

Marshall, J. (1974, reprint 2000). *George and Martha*. New York: Houghton Mifflin.

Marshall, J. (1982a). *George and Martha one fine day*. New York: Houghton Mifflin.

Marshall, J. (1982b). *George and Martha encore*. New York: Houghton Mifflin.

Marshall, J. (1986). *George and Martha tons of fun*. New York: Houghton Mifflin.

Marshall, J. (1991). *George and Martha round and round*. New York: Houghton Mifflin.

Martin, B., Jr. (1998). *Snowflake Bentley*. Illustrated by M. Azarian. New York: Houghton Mifflin.

Martin, B., Jr., & Archambault, J. (1988). *Listen to the rain*. Illustrated by J. Endicott. New York: Henry Holt.

Marzollo, J. (1995). *I spy school days: A book of picture riddles*. Pictures by W. Wick. New York: Scholastic.

Master Communications. *Families of the World* (series) (1990–2002) [Video].

Mazer, A. (1991). *The salamander room*. Illustrated by S. Johnson. New York: Dragonfly Books.

McCue, L. (1990). *Puppies love*. New York: Random House.

McCully, E. A. (1992). *Mirette on the high wire*. New York: G. P. Putnam's Sons.

McCully, E. A. (1997). *Starring Mirette & Bellini*. New York: G. P. Putnam's Sons.

McCully, E. A. (2000). *Mirette & Bellini cross Niagara Falls*. New York: Putnam Publishing Group.

McLoughlin Bros. (1980). *The magic mirror: An antique optical toy*. New York: Dover Publications.

Meddaugh, S. (1997). *Cinderella's rat*. New York: Houghton Mifflin.

Menzel, P. (1994). *The material world: A global family portrait*. Garden City, NY: Doubleday.

Mikula Web Solutions, Inc. (2005). The butterfly website. Retrieved from http://butterflywebsite.com

Miller, J. (1998). *On reflection*. New York: Yale University Press.

Millson, F. (1996). *Light and color*. New York: Troll Communications.

Mooney, M. (1994). *A matter of balance*. Illustrated by S. Kretschmar. Worthington, OH: Voyages.

Mora, P., & Mora, F. X. (2001). *Listen to the desert*. New York: Clarion Books.

Morrison, P., & Morrison, P. (1994). *Powers of ten: A book about the relative size of things in the universe and the effect of adding another zero*. San Fransisco: W. H. Freeman & Company.

Munsch, R. N. (2001). *Love you forever*. Illustrated by S. McGraw. Buffalo, NY: Firefly Books.

Munsch, R., & Martchenko, M. (1981). *Jonathan cleaned up then he heard a sound: Or blackberry subway jam*. Buffalo, NY: Annick Press.

Murphy, P., Doherty, P., & Merrill, J. (1993). *Bending light: Dozens of activities for hands-on learning*. Boston: Little, Brown and Company.

Nieto, S. (2003). *Affirming diversity: The sociopolitical context of multicultural education*. New York: Allyn & Bacon.

Ohanian, S. (1999). *One size fits few: The folly of educational standards*. Portsmouth, NH: Heinemann.

Paint Shop Pro 9. (2004). Jasc Software, Inc. Retrieved from http://simsub. digitalriver.com/cgi-bin/se/jasc/ psp91117/0/ keyword/paint_shop_ pro_exa

Paul, A. W. (1992). *Shadows are about*. Illustrated by M. Graham. New York: Scholastic.

Pearson, T. C. (2002). *Bob*. New York: Farrar, Straus and Giroux.

Perry, S. (1995). *If . . .* Venice, CA: Children's Library Press.

Pfeffer, W., & Keller, H. I. (1999). *Sounds all around*. New York: HarperTrophy.

Piaget, J. (1965, originally published 1932). *The moral judgment of the child*. New York: Free Press.

Piaget, J. (1977, originally published 1975). *The development of thought*. New York: Viking Press.

Reggio Children. (1992). *Amusement park for birds*. [Video]

Reggio Children. (2002). *Not just any place*. [Video].

Reggio Children. (2005). *Hundred languages of children* (Catalogue of the exhibition, updated ed.). Reggio Emilia, Italy: Reggio Children.

Reggio Children USA. (1980). *Portrait of a lion*. [Video].

Reggio Emilia. (1999). *Everything has a shadow except ants*. Reggio Emilia, Italy: Reggio Children.

Reggio Emilia. (2000a, b). *Light: Children's thoughts, images, and explorations*. Reggio Emilia: Diana Municipal Preschool.

Reider, K., & Von Roehl, A. (1999). *Snail started it*. New York: North-South Books.

Rodgers, D. B., & Chaillé, C. (1998). Being a constructivist teacher educator: An invitation for dialogue. *Journal of Early Childhood Teacher Education, 19*(3), 203–211.

Rodgers, D. B., & Dunn, M. (1997). And never the twain shall meet: One student's practical theory encounters constructivist teacher ed practices. *Journal of Early Childhood Teacher Education, 18*(3), 10–25.

Ross, G. (Director). (2003). *Seabiscuit*. [Motion picture].

Royston, A. (2001). *Pulleys and gears (machines in action)*. Portsmouth, NH: Heinemann.

Ruef, K. (1998). *The private eye: "5X" Looking/thinking by analogy—A guide to developing the interdisciplinary mind*. Chicago: University of Chicago Press.

Ryan, P. M. (2001). *Hello ocean*. Illustrated by M. Astrellam. Watertown, MA: Charlesbridge Publishing.

Ryder, J. (1990). *Under your feet*. Illustrated by D. Nolan. New York: Simon & Schuster Children's Publishing.

Ryder, J. (1996). *Night gliders*. New York: Troll Communications.

Sabbeth, A. (1997). *Rubber-band banjos and a java jive bass: Projects and activities on the science of music and sound*. New York: Wiley.

Santore, C. (1997). *William the curious: Knight of the water lilies*. New York: Random House.

Sayre, A. P. (2002). *Secrets of sounds: Studying the calls of whales, elephants, and birds*. New York: Houghton Mifflin.

Schuett, S. (1995). *Somewhere in the world right now*. New York: Dragonfly Books.

Scieszka, J., & Johnson, S. (1991). *The frog prince continued*. New York: Viking.

Scieszka, J., & Smith, L. (1992). *The stinky cheese man and the other fairly stupid tales*. New York: Viking.

Scieszka, J., & Smith, L. (1999). *The true story of the 3 little pigs!* New York: Viking.

Seuss, Dr. (1996). *Mr. Brown can moo, can you? Dr. Seuss's book of wonderful noises*. New York: Random House Books.

Shannon, D. (2000). *The rain came down*. New York: Blue Sky Press, Scholastic.

Shapiro, B. (1994). *What children bring to light: A constructivist perspective on children's learning in science*. New York: Teachers College, Columbia University.

Showers, P. (1985). *What happens to a hamburger?* Illustrated by A. Rockwell. New York: Harper's Row.

Simon, S. (1983). *Hidden worlds, pictures of the invisible*. New York: William Morrow & Co.

Slepian, J., Seidler, A., & Freem, E. P. (1992). *The hungry thing goes to a restaurant*. New York: Scholastic.

Slepian, J., Seidler, A., & Martin, R. P. (1990). *The hungry thing returns*. New York: Scholastic.

Sonnenfeld, B. (Director). (1997). *Men in Black*. [Motion picture].

Spier, P. (1979). *Crash bang boom*. New York: Doubleday.

Spier, P. (1988). *People*. New York: Doubleday Books for Young Readers.

Stevenson, R. L. (2002). *My shadow*. Illustrated by M. Felix. Mankato, MN: Creative Editions.

Stomp. (1996). Retrieved from www.stomponline.com/show3.html

Sweeney, J. (1996). *Me on the map*. Illustrated by A. Cable. New York: Crown Publishers.

Swinburne, S. R. (1999). *Guess whose shadow?* Honisdale, PA: Boyds Mills Press.

SymmeToy. (2003). Hufnagel Software. Retrieved from http://www.hufsoft.com/software/page4.html

Symmetry. (2005). Retrieved from http://www.teachers.ash.org.au/mikemath/movies/symmetry1.html

Taback, S. (1997). *There was an old lady who swallowed a fly*. New York: Viking Books.

Taback, S. (1999). *Joseph had a little overcoat*. New York: Viking Children Books.

Taback, S. (2002). *This is the house that Jack built*. New York: G. P. Putnam's Sons.

Teel, S., & Teel, M. (2002). Kids snow page. Retrieved from http://ccins.camosun.bc.ca/~jbritton/snow/snow.html

Tompert, A., (1988). *Nothing sticks like a shadow*. Illustrated by L. M. Munsinger. New York: Houghton Mifflin/Walter Lorraine Books.

Topal, C. W., & Gandini, L. (1999). *Beautiful stuff: Learning with found materials*. New York: Sterling Publishing.

Trivizas, E., & Oxenbury, H. I. (1997). *The three little wolves and the big bad pig*. New York: Simon & Schuster.

Twentieth Century Fox. *Home alone* (1990). [Motion picture].

Van Allsburg, C. (1988). *Two bad ants*. New York: Houghton Mifflin.

Vecchi, V. (Ed.). (2002). *Theater curtain: The ring of transformations*. Reggio Emilia, Italy: Reggio Children.

Warner Bros. (1985). *Pee-wee's Big Adventure* [Motion picture].

Wells, R. E. (1996). *How do you lift a lion?* Morton Grove, IL: Albert Whitman & Company.

White, E. B. (1974). *Charlotte's web*. Illustrated by G. Williams. New York: Harper Collins.

Wiesner, D. (1991a). *Free Fall*. New York: HarperTrophy.

Wiesner, D. (1991b). *Tuesday*. New York: Clarion Books.

Wiesner, D. (1992). *June 29, 1999*. New York: Clarion Books.

Wiesner, D. (1999). *Sector 7*. New York: Clarion Books.

Wiesner, D. (2001). *The three pigs*. New York: Clarion Books.

Wilde, S. (1992). *You kan red this!* Portsmouth, NH: Heinemann.

Williams, D. (2002). *Peter Pan*. (J. M. Barrie, original author). Random House: RH/Disney.

Wolfe, M. F. (2000). *Rube Goldberg: Inventions!* New York: Simon & Schuster.

Wood, A. (2000). *The napping house*. Illustrated by D. Wood. San Diego: Harcourt.

Wood, J. N. P., & Brown, D. I. (1990). *Survival: Could you be a mouse?* Nashville, TN: Ideals Publishing.

Works, M. (1991). *Peter Pan* (Disney Classic Series). New York: Mouse Works.

Wurm, J. P. (2005). *Working in the Reggio way: A beginner's guide for American teachers*. St. Paul, MN: Redleaf Press.

Yolen, J. (1987). *Owl moon*. Illustrated by J. Schoenherr. New York: Philomel Books.

Yolen, J., & Stemple, J. P. (1995). *Water music*. New York: Wordsong Boyds Mills Press.

Young, E. (1989). *Lon Po Po: A Red-Riding Hood story from China*. New York: Philomel Books.

Zolotow, C. (1992). *This quiet lady*. Illustrated by A. Lobel. New York: Greenwillow.

Zolotow, C. (1993). *The moon was the best*. Pictures by T. Hoban. New York: Willow Books.

Zolotow, C. (1995). *When the wind stops*. Illustrated by S. Vitale. HarperCollins.

Zolotow, C. (2000). *My friend John*. Illustrated by A. Harvery. New York: Doubleday.

Zubrowski, B. (1992). *Mirrors: Finding out about the properties of light*. New York: Morrow Junior Books.

Zubrowski, B., & Doty, R. I. (1995). *Shadow play: Making pictures with light and lenses*. New York: Boston Children's Museum Activity Book/Morrow Junior Books.

Index